KU-713-560

ENCOUNTERING
EVIL

live options in theodicy

STEPHEN T. DAVIS, editor

JOHN B. COBB, JR.

DAVID R. GRIFFIN

JOHN H. HICK

JOHN K. ROTH

FREDERICK SONTAG

T. & T. CLARK LTD.
36 GEORGE STREET, EDINBURGH

Unless otherwise indicated Scripture quotations are from the Revised Standard Version of the Holy Bible, copyright, 1946, 1952, and © 1971, 1973 by the Division of Christian Education, National Council of the Churches of Christ in the U.S.A. and used by permission.

News items on the first page of the Introduction are compiled from the Los Angeles Times, the Los Angeles Times-Washington Post News Service and major wire and supplementary news agencies. Copyright, 1980, Los Angeles Times. Reprinted by permission. "Distemper Outbreak Puzzle Experts," by Mike Sturman, published March 16, 1980. "Laser Will Attempt to Shoot Down Missile," by Robert C. Toth, published March 16, 1980. "A retired banker and his wife . . . " under "The Nation," published March 16, 1980, page two, part one. "Oil from the wrecked tanker . . . " under "Energy & Environment," published March 16, 1980, page two, part one. "A two-bit bet in a Long Beach . . . ," under "The Southland."

© copyright John Knox Press 1981

Printed in the U.S.A. by
R. J. Carroll, Inc.

for

T. & T. CLARK LTD., EDINBURGH

0 567 29107 3

All Rights Reserved. No part of this publication may be reproduced, stored in a retrieval system, or transmitted, in any form, or by any means, electronic, mechanical, photocopying, recording, or otherwise, without the prior permission of T. & T. Clark, Ltd.

KING ALFRED'S COLLEGE

214
DAV

100193

Contents

Introduction

We live in a morally ambiguous world. Most of us experience moments of contentment, happiness, even joy. But there is much unhappiness, discontent, and pain in the world as well. There is undeserved suffering, grinding poverty, excruciating pain, irrational acts of violence, and sudden sinister twists of fate.

Here, for example, are five news items from the *Los Angeles Times* of March 16, 1980:

> A retired banker and his wife in Sheridan, Indiana were charged with reckless homicide in the "slavery" death of a 74-year old man, one of three mentally retarded persons who worked for them and lived in a filthy trailer behind their home.

> Oil from the wrecked tanker Tanio spread along 40 miles of Brittany coastline, polluting picturesque bays and tourist beaches. The French army was asked to send reinforcements to join the 1,100 troops already helping villagers with the cleanup. About 21,000 barrels of oil spilled into the sea when the Tanio broke in two during a storm.

> A two-bit bet in a Long Beach pool hall led to an argument that resulted in the slaying of one Long Beach man and the critical wounding of another. Police said the victims were playing pool with a third man, betting 25 cents a game, when the third man left in anger. He returned, armed, and shot both his opponents.

> The source of a mysterious outbreak of canine distemper in the Monrovia area, which has resulted in the death of nine raccoons in the last two weeks, has authorities puzzled and concerned for the safety of local domestic animals. Local pet owners are being advised to have their dogs immunized against the disease, which is almost always fatal.

> An aerial test of a lazer beam "death ray" weapon will occur soon at White Sands missile range in New Mexico. A modified KC-135, an Air Force version of the Boeing 707, will fire a lazer beam from an infrared light and attempt to destroy an air-to-air missile. The demonstration will introduce into a realistic battle situation a weapon that shoots packets of energy rather than explosive projectiles. Lazers seem certain to become the first of a new class of such weapons.

Most of us feel sorrow and revulsion when we hear items such as these. We share a feeling that our world would be a better world if they did not occur. So some perfectly sane and intelligent questions that can be asked are: why do they happen? why is our world so full of violence and suffering? is there a reason?

This very "Why?" question forms the subject matter of this book, viz., the problem of evil. One way to introduce the problem of evil is to ask for whom it is a problem. The usual answer is that the problem of evil is a problem for *theism*. But what exactly is theism? Let me attempt to define the term. Although not intentionally polemical, it should be noted that the definition I will offer is not neutral either. Doubtless many will disagree with it, including some of the contributors to this book. Nevertheless, let me define "theism" as *the belief that the world was created by an omnipotent and perfectly good personal being.* Theism takes many forms. There are Christian theists, Jewish theists, Moslem theists, and many other theists. What holds them together, I believe, is their common commitment to the view of God stated above.

It might be helpful to comment briefly on five facets of theistic belief.

(1) There is one God.

Theism, as I here define it, is a form of monotheism.

(2) God created the world.

Theists claim that the world came into existence because of a decision on God's part and so is dependent on him. The world is a contingent thing.

(3) God is omnipotent.

What this statement means is highly controversial among theists. Let me suggest that God is omnipotent at a certain point in time if and only if for any logically possible state of affairs the statement that "God brings about that state of affairs" is coherent, God can bring about that state of affairs at that time.

(4) God is personal.

Theists say that God is a conscious being who has thoughts, intentions, desires, and will. In addition, unlike the God of the eighteenth century Deists, he is concerned about and deeply interested in his creatures. Accordingly, he continues providentially to influence the world even after creation.

(5) God is perfectly good.

This statement too is controversial as to its precise meaning. Let me provisionally suggest it means that God never does what is morally wrong; all his intentions and actions are morally right. In addition, theism claims that God is benevolent and loving toward his creatures; he never causes any sort of suffering unless there are overriding moral reasons for him to do so (e.g., it will lead to greater good if he does so).

There is little doubt that the problem of evil is *the* most serious intellectual difficulty for theism. The heart of the problem is the simple question: why does God permit evil? Of course, this is a *practical* as well as intellectual problem: the question deeply troubles all sorts of people. Many sensitive theists are caused to have doubts by the problem of evil, perhaps even to question the truth of theism. For such a person, responding to the problem of evil is a spiritual as well as intellectual necessity. But the question interests non-theists as well: many such people say that the problem of evil is the main obstacle preventing them from embracing theism. Such people too will be deeply interested in responses to the problem of evil.

Although non-theists can be bothered by the question, Why does God permit evil?, it is important to see that the problem of evil is only a problem in the broad context of theistic religion. Those who deny that God is perfectly good have less trouble answering the question — evil exists because God's demonic side leads him to create evil. It is also easier for those who deny that God is omnipotent — evil exists, they can say, because it is not in God's power to prevent the existence of evil. Theists can take neither route. Accordingly, it is much harder for them to answer the question.

The problem is this: if God is omnipotent (as defined above) he must be *able* to prevent evil (the state of affairs of there existing no evil seems precisely the sort of state of affairs an omnipotent being can bring about). And if God is perfectly good he must be *willing* to prevent evil. But if God is both able and willing to prevent evil, why does evil exist? Why do children die of inoperable cancer of the throat? Why do innocent people suffer in prison? Why do earthquakes and tornadoes and famines cause pain and death? Why do people lie, steal, and kill? Thus, in an oft-quoted passage, David Hume asks about God: "Is he willing to prevent evil, but not able? Then he is impotent. Is he able, but not willing? Then he is malevolent. Is he both able and willing? Whence then is evil?"[1]

But even this is still a bit vague. Precisely how is the problem of evil a problem? Precisely how does it constitute a threat to theism? Surely the problem must be more than just a set of questions that embarass theists. It appears that two main approaches are taken by those who use the problem of evil to criticize theism. The first approach is *logical*: it says that theists are in some sort of logical difficulty because they hold all three of the following statements:

> *(3) God is omnipotent,*
>
> *(5) God is perfectly good,*

and

> *(6) Evil exists.*

But these three statements — so the critic claims — form an inconsistent set of statements. That is, they cannot all be true; the truth of any two of them implies the falsity of the third. Theism is thus a contradictory position because it involves acceptance of the following logically inconsistent statement:

> *(7) God is omnipotent, and God is perfectly good, and evil exists.*

(which is merely the conjunction of [3], [5], and [6]). Theists simply contradict themselves.

The second approach is *epistemological:* it says not that the existence of evil is *logically inconsistent* with the existence of a perfectly good and omnipotent God but rather that it *constitutes powerful evidence against* the existence of such a God. That is, the existence of evil in the world constitutes very good reason to disbelieve or at least seriously doubt the existence of the God of theism.

Both approaches are serious *prima facie* threats to theism, but a second distinction should be made. Some critics of theism emphasize that the problem of evil is created for theism given the existence of *any* amount of evil in the world, however small. Other critics emphasize the problem of evil as being created by the *actual amount of evil* that exists in the world. What is said to constitute a threat to theism is not that evil exists but that *too much* evil exists. Still other critics emphasize *surd* evil — evil that is superfluous or morally unjustified. The problem of evil, they say, is created by the fact that at least some of the evil that exists in the world is surd evil.

A third distinction should also be made — between two sorts of evil, *moral evil* and *natural evil.* Roughly, moral evil is wrongdoing or suffering brought about by moral agents such as human beings. Moral evil is often called "sin"; it includes such things as pride, envy, lying, murder, selfishness, robbery, greed, etc. Roughly, natural evil (sometimes called physical evil) is pain and suffering brought about by such natural events as earthquakes, diseases, famines, floods, etc. (It should be pointed out that these terms are sometimes defined in a slightly different way, viz., such that *moral evil* means sin [having exclusively to do with intentions, not consequences] and that *physical evil* means suffering [whether caused by human or non-human agents]. However, our terminology in this book will reflect the first way of making the distinction.)

The word "theodicy" appears in the subtitle of this book. Derived from two Greek words Øeós (God) and δικζ(justice), theodicy is the word traditionally used in theology for an argument that attempts to show that God is righteous or just despite the presence of evil in the world. That is, it tries to show that God can be omnipotent and perfectly good despite evil. However, some of the "theodicies" contained in this book do not involve attempts to retain belief in divine omnipotence and perfect goodness (not all the contributors are theists, as I have defined the term). Furthermore, in the case of some contributors to the book, opinions will differ whether they can legitimately call themselves theists (as I have defined the term). Some may fairly call themselves theists because they accept the belief stated in the fourth paragraph of this introduction, even though they disagree with some of the comments I made on it in the fifth paragraph. Accordingly, I propose to use the word theodicy in a broader way. For our purposes, let us say that a theodicy is *any* response to the problem of evil from the perspective of Judeo-Christian religious belief, broadly construed. In this sense, all the contributors to this book are "theodicists" because all have religious beliefs within that tradition and all are deeply concerned about responding to evil from the perspective of those beliefs.

This book about the problem of evil was written by a group of philosophers and theologians who teach at the Claremont Colleges in Claremont, California. All of us have previously written on the problem, and it seemed worthwhile to pool our wisdom, so to speak, into a book in which our various theodicies are presented and jointly criticized. Let me introduce the main contributors to the book. David R. Griffin is Professor of Philosophy of Religion at the School of Theology at Claremont and Executive Director of the Center for Process Studies. John H. Hick is Danforth Professor of Philosophy of Religion at Claremont Graduate School. John K. Roth is Professor of Philosophy on the Russell K. Pitzer Fund at Claremont Men's College. Frederick Sontag is Robert C. Denison Professor of Philosophy at Pomona College. Stephen T. Davis, the book's editor, is Associate Professor of Philosophy and Religion at Claremont Men's College. A bibliography in the rear of the book lists all our previous writings that are relevant to the problem of evil.

The design of the book is as follows. Each chapter consists of three sections. The first and longest section is the contributor's theodicy. It is his attempt to explain his latest thinking on the problem of evil, for in the case of many if not all of us, our previous writings have been subjected to criticisms which have caused us to do at least some rethinking. The second section in each chapter consists of critical responses to the theodicy contained there written by the other four main contributors. The third section in each chapter consists of the contributor's attempt to defend his theodicy against the criticisms of the others.

Our method in writing the book was as follows: the theodicies were written first and during the same period. They were then collected and distributed to the five contributors, at which point the critiques were written. These too were then collected and distributed, at which point the final responses to the critiques were written. With the exception of the editor, no one saw anyone else's work at any point in the process till everyone did.

This result of all this, I believe, is fascinating and illuminating. Besides the high caliber of the contributors to the book, there are two reasons for this. The first is the great variety of approaches represented here. The reader will find stylistic, methodological, and substantive differences among the authors, as well as disagreement on other fundamental issues in theology besides the problem of evil. Griffin, for example, is a Process thinker, i.e., one who approaches theology from the perspective of the thought of Alfred North Whitehead and Charles Hartshorne. Hick is a philosopher of religion and theologian who approaches religious issues from a global perspective, alert and open to the concerns of the world's various religions and cultures. Roth is a liberal Protestant who writes from an existential perspective that has been heavily influenced by Jewish thinking and by the Holocaust. Sontag is a philosopher and philosophical theologian of wide interests who writes from the perspective of existential metaphysics. And I am an analytic philosopher by training and an evangelical Christian by persuasion.

The second reason I believe many will find this book fascinating and illuminating is the give-and-take found in the discussion sections. This is not an ordinary anthology containing just a collection of articles on some subject. Instead, each contributor subjects the other theodicies to searching criticism and is forced to defend his own. Our hope is that the reader's understanding of the problem of evil will be significantly deepened and that, finishing the book, the reader will be helped to decide which approach to the problem of evil, if any, is most promising.

We are also fortunate in that John B. Cobb, Jr. has written a perceptive and helpful postscript. Cobb is Ingraham Memorial Professor of Theology at the School of Theology at Claremont and Avery Professor of Religion at Claremont Graduate School. He has done a skillful job of summing things up, looking at the problem of evil from the perspective of practical theology, and suggesting further fruitful insights from his own perspective.

One interesting fact to emerge from recent discussions of the problem of evil is that the paradigm evil event to which virtually all theodicts now refer — including all the contributors to this book — is the Holocaust, i.e., the murder of six million Jews and others by the Nazis during World War II. At one time the paradigm evil event referred to by theodicists was the infamous Lisbon earthquake of November 1, 1755. Followed by fires and even a flood of the Tagus, the disaster destroyed the city and killed tens of thousands of people. The Lisbon earthquake is an example of natural evil; the Holocaust, of moral evil. Although both are apt symbols of human suffering, it is perhaps fitting that the one has replaced the other in our minds as *the* evil event. For we twentieth century people — with the advances in technology we have seen, with the rise of mass organization and totalitarian political ideologies — are acutely conscious of the tremendous power human beings have to inflict suffering on each other.

Let me then pose this question for the authors and readers of this book: are there any theodicies, represented here or elsewhere, which are credible when they try to account for the Holocaust?

1 A Theodicy of Protest
JOHN K. ROTH

Jesus gazed at them. "For men," he said, "it is impossible, but not for God: because everything is possible for God."—Mark 10:27 (The Jerusalem Bible)

He is almighty, isn't He? He could use His might to save the victims, but He doesn't! So—on whose side is He? Could the killer kill without His blessing—without His complicity?—Elie Wiesel, *The Trial of God*

And the Lord repented of the evil
which he thought to do to his people.—Exodus 32:14

I. We Are Consumed

Seventy million human beings have been uprooted, enslaved, or killed in the twentieth century alone. Albert Camus made that estimate when he published *The Rebel* in 1951. What the figure should be today, God only knows. It is all-too-clear, however, that wars persist, scarcity continues to take its mammoth toll, and human misery, so graphically written on the faces of refugee children, rages unabated. Granted, even if the twentieth century is one of unprecedented mass death, it is not so different from others that have gone before. But that fact gives no comfort, especially if one cannot escape the conviction that such waste is wrong, either because it is contrary to God's will or because it reveals life's fundamental absurdity.

Usually "theodicy" refers to human vindications of God's justice in permitting evil to exist. Most theodicies of the Protestant Christian variety belong in that tradition. The outlook developed here is related to it, too, but the breaks with classical Christian Protestantism are no less important than the lines of continuity. My approach underscores God's sovereignty. It allows for his disappointment with human life gone wrong. It also holds out for the possibility of grace experienced through faith and for the hope of God's salvation. At the same time, and precisely because the accumulated devastation of history is so vast, this perspective echoes voices that are Jewish as well as Christian, some of them far older than those of Martin Luther or John Calvin. The Jewish voices belong to a dissenting spirit that quarrels with God over *his* use of power. That confrontation is rooted not so much in rejection of God but rather in recognition that such defiance is crucial in struggles against despair. Jewish insight, ancient and contemporary, calls for men and women—particularly Christians—to consider a theodicy of protest.

What does "evil" mean? That question itself is a crucial element in the problem of evil. The word often functions as a noun, suggesting that evil is an entity. In fact, evil is *activity,* sometimes *inactivity,* and thus it is a manifestation of power. Evil power displays are those that *waste.* That is, evil happens whenever power ruins or squanders, or whenever it fails to forestall those results. Evil comes in many shapes and sizes. The kind that concerns us here ignores and violates the sanctity of individual persons. Everyone inflicts that sort of pain and yet some individuals and societies are far more perverse than others. The measure is taken by the degree to which one's actions waste human life.

Prior to death, and perhaps beyond, existence is in process. Because things move and change, waste may not be simply waste, nor evil simply evil. Capitalizing on that fact, some writers mute screams of pain by hearing them as *instrumental.* Destruction then becomes a means to what is new and better. Or, if not all havoc readily fits that scheme, ruins may still provide occasions for atonement, forgiveness, and magnificent attempts at redemption. To the extent that evil can be interpreted as instrumental, as somehow transcended by a better situation overall, power's waste is rendered less radical.

Eschatological hopes hinge on some version of an instrumental view of evil. They differ, however, in their optimism about evil's being overcome by good. Most Protestant theodicies affirm that this overcoming, at least from a divine perspective, will be complete. A protesting theodicy affirms that any overcoming of this kind, at least from a human perspective, should be less well regarded. The reason is clear: too much has been lost.

Theodicy consists of fallible options. That result is unavoidable because we are dealing with thoughts, emotions, and choices organized by finite human minds. It is equally true that such minds exist only in social contexts that decisively influence what they are. Therefore, it is not accidental that I speak of a theodicy of protest. Before proceeding with a more detailed discussion of points only mentioned thus far, let me note some factors that produce this personal outcome.

My father is a Presbyterian pastor. I was raised in a home where God was alive, and his reality abides with me still. Early on I was introduced to theology and philosophy in my father's sermons, which emphasized human responsibility, social justice, and the sovereignty of God. Later encounters with Søren

Kierkegaard would do much to deepen my understanding—and my questioning—of those ideas.

In the latter half of the 1960s, while I was in my late twenties, the "death of God" was bandied about. Although I could not agree with the facile optimism that proclaimed God's demise as a joyous event signifying humanity's freedom and coming-of-age, I was profoundly moved by Richard L. Rubenstein's *After Auschwitz*. This book and its Jewish author placed the Holocaust, the mass murder of the Jewish people during the Nazi era, firmly on the American theological agenda. Rubenstein affirmed the death of a traditional God of history, but he neither rejected all views of God nor saw that the "death of God" was any cause for celebration. If Rubenstein's constructive proposals did not always persuade me completely, his straightforward insights about the religious crisis lurking in the Holocaust sent me on a quest. Could my own religious and philosophical experience muster a response that would work better for me? My journey is still under way.

Other currents were touching me as well. The finite, limited Gods of William James, A. N. Whitehead, and other "process theologians" offered some appeal. But as I wrote about American religious thought with my colleague Frederick Sontag, I became disenchanted with the sanguine assumptions about human nature and history that are required by those outlooks if trust in redemption is warranted.[1] Nonetheless, religious hopes remained in my bones, as they still do, and thus my convictions about human frailty and failure forced me to reconsider the power of God.

As it happened, the context in which that reconsideration took place was again provided by the consuming fire of Auschwitz, seen this time through the writings of a Jewish survivor, Elie Wiesel.[2] Wiesel's authorship shows that life in a post-Holocaust world can be more troublesome with God than without him. And yet Wiesel will not let God go, any more than he will give up on humankind, although he has good reason to do both. Instead he dissents, seeking to check despair not by acquitting or ignoring God but by putting him on trial.

The verdict reads "guilty," but that word is not the end. Wiesel's thought has a method, and the method is that of a protestant. Never failing for questions, he keeps asking, "What is the next step?" Reaching an apparent conclusion, he moves on. "And yet? And yet." . . . "In spite of this, something more must be noted." . . . "How is one to believe? How is one not to believe?" . . . Those are the forms of his thinking. They enable Elie Wiesel not to discount the waste that indicts God, but to stand with Moses in acknowledging God's sovereignty even as he argues against God for the sake of his people.

Wiesel's point is not to locate a divine scapegoat, nor does he think that any problems are solved by blaming God. On the contrary, his work demands human responsibility. And yet Wiesel understands that much also depends on God's reality or lack of it, on what God can and cannot do, will and will not do. More than once Elie Wiesel has said that he opposes two things: indifference and absurdity. Religously speaking, his aim is to map out boundaries of meaning in the wake of Auschwitz. To deny God outright could go too far. But to affirm his total goodness, to apologize for God, to exonerate him on grounds of weakness—these steps go too far as well.

The quotations at the outset of this essay were chosen with care. A protesting theodicy puts God on trial, and in that process the issue of God's wasteful complicity in evil takes center stage. The God interrogated is one for whom everything is possible, an awesome biblical announcement. According to the Gospel narrative, when Jesus made that claim he did so where entry into the kingdom of God was at issue. One implication of that discussion is that God can bring about good ends that are completely beyond human energies. I agree, but not unequivocally. For those ends to occur in the fullest measure possible, human repentance will have to be matched by God's. Even then there will be too much waste left over. Unlike some theodicies, this one is *not* too good to be true.

II. How Long, Lord, Before You Relent?

A. *History*. Protestant theology usually holds that God cares about history. My theodicy of protest begins by probing that assumption, and it does so by agreeing with Hegel: history is "the slaughter-bench at which the happiness of peoples, the wisdom of states, and the virtue of individuals have been sacrificed."[3] Granted, that appraisal does not contain all that should be said, but that fact itself produces more problems than it solves.

According to Genesis, God called the creation good. In some sense, everyone agrees. Corrupted though the world may be, our lives are not without optimism. It persists in the experience that life is worth living. If it were not, nobody would bother with theodicy. We do not inhabit a perfect world, but neither is this one the worst that might be. Therefore, questions about history's meaning and destiny loom large. One way to summarize those questions is to ask: if creation is good, and yet history is largely a slaughter-bench, how "cost-effective" are God's decisions?[4]

Theodicy must reckon with God-as-economist, and the question posed above deals with his waste. When Jews and Christians say that history should be understood in terms of creation, they imply that God's purposes affect what comes to be. So consider a dilemma: either those purposes necessitate every jot and tittle of history, or they are compatible with alternatives that would reduce the slaughter-bench qualities of human life. On all counts there are good grounds for protest.

In the former instance, for example, God's economy might be without waste, but the issue of whether God was bound to pursue only those particular purposes, with their exact and horrendous historical consequences, surely calls into question the freedom—divine and human—so central to the biblical records.

On the other hand, if God is not so determined, his purposes permit multiple routes to their achievement. Indeed the purposes themselves may have a flexible quality. Such largess, however, is not merely lavish. The slaughter-bench makes God's luxury wasteful. And one point more: no matter what horn of the dilemma is seized, any ways in which God could rationally justify his economy as purely cost-effective in pursuing goodness that we can appreciate . . . well, those ways are beyond imagining. This result testifies that such a wasteful God cannot be totally benevolent. History itself is God's indictment.

B. *Responsibility.* Most people want a totally good God or none at all. In religious circles, then, it has not been popular to put God on trial. For centuries human beings have taken themselves to task in order to protect God's innocence, and not without reason. Even at the price of an unwarranted guilt-trip, the desire runs strong to separate good and evil neatly. Life is simpler that way. And so theology puts Father in the right and his children in the wrong. At least that tendency held until the idea of sin was replaced by an "I'm OK, You're OK" psychology.

A protesting theodicy finds both of those views wanting. Nobody is OK. Otherwise the slaughter-bench would not be so drenched. And when one says "nobody," God is included as well as humanity. Whether considered in terms of violation of God's will, or simply in terms of goodness that is known and left undone, sin abounds in human life. But Camus is also correct: "man is not entirely to blame; it was not he who started history."[5]

It is irresponsible to assign responsibility inequitably. God must bear his share, and it is not small unless he could never be described as one for whom all things are possible. God's responsibility is located in the fact that he is the one who ultimately sets the boundaries in which we live and move and have our being. True, since we are thrown into history at our birth, we appear in social settings made by human hands, but ultimately those hands cannot account for themselves. To the extent that they are born with the potential and the power to be dirty, credit for that fact belongs elsewhere. "Elsewhere" is God's address.

Do not take lightly what God's responsibility entails. It means: in the beginning . . . Auschwitz, Hiroshima, and the words of a nine-year old girl, one of the Vietnamese refugees, who recently was heard to say, " 'I prayed that my death would be quick and merciful.' "[6] The point is not that God predestined or caused such events directly. Some theodicies have taken that position, but not this one. It rejects such conclusions because it assumes the reality of human freedom. At the same time, that freedom—much as some thinkers would like—does not remove God from the dock.

C. *Freedom.* Richard L. Rubenstein's penetrating study of the Holocaust, *The Cunning of History,* makes the following observation: "Until ethical theorists and theologians are prepared to face without sentimentality the kind of action it is possible freely to perpetrate under conditions of utter respectability in an advanced, contemporary society, none of their assertions about the existence of moral norms will have much credibility.''[7] The inference I want to draw from Rubenstein's assertion is this: human freedom has been used as God's defense; in fact, it is crucial in his offense.

Using freedom as a defense for God is a well-known strategy. Moving from the idea that freedom is a good, the argument has usually been that God gave freedom to human life in innocence. The gift, to be sure, did include a capacity for self-perversion. God knew that fact and perhaps even that liberty would be abused. Still, the apology continues, God's gift is justified. Only with the freedom we were given can men and women truly be the children of God. Moreover, where sin infests us, God's own freedom is gracious enough to offer forgiveness and love that can release us to try again and also rectify every wrong. On all counts, apparently, God's benevolence is validated even as humanity's is not.

Already the cost-effectiveness of God's creative acts has been challenged. In that challenge a critique of the gift of freedom was implied. To make the critique explicit, the nature of our freedom must be focused. In a word, our freedom is both too much and too little. It is far more an occasion for waste than a defense of God's total goodness can reconcile.

On one hand, freedom constitutes an insufficient defense for God because of its paucity. Two areas of life make this fact evident. First, as Descartes emphasized long ago, human ignorance wreaks havoc everywhere. In his optimism about human reason, however, Descartes underplayed his hand: too often our freedom is helpless to dispel ignorance in time to save countless victims from their tragic fate. Cancer, for example, kills thousands every year. If we could, we would use our freedom to stop its waste, but a shroud of unknowing is more than the powers of our freedom can presently penetrate. Granted, that situation may give opportunity for us to use freedom nobly in a struggle to obtain knowledge or in a battle with pain and death. Meanwhile the mound of corpses rises.

Evidence of the paucity of freedom is not restricted to our struggles against natural forces that can kill. It also exists in the social structures that bind our lives. Rubenstein's example of the Holocaust offers a telling case. The Holocaust was no sport of history. When the fury of Auschwitz was unleashed, the powers at work there were so deeply entrenched that none of humanity's countervailing energy, individual or collective, could halt them before millions perished.

To think of millions, however, may not make the point sharp enough. Consider, therefore, *Sophie's Choice*. Sophie Zawistowska is a Polish survivor of Auschwitz. As William Styron tells her story, his brilliant novel becomes a commentary on the powerlessness of individual freedom as it faces overwhelming forces of social domination. For a time, Sophie has been a privileged prisoner, assigned to secretarial duties in the house of Rudolf Höss, the commandant of

Auschwitz. Urged to use her position to assist the underground resistance movement, Sophie will try to steal a radio from Höss' house.

Sophie knows where one can be found, a small portable that belongs to Höss' daughter, Emmi. She passes the girl's room every day on her way upstairs to the office where Höss does his work. Once she tries for the radio, but Emmi catches her, and Sophie is nearly undone. Her sense of failure runs deep, only less so than the realization that she will never regain her courage to steal the radio again. Sophie knows "how, among its other attributes, absolute evil paralyzes absolutely."[8]

She knows the frailty of freedom not simply because of the incident with the radio, but because of the setting that surrounds it. And nothing is more important in that setting than her children, Jan and Eva. Jan is alive somewhere in the children's camp at Auschwitz. Höss has promised that Sophie can see him, and her attempted theft took place with the knowledge that she would jeopardize her chance to embrace the boy whose life gives hers a reason for going on. Sophie is not without courage, far from that, but once is enough. She cannot put the radio ahead of her need for Jan.

Who could blame Sophie, especially when Eva is remembered? Eva is gone, gassed. And Sophie's freedom, or the lack of it, shows how pathetic a "free-will defense" for God can be. Eva's life was lost because Sophie was left free to choose. As she disembarked from the stifling train that brought her and the children from Warsaw to Auschwitz, a selection took place. An SS official—Styron calls him Dr. Jemand von Niemand—decided to make freedom real, dreadfully so, by forcing Sophie's choice. Instead of losing both Jan and Eva to the gas, which was the fate of most young children there, Sophie could pick one of hers to live. "*'Ich kann nicht wählen!'* she screamed."[9] I cannot choose . . . and then so as not to lose them both, Sophie let Eva go. Sophie's choice stayed with her. She experienced liberation in 1945, but only fully in 1947 when she gave up her own life—also by choice.

It is only a story. But there is truth in it because paralysis and untimely death are results of freedom that is allowed, like Sophie's, to be too little. Of course there was heroism in Auschwitz, her kind not least, and ultimately the death camps died. The price, however, was horrible, and even to suggest that there could be no adequate display of human virtue—or no sufficient glory in heaven—without such testing odds . . . well, that proposition mocks the victims far more than it honors them. Sophie's choice accuses God and rightly so.

The matter does not end there, however, because the freedom God gives us is also too much and too soon. That fact follows as a corollary from what has gone before. So often the waste of human life is our own making. Cancer illustrates that we are free to abuse our bodies until things go too far, and the Holocaust shows that human beings can and will do anything to each other. We have more power, more freedom, than is good for us. Perhaps there was an Eden where all the factors of freedom were in healthy equilibrium. In present history, however, that dream is a myth at best. Our condition smacks too much of the feeling that we are "damned if we do, and damned if we don't"—not in some hell to come, but here and now.

Freedom's defense for God looks more and more like a ploy by the devil's advocate. That defense cannot avoid saying: only if freedom has the potential to be what it has become can there be a chance for the highest goods. But can the end justify the means?—that is the question. A protesting theodicy is skeptical because it will not forget futile cries. No good that it can envision, on earth or beyond, is worth the freedom—enfeebled and empowered—that wastes so much life.

D. *Excuses*. Perhaps Stendahl was right: God's only excuse is that he does not exist. Not so, suggest some contemporary voices. God, they say, has been mistakenly viewed as all-powerful. In fact, his creative activity reveals limitations in his existence, and thus the claim that he is totally benevolent can be preserved. In effect, then, this God's excuse is that he always does the best he can. Originally, he brought order out of chaos—uncreated, primordial, resistant—and fashioned a world of beauty and richness. Within that setting he lured humanity into existence, endowed with freedom to choose. But if God's authority can minimize the confusion that we produce with our liberty, it is also true that he cannot both intervene directly and still retain the integrity of free human creatures. This God holds his breath, as it were, while we act . . . and then the best he can do is to pick up the pieces so that survivors can try again.

Such a view would be fine if the pieces were not so many and so bloody. This God of weakness may indeed be excused, not least because he is hardly worth bothering about. He is simply too ineffectual to forestall waste decisively, unless of course one holds that he has some heretofore unwitnessed potential for eschatological power. On what ground, however, could such a claim be based? Most versions of Jewish and Christian faith would locate that ground in historical events: the exodus or the resurrection, for example. But to speak of a God who leads people out of bondage or who raises persons from death is surely *not* to speak of a God who, by history's on-going testimony, is always doing the best he can. God's saving acts in the world are too few and far between.

If God raised Jesus from the dead, he had the might to thwart the Holocaust long before it ended. Coupled with the view that resurrection is not merely the release of an immortal spirit from a lifeless physical body, but rather the recreation of a person for whom all life has ceased, that premise governs a theodicy of protest. In doing so, it makes God harder to excuse. But that fact, in turn, leaves us to ask: why should anybody bother with a God like this one, who seems so infrequently to do the best that is within God's power?

E. *Despair*. Things are not going very well. A protesting theodicy does not say that God's love controls the universe, nor does it hold that there is any good sense in claims that find this world to be the best one possible. Thus, it must reckon with despair.

To despair is to lose or give up hope. For our purposes two dimensions of that experience are of special significance. First, this theodicy of protest despairs over the hope that history is evolving toward a Kingdom of God on earth. That claim does not deny that there is progress, which one writer defines as "a condition that is better by far than what it replaces after accounting for any side effects."[10] What it affirms, however, is that all progress is cunning, and so one can agree when Rubenstein states: "the Holocaust bears witness to *the advance of civilization*."[11] Far from assuming that things will get better and better if only we work well enough together, this outlook supposes that human life is always under siege. All gains are precarious, periodic, and problematic. Life is one damned problem after another. Many of them are killing.

And yet the human prospect is not hopeless, nor is it without reasons for joy and thanksgiving. In fact, that prospect can be enhanced to the degree that the widespread experience of despair is turned on itself to yield a spirit of dissent. The logic of this reversal makes a straightforward appeal, namely, that once we realize how strong the good reasons for despair really are, then short of abdicating to waste there is little left to do but to turn and fight. Such responses have no utopian illusions. They stand instead with this conviction: unjustifiable waste is everlastiing, but it deserves no more victories.

Second, our theodicy of protest despairs over the hope that there will be any future good "so great as to render acceptable, in retrospect, the whole human experience, with all its wickedness and suffering as well as all its sanctity and happiness."[12] Put another way: no matter what happens, God is going to be much less than perfectly justified. But wait, someone may say, even if it is true that we cannot now fathom how God could possibly salvage this mess in a way that justifies him perfectly, surely that task can be fulfilled. Indeed the very claim that with God all things are possible would seem to demand such an option. People can believe in that optimistic outcome if they wish, but dissenters demur and the reason is simply history itself. The irretrievable waste of the past robs God of a perfect alibi. Only if he obliterates truth by wiping out the memory of victims can a protesting "Why?" be stilled forever. So long as that question can sound, the whole human experience stands as less than acceptable.

And yet the human prospect is not hopeless, nor is it without reasons for joy and thanksgiving. Life can be less unacceptable. We know that to be true because from time to time there are works of love that people do. Those realities, linked with despair that finds love not enough, may lead us to affirm life by refusing to give despair the final say. In those experiences, one may discover that the issue of whether God is without any justification depends on what he does with the future, his and ours.

III. May Your Blessings Be with Us

A. *Power*. Dissenting moods are at the foundation of my approach to theodicy. But those moods also seek to turn dissent into a religious response that can make more sense out of life, not less, without abandoning honesty in facing life's harshest facts. To fill out that response, particularly with regard to its views about what God might be like, requires first a further assessment of power.

This theodicy of protest affirms the existence of an omnipotent God.[13] That is, God is bound only by his will. Nothing except it determines what he shall do or become. All possibilities are within God's reach, and so he could have created very differently. Likewise, his relation to our world could take many forms even now. The one he establishes may have its reasons, but it is contingent nonetheless.

Why make these affirmations? My answer resides in choices made from experience. In a word, I find that the world cannot account for itself. It demands a creator. My understanding of what that creator might be comes to me through the tradition carried forward in Jewish and Christian Scripture. Much, but not all, of that tradition continues to ring true in my life, and thus I work to reconcile those aspects with notes of dissonance. The struggle, more than the result, unfolds here.

If God is sovereign, bound only by his will, then apparently he chooses to be the creator and master of this universe. Although he could intervene dramatically at any point in present history, he elects to let freedom work out its own course as it lives in individuals and communities. Thus, God's "plan" for history is virtually no plan at all. It can release the worst as well as the best that is in us, and therefore the presence of this God may feel like the absence of all gods.

God could predetermine the future; he declines so as to make freedom real. But if the future is in the making, the past is not, at least not enough. Having committed himself to what took place, God can respond to that choice, but his own omnipotence also binds him. Choosing as he wills, he cannot take back the wasted past completely. Therefore, no good that God can do will totally fill the void.

Everything hinges on the proposition that God possesses—but fails to use well enough—the power to intervene decisively at any moment to make history's course less wasteful. Thus, in spite and because of his sovereignty, this God is everlastingly guilty and the degrees run from gross negligence to murder. Perhaps we should feel sorry for a God so soiled. Not so, says Berish, one of the characters in Elie Wiesel's *The Trial of God*: "If I am given the choice of feeling sorry for Him or for human beings, I choose the latter anytime. He is big enough, strong enough to take care of Himself; man is not."[14]

God's guilt could be reduced to the extent that he lacks power. But to the extent that God lacks power, he may also be ineffectual. Short of no God at all, what people have to ask religiously, therefore, is whether we should settle for an innocent but ineffectual God or whether we should run the risks of relating to a God who is really master of the universe but much less than perfectly good by any standards that we can comprehend. Are there any good reasons why such risks should be accepted?

B. *Suffering.* History refutes more than it confirms God's providential care. And yet there are moments, personal and collective, that hint of something more. Promise lives, for example, in the messianic hopes of Judaism and Christianity. Although interpretations of those hopes are pluralistic and often at odds, a core in both affirms that God can and will intervene to heal and restore. Persons who hunger and thirst after righteousness cannot be filled by those claims alone, but to share in their hope is better than nothing. However, to do so without abandoning the world's victims, confrontations with suffering are required.

A Jewish confrontation with suffering occurs in the continued delay of the Messiah's arrival. Whether that arrival is equated with the collective transformation of Jewish and human spirit, achieved by men and women themselves, or whether it is regarded as God's intervention in the midst of human recalcitrance, the waste keeps piling up. The messianic promise is not easy to accept. It may, in fact, be impossible to believe except as one embraces it as an expression of defiance over what has been permitted. Suffering brought on by such acts of commitment may be redemptive, but if so, those same experiences testify that most suffering is not.

At least once, most Christians say, the Messiah came in Jesus of Nazareth. His life, death, and resurrection may make all the difference in the world for those who accept him, but such promise also enjoins face-to-face encounters with suffering. One of those encounters is prompted by a question: was God really serious about making all things new in Christ when Calvary could lead to the crematoria of Auschwitz?

If God suffered in Christ—as a blood sacrifice to appease his own wrath over human sin, as a sign of grace to show that nothing can separate the world from his love, as atonement for his own injustice toward men, women, and children, for whatever reason—good sense remains in question. God suffers with humanity, according to Christian claims. But the mass of agony does not have to be, and if God is only a suffering God, then we do indeed need a God to help us. The very idea of a suffering God provokes one to insist: what is going on here?

God's promises call for protests. And yet the same realities that make one dissent against the promises can also be the facts that impel us to struggle toward them—unless, of course, we are willing to let suffering rage with impunity or to resign ourselves to death as the end-in-itself. To see how that tension might be real, consider God's servant Job.

C. *Trust.* "Though he slay me, yet will I trust in him" (Job 13:15).[15] Job's ancient declaration is crucial for a theodicy of protest. Indeed his entire story is at the heart of the matter. Some interpretations highlight Job's "repentance" for daring to question God, stressing how he seemed to receive back his fortune as well. But if one concentrates on the statement quoted above, the situation is different and also more honest.

At this point Job argues. Yes, things are wrong, but the wrong is not his doing, nor is it obviously owing to the other victims, whose loss has plunged Job into a defiant grief. Or, at the very least, there is a serious disproportion between crime and punishment. It cannot and must not be accepted. And yet Job's argument is no rejection of God. Rather it trusts that God will vindicate him.

Job's trust is bold, even extreme. It entails God's confession that he has treated Job unfairly, yes brutally, for according to the story it was only by God's choice that Job was all but destroyed on the pretense of testing his faithfulness. Job was faithful all right, almost with a vengeance. But did he win or lose? God thundered back with his non-answer, challenging Job with a who-do-you-think-you-are.

Then came Job's repentance. Elie Wiesel suggests, however, that Job's humility was no simple resignation. Wiesel reads it instead as resistance and rebellion masked in hasty abdication. Ultimately God cannot be defeated, which is both our hope and our despair, but in confessing—when God, with greater reason to do so, did not—Job "continued to interrogate God."[16] A protesting theodicy takes heart from that reading, not least because it implies that Job did not give up. Whatever the form of his protest and so long as it lasted, he could still be saying, "Though he slay me, yet will I trust in him."

D. *Hope*. Carl Jung's *Answer to Job* states that "God is not only to be loved, but also to be feared."[17] These days it is religiously unfashionable to talk about fearing God. His love is more in vogue, and religious observance tends to drown out all sense of awe and judgment in gluts of celebration. A theodicy of protest both *acknowledges* and *yearns* for the love of God. It does the former because life is a created gift, one that is basically good and able to become even better. To that assumption it adds risk-filled acceptance of the biblical promises that there shall yet be life more abundant. The yearning moves from that same base, but it is rooted even more in the apprehension that there is too little love to be seen. Men and women do not love as well as they can, but neither does God, and therefore Elie Wiesel is right again: " 'To have hope in God is to have hope against God.' "[18]

Such a God has no simple nature. He is tugged and pulled by multiple desires, but he is not at their mercy. They are controlled by his own acts of will. This God is no bumbler. He knows what he is doing, and that reality is the problem. Our protests do him no harm. Indeed, his license gives us a mandate to say what we feel, and we must . . . so long as we speak for the sake of human well-being. When dissent is raised in that spirit, its rebellious care may grip God's heart.

Still, the fact remains: the net result of God's choices is that the world is more wild and wasteful than any good reason that we can imagine would require it to be. Thus, to be for such a God requires some sense of being against him as well. To defend the good as we know it best—especially to carry out God's own commandments that we should serve those in need, heal the sick, feed the hungry, forestall violence—we must do battle against forces that are loose in the world because God permits them.

Job, says Elie Wiesel, "did not suffer in vain; thanks to him, we know that it is given to man to transform divine injustice into human justice and compassion."[19] Neither individually nor collectively can human beings fulfill that task completely. The odds set by God are too high. Nonetheless, it remains possible to be for God by being against God, and the way that we do so best is by giving life in care and compassion for others. Then there is reason for hope on earth and perhaps beyond.

E. *Answers*. Most theodicies have a fatal flaw: they legitimate evil. They do so by saying too much or too little as they answer questions posed by waste. The first tendency is illustrated in theories that would make all suffering deserved. The second is found in attempts to insure totally happy endings by appealing to God's unfathomable wisdom and goodness, even though we have not the vaguest notion of how such endings could possibly be. There is a sense, then, in which this theodicy of protest is *anti-theodicy*. It has no desire to legitimate waste. It must be wary of answers or of the lack of them—including its own.

It is no legitimation of evil to acknowledge its existence. This theodicy does so without blinking, and that quality is one of its greatest assets. A possible trap, on the other hand, may lie in its insistence that God is guilty and even without apology for apparent refusal to change his worldly ways in the foreseeable future. Without caution that outlook could become a form of scapegoating, one that places a premium on blaming God, leaving the impression as it does so that there is really not very much that human beings can do.

We do face great odds. Still, there is much that we can do. Indeed we shall have to act or there will be too little action on humanity's behalf. The world—too much no doubt—is in our hands. For if God listens and answers, it is usually in silence. If he is judge or ally, it is less by intervention that metes out justice in total equity and more by letting events fall as they may to reveal the corrupt absurdity, as well as the grandeur, of what we do together. The future is more open than it ought to be. We have all that we can do and then some, and if we fail to act well, the waste will only increase.

" 'My God, my God, why have you deserted me?' " (Matt. 27:46).[20] Jesus' question is contemporary. It evokes others: can we learn not to blame God as a way of covering over our responsibilities? Can we learn to be boldly honest with God and with ourselves as a means to deepen compassion? A theodicy of protest must keep raising those questions for itself. It must also keep struggling to answer them affirmatively. Coupled with those emphases, its vision of an omnipotent God, whose nature is a self-controlled mixture that gives us freedom and that may yet reduce evil's waste, is an option that can set human souls on fire for good.

IV. Lord, You Have Been Our Refuge Age After Age

As William James summed up *The Varieties of Religious Experience,* he observed that "no two of us have identical difficulties, nor should we be expected to work out identical solutions." A few sentences later, he went on to say: "the divine can mean no single quality, it must mean a group of qualities, by being champions of which in alternation, different men may all find worthy missions."[21] Such wisdom informs all sound theodicies. Human religious needs are diverse. No single response can encompass them all or nourish every spirit. Thus, every good theodicy will be, in part, an anti-theodicy. It will disclaim the full adequacy of its own outlook and that of every other as well.

Imperfect as it is, the theodicy explored here does originate in felt needs. Two are fundamental: a sense that human affairs are far worse than any good reason can justify or than our powers alone can alter; and, second, a yearning that refuses to settle for despair that the first feeling generates. A God encountered in Jewish and Christian experience makes possible an option that keeps hope from dying, without making the dreary facts unreal. But this God offers little tranquillity because he defers rescue. He allows us—and thereby participates in—our own undoing.

Life is outrageous. Hardly anyone will deny that conclusion outright. Tragedy, pain, injustice, premature death—all of these and more waste us away. No explanation seems quite able to still our anger, hostility, and sadness. A theodicy of protest believes not only that such emotions are profoundly real, but also that they are in many cases justified. Any religious perspective that fails to give them expression diminishes the human spirit. Whether unintentionally or by design, the Christian emphasis on God's love has had a repressive effect in this regard. It strains to make everything fit the care of a Father who is love itself. For some persons that strain is too much. There may be others for whom an open admission of that fact would bring healthy release. Although the faith of us Christians would not be rendered easier, it would be quickened by quarreling with the claim that "God is love," even as we refuse to let it go (1 John 4:8).[22]

Annie Dillard's poetic book, *Holy the Firm,* is a meditation prompted by the crash of a small airplane. Miraculously no one was killed. But Julie, a seven-year-old flying with her father, has had her face burnt beyond recognition.

There is a small church in the Puget Sound country where Annie Dillard lives. She believes that its minister, a Congregationalist, knows God. "Once," she writes, "in the middle of the long pastoral prayer of intercession for the whole world—for the gift of wisdom to its leaders, for hope and mercy to the grieving and pained, succor to the oppressed, and God's grace to all—in the middle of this he stopped, and burst out, 'Lord, we bring you these same petitions every week.' After a shocked pause, he continued reading the prayer." For his protest, Annie Dillard adds, "I like him very much."[23]

These vignettes suggest that a theodicy of protest has a place in Christian life. Indeed it should take that life back to some of its most important origins. For instance, the sub-headings in this essay are phrases from Psalm 90.[24] Like many others, that psalm is full of lamentations and awesome questions. It can even be read to include dissenting cries over what God has done and left undone. And yet all of these moods are also lifted up not as rejections of faith and hope, but because God is encountered as one whose good promises can be real. Such outlooks are not restricted to the psalms. We have seen them in Job. Anyone who studies the life of Moses or Abraham, Jeremiah or Ezekiel, will find them there, too.

Of course, Christians can ask whether these Jewish expressions have not been superseded by the New Testament, which apparently plays down such themes if they are present at all. A second reading, however, reveals notes that may not stand out at first glance. Jesus brings signs of what good can be. He urges people to give their lives for others, and at least some people try. But the world does not yield, then or now, and Jesus himself ends up crucified, God-forsaken. So goes one part of the Christian story, balanced by another that stresses resurrection and victory to come in spite of losses now. Promises, glimpses, *and* failure, waste—taken together, as they must be, those realities make the New Testament a source of protesting faith as well. If that is the case, then Christian churches can enhance the disclosure of those feelings by reaffirming Jewish voices that set them out forthrightly. By doing so, Christian preaching may offer less cheap grace and inspire more the fear of God that provokes righteous rebellion. In a similar spirit, prayer, like that of Annie Dillard's preacher, will aim less at peace of mind and more at seeking God's strange ways in the disruption of our plans.

William James distinguished between outlooks that are healthy-minded and sick-souled. The former find that, at worst, evil is instrumental; disagreement drives the latter. The late twentieth century is a time for sick souls. If there are those who can look evil in the eye and still be healthy-minded ... well, that possibility may be a sign of hope in itself. But healthy minds are not for everybody. The theodicy outlined here is one for sick souls who know that their sickness cannot—must not—be cured, and who likewise refuse to acquiesce because to do so would accomplish nothing.

Long ago a Jewish family was expelled from Spain. Plagued at every turn, they could find no refuge, except that sleep turned into death for them, one by one. At last only the father was left, and he spoke to God:

"Master of the Universe, I know what You want—I understand what You are doing. You want despair to overwhelm me. You want me to cease believing in You, to cease praying to You, to cease invoking Your name to glorify and sanctify it. Well, I tell You: No, no—a thousand times no! You shall not succeed! In spite of me and in spite of You, I shall shout the Kaddish, which is a song of faith, for You and against You. This song You shall not still, God of Israel!"[25]

That Jewish story summarizes well one strand of a protesting theodicy. An ageless dialogue sounds out another. God's creation is at stake. It is far from perfect, and thus . . .

"Could you have done better?"
"Yes, I think so."
"You could have done better? Then what are you waiting for? You don't have a minute to waste, go ahead, start working!"[26]

A theodicy of protest is for those who need it. Like the victims of waste in our own day, who knows how many they may be?

Critiques

Critique by Stephen T. Davis

Roth's eloquent and evocative essay expresses an attitude all sensitive theists should feel—horror, deep sadness, and even outrage at the excesses of evil in human history. Despite massive differences between his God and mine and consequently between his theodicy and mine, there is much in Roth's essay with which I can strongly identify. For example, I agree that God is ultimately responsible for what has happened in the world; that this could have been a much better world than it has thus far turned out to be; that no theodicy has all the final answers; that whether or not God is justified in creating this sort of world depends on what he does with the future; and that we need to trust in God despite the theological and spiritual problem created by the presence of evil in the world. I also applaud the note of moral imperative in Roth's theodicy—I too think we need to "turn and fight" against evil.

The essential difference between Roth's theodicy and mine is that his response to the problem of evil involves giving up something I regard as religiously essential, central to Scripture and Christian tradition, and personally precious, viz., the notion that God is perfectly morally good. Roth explains the presence of excessive waste in human history by positing, so to speak, a demonic or dark side to God which allows or causes it. I suspect there is little I can do to deflect Roth from this path; it is, I believe, something of a gut-level, emotive (I do not intend these words in any pejorative sense) reaction to the suffering he sees in the world, especially the outrages of the Holocaust.

Nevertheless, I will offer two criticisms of Roth's theodicy, the first of which concerns omnipotence and the second of which concerns hope.

(1) We must first notice that Roth needs a strong view of divine omnipotence to insure that God is (unlike a finite God) indictable for evil, i.e., so that God cannot be excused on the grounds that he is not strong enough to prevent evil. Thus Roth says that God is "bound only by his will" and that with him "everything is possible." God is, Roth believes, powerful enough to have prevented the Holocaust and indeed to intervene against *any* wasteful event in history. As Roth admits, his entire program in theodicy hinges on this strong view of God's power. Thus the essential puzzle I have with Roth's argument is that he apparently goes on to weaken God's omnipotence in order to rule out the possibility that God can retain his perfect goodness by redeeming all evil. The notion that God can redeem all evil, Roth says, is "beyond imagining"; no good "that can be envisioned," however great, can do so; "we have not the vaguest notion" how history could reach a totally happy ending.

But surely this is to go back on the strong view of omnipotence sketched above. Surely everyone will admit that *some* of the evil we see in the world is redeemable. But if God is omnipotent, i.e., is limited only by his will, why can't we say *both* that his will is wholly good *and* that he can and therefore will one day redeem all evil? If Roth is correct when he says that "all possibilities are within God's reach," then at the very least he owes us an explanation why redeeming all evil is not possible and thus won't be achieved by God (and thus requires abandoning the notion of divine perfect goodness).

Of course Roth is within his intellectual rights if his response is a personal one, i.e., if he says simply that the best judgment he can make in the light of all the evidence is that there has been too much waste for it ever to be redeemed. I agree with Roth that some evil is "irretrievable" *in the sense that* the past is set and irrevocable. Nothing that God or anyone else can now do can alter, for example, the fact that six million people died. But it does not follow from this that an omnipotent being cannot successfully "retrieve" all evil *in the sense that* he will one day achieve such great goods that all past evils will pale into insignificance, even for the victims and sufferers. I believe three factors—Roth's strong stated view of omnipotence, his commitment to Scripture and to the Christian tradition, and his emphasis on hope—should lead him to recognize this.

The point, in sum, is this: Roth says he cannot understand how God could possibly redeem and render acceptable all the waste that has occurred (and I must admit that I cannot understand it either). But an omnipotent being is not bound by the inability to understand that Roth and I share. I do not claim to understand how God can render the Holocaust acceptable, any more than I claim to understand how he raised Jesus from the dead. But my lack of wit does not limit God. Perhaps he will one day do the one, just as I believe he once did the other.

(2) Religious hope runs like a drum-beat throughout Roth's essay. Clearly hope is crucial to his obviously deep and sincere religious beliefs. Of course, as seen above, Roth does not hope for a total redemption of all evil, but he does think there is ground both for present joy and thanksgiving and for hope of "life more abundant" in the future. God's good promises can be real, he says; Judaism and Christianity both affirm that "God can and will intervene to heal and re-store." What exactly does Roth hope for? In precisely what sense will God "heal and restore"? Perhaps Roth hopes, just as Hick and I do, for a good eschaton in which all will be well. He will only insist that no matter how good it is it will never justify the evils that have occurred as history moved toward it.

But my question is this: if God truly has a demonic side, what ground is there for hope? Surely a partially evil God may well decide perversely to give us "life *less* abundant." I think Roth sees the problem; I take it this is why he calls trusting in God a *risk*. But surely with Roth's God the risk is too great. If God is partially demonic the risk that he will be in a testy mood when the eschaton dawns is too much to take. I will trust such a God no more than I will trust a momentarily calmed manic-depressive who is holding a gun. If God is, as Roth says, a grossly negligent murderer, I will no more worship him than I will worship a Caligula or a Stalin. I will only worship and trust a being I believe is wholly good.

Critique by Frederick Sontag

The trouble with Roth's Theodicy of Protest is that it won't "sell in Peoria." The religious consciousness searches, whether consciously or unconsciously, for a "solution" to the problem of evil. Most religions that attract followers give answers, and they draw their devotees because they offer them a source of relief. I do not say this attitude is right, or the situation desirable, but it is a fact of life. If a theodicy wants to provide a solution to the problem of evil, it must recognize the psychological needs of the people to whom it speaks. A Theodicy of Protest simply puts the burden back on the individual believer. God is neither relieved of responsibility nor is all made right with the world. We cannot accept either nature or God as they are. To ask us to do so is too hard a line for the average weak human being to accept. If one is looking for a religious solution, one is not likely to want to settle for a more difficult situation than one began with before protesting.

Along with this problem goes the secularist trend. For two centuries or so many have been opting for "anthropodicy" rather than "theodicy." That is, the rise of natural science and the Enlightenment combine to argue that evil is a human problem and should be met and dealt with as a human responsibility, not

God's. Ironically, when one considers theodicy as an alternative, the naturalist tends to be conservative and to view God in a pietistic sense. Thus, a Theodicy of Protest, which sees God as stern and strong, seems incomprehensible. Moreover, a Theology of Protest has a core of mystery about it which neither the rationalist nor the naturalist can buy. They think God should be absolved of responsibility for evil (whether they believe in God or not) and so reject both his involvement and the sense of mystery entailed. A Theology of Protest is neither a popular nor saleable item.

It may nevertheless be correct. And we ask: should strong religious belief always be a minority affair (a remnant) vs. a popular and easier belief? Zen Buddhism is small but strenuous and influential. Pure Land Buddhism is easier and more popular. Hasidism is not "main line" Judaism, but it is important. The Jobs of the world, who remain faithful in spite of a divine threat against their lives, are a rarity. Roth wants to stress God's sovereignty, but this involves God in responsibility too. Plato long ago proposed that the gods be responsible not for everything but only for the good. David Griffin wants to return to that, and it is a tradition which has dominated our notions of divine perfection. The issue is: must what is perfect be all-good? Roth sides with the Jewish voices who protest God's use of power, but some among us will prefer to reject God altogether as an explanation of evil. On the other hand, the piously religious prefer a God who solves (or dissolves) the problem of evil for them and makes all right with the world.

The "waste" we find in the world is the chief dilemma, and most theodicies ignore this issue rather than account for it (cf. Davis). The naturalist has an easier time, because a process of evolution which is not in divine control can be wasteful without implicating any divinity in faulty planning. The problem with this naturalist preference for anthropodicy in a post-scientific, post-Marxist world, is that evil should have abated if their anthropodicies and programs for the elimination of evil had worked. But after a century of trying—Roth is right—the Holocaust makes naturalism less acceptable, unless of course it abandons all pretense to bring about improvement and any claim to produce a utopia. Holocausts also make easy religious solutions less acceptable, if the religious face up to them. But at the moment we do not seem quite ready to abandon the romantic picture of the future which the modern world proposed when it took over control from God.

Why did God create a wasteful world that incites us to rebellion?—that is the mysterious question Roth must answer or else join the ranks of the antireligious. We already know that nature is not benevolent, but it is a greater mystery if we find that our Creator-God is not. At this point we come up against the contrast of Judaism and Christianity. It is not an accident that Roth cites Elie Wiesel and Richard Rubenstein. Jewish religion has a greater tolerance for evil and a propensity to accept harshness in God. But Christianity came out of Judaism, rather then remaining within it as another sect, just because they had an answer to that situation in the form of a new revelation. God is love and he overcomes death is their announcement, and this new life is offered to all peoples, not one. Thus, one is a Christian because one feels one has a joyous answer to the age-old religious struggle with the divine. God will make all things new. The contrast, as well as the difficulty, comes over whether this is the way the world is now, or whether we accept it as a promise for future transformation.

God has given us freedom, but it is "too much too soon." However, those who hear Christianity's good news are quite willing to compromise freedom, both for God and for all people in order to accept the security of a perfectly kind God rather than a harsh one. Having accepted the justification of oneself before God which the Christian forgiveness of sin offers, he or she transfers this across to God and assumes that God is fully justified too (vs. Roth's position). For the new believer to feel justified but to decide that God is not requires a forgiveness on his or her part that is hard for humans to achieve. It is much easier to see the whole of history as "God's plan" than it is to assume that God gave it to us open-ended and wanted us (along with the existentialists) to accept responsibility for its outcome.

Roth accuses most theodicies of "legitimating" evil, but that is quite natural. The human psyche needs security against the dark forces that threaten it from the unconscious. If "the religious solution" offers the psyche protection from devastating forces, as Carl Jung argues, then those who accept this option, vs. a naturalist anthropodicy, do so because they want the problem of evil laid to rest and explained once and for all. Sun Myung Moon attracts followers around the world because he has a definitive plan to conquer evil and usher in God's kingdom. A Theodicy of Protest does not solve the problem but instead asks us to accept an awful burden. Few will do that if they can avoid it. If we can decide that evil is necessary in order for the good in the world to exist or if it is unavoidable, this calms our fears. To say that evil or wanton destruction did not need to be as it is places a burden of freedom on both God and humans that at least men and women have difficulty in accepting. Thus, a Theodicy of Protest may be a correct (or at least a probable) insight into God's plan, but it can never hope to be greeted by popular acclaim, particularly not among the religious.

Critique by David R. Griffin

Roth and I agree that all evil cannot be explained away as merely apparent, and that therefore the traditional doctrine of omnipotence cannot be consistently held with the doctrine that God is totally good. And we agree that this is true even with Hick's addition of the doctrine of divine self-limitation. We only disagree in that Roth rejects the doctrine of God's total goodness instead of the traditional doctrine of omnipotence. One reason is that he believes this option provides a better basis for hope: if the reason for evil were an ontological limitation on God's power, we could never expect a radical reversal in the relation between good and evil; but if the excessive evil is due to a moral problem in God, we can regard this as a merely contingent fact that may be overcome. In fact, our very protest may, Roth seems to say, be a factor in effecting the needed conversion in God.

I will mention three of the major problems I have with his view. First, I see no basis for hope that a partly evil deity could be led to repent. In our case, conversions usually involve coming to adopt a larger perspective on things. But God by definition already has an all-inclusive perspective. We have experienced the difficulty of trying to change the mind of a president who thought he was in control of the facts: our protests fell on deaf ears, since he was convinced in advance that our protests were based on ignorance of the total picture.

Also, how long has God had this moral defect? Presumably forever. That's a long time! And many would say that that which has been forever is necessary. This makes very questionable Roth's suggestion that a moral problem in God would be merely contingent. The moral problem of a lack of total goodness in God may be just as irreversible as the ontological limitation on God's control hypothesized in my essay.

Second, I believe Roth's position contradicts the very nature of religion. Vital religion, as I understand it, is driven by the desire to be in harmony with what is taken to be the Holy Reality. The extra-ordinary moral concern in cultures decisively affected by Judaism, Christianity, Islam, and Zoroastrianism is due to the fact that the Holy One worshiped by devotees of these religions has been perceived to be a Just and Righteous God. It is true that many of the doctrines of the theologians of these traditions have implications, when examined closely, that make God's goodness questionable. But the ordinary believers have always held God's holiness to include, as a central element, goodness without qualification. When this belief has been challenged by the problem of evil, theologians and ordinary believers have taken comfort in the assurance that in some way, perhaps totally mysterious to our finite minds, God is nevertheless totally good.

This conception, and the intimately related *perception* that goodness is holy, have been fundamental to the more-than-normal drive in these cultures to reform the structures of society to make them more just. And yet Roth now urges us to adopt a position in which we would consciously be working for justice in opposition to God. We are to be "for God by being against God," to "turn divine injustice into human justice." This attitude is psychologically possible in the short run, i.e., for people whose perceptions and aims were originally molded by the drive to be in harmony with the Holy One whose goodness, when it differed from our conceptions of justice, did so by going beyond it, not by falling short of it. But, if my understanding of religion is correct, the attitude Roth advocates is psychologically impossible in the long run: the belief that God is not perfectly good will eventually undercut our own concern for moral goodness. The religious drive to be in harmony with Roth's God, rather than countering our own evil tendencies, will actually give support to them. This is the most unfortunate aspect of Roth's position: directly counter to his intentions, his position *does* legitimate evil, since it says that deity itself, the Holy One, the one with an all-inclusive perspective, fosters it unnecessarily.

My third criticism: Roth rightly points out that everything in his position hinges on the proposition that God has totally determined the basic structure of the world, and has the power to intervene to prevent any specific evils. But he provides no good reasons for affirming this all-important proposition. In part he seems to affirm it because of the biblical statements that all things are possible to God. But this cannot provide a sufficient basis for several reasons. First, Roth believes that God gave freedom to human beings, and humans could have used their freedom to write false statements in the Bible. Second, even if that statement were divinely inspired, that would provide no assurance of its truth, since Roth's God might have inspired that idea while in one of his more demonic moods. Third, there are many statements in the Bible, such as those affirming God's total goodness, that Roth rejects.

One of Roth's explicit arguments for affirming the traditional doctrine of omnipotence is this: "If God raised Jesus from the dead he had the might to thwart the Holocaust." This is an extremely weak argument. For example, it is not immediately self-evident that the *kind* of power needed for the two types of events is the same. In any case, we have far too little knowledge of what precisely happened in the event we call "the resurrection of Jesus from the dead" to make sweeping ontological inferences from it.

When Roth raises the question as to why he affirms that "God is bound only by his will," and that "all possibilities are within God's reach," his answer is extremely vague. He gives no analysis of the nature of possibility; we are not told, for example, if it is possible for God to create things whose description involves logical contradictions, such as round squares. In any case, his answer seems to reduce to the assertion that much of the tradition carried forward in the Bible continues to ring true in his life, and that this tradition has made those affirmations about God's power. But of course that provides no answer as to why he chooses to reaffirm this tradition's affirmations about God's power instead of its affirmations about God's total goodness.

Roth describes his position as an anti-theodicy. It *is*, but for a more important reason than the one he gives. The task of theodicy is to show how, in spite of evil, there is a power worthy of worship. The being Roth calls God is not one I can consider worthy of worship. Of course, Roth thinks the same of the God I portray. Since this God does not have the kind of coercive power needed to prevent natural and moral evil, Roth sees this God as "weak" and "ineffectual," and hence as "hardly worth bothering about." The contrast between Roth's position and mine raises clearly the question: what is it we should be "bothering about" in our religious activity, if we have to choose overwhelming power or overwhelming goodness?

Critique by John H. Hick

What Roth offers is, as he himself says, not so much a theodicy as an anti-theodicy. Such an anti-theodicy—crying out to God in protest and accusation, and yet assuming in that very act that God is both real and good—is a necessary complement to all attempts to produce a Christian theodicy. For when the theodicist has said all that he can say—showing, for example, how God might create humankind as an imperfect and immature creature who may in one's own freedom, in response to divine grace, develop spiritual potentialities and so eventually come to the heavenly Father; and how such a creature might require as the scene of his pilgrimage a hard and challenging environment rather than a paradise; and how it is that in such a person-making world the apparently random incidence of evil must remain mysterious to us; and how the whole harsh, blood-stained and tear-stained creative process may nevertheless be justified by the limitless good to which it leads—when all this and much more has been said the haunting question remains, is such a process really worthwhile? Is existence worth having on these terms? This was also Dostoevski's question. Ivan, in *The Brothers Karamazov*, says,

> Imagine that you are creating a fabric of human destiny with the object of making men happy in the end, giving them peace and rest at last, but that it was essential and inevitable to torture to death only one tiny creature—that baby beating its breast with its fist, for instance—and to found that edifice on its unavenged tears, would you consent to be the architect on those conditions? Tell me, and tell the truth.[27]

Any answer to this question will arise out of faith or lack of faith in God. If we are led by our own religious experience to make the ultimate affirmation of the reality and love of God, then we can only believe that his creative work *is* in the end worthwhile. But we cannot profess to foresee, except in the utmost generality, *how* this is going to be so. We can only live in faith and hope—faith being a present awareness of existing in the presence of God, and hope being that faith projected onto the future. And because we are spiritually weak, because our faith is a wavering rather than a steady state, the note of protest and accusation remains a natural, indeed an inevitable, ingredient of our being. Such protest is an acknowledgment of the sheer mystery which surrounds us, in the face of which we both believe and doubt, both praise and protest. The two go together, for the other side of protest is belief: in accusing God one implicitly affirms his presence.

It is a reflection of our human limitations that different writers on theodicy generally voice these two different aspects of our situation, some constructing theodicies and others articulating the persisting protest. Being the limited creatures that we are, we function in terms of specialized vocations. Thus, in relation to the theodicy issue, Davis and I both feel a vocation to try to develop constructive theories, whilst Roth evidently feels a vocation to bear witness to the insufficiency of any theodicy, and to voice the protest and accusation which has been part of people's response to the problem of evil since the time of Job.

I therefore see considerable wisdom in Roth's emphasis that "Human religious needs are diverse. No simple response can encompass them all or nourish every spirit." It may well be that we—the Christian community as a whole, or more widely the world religious community as a whole—need a variety both of theodicies and of anti-theodicies, or theodicies of protest. The Irenaean theodicist should be particularly open to a brother anti-theodicist, since the Irenaen type of theodicy concludes that God alone is ultimately responsible for the existence of the actual universe, including all its evil. Monotheism means that "the buck stops" only at the throne of God. In moments of deep anguish, with the redeeming future beyond our horizon we can only cry out in protest; and that protest must be directed in faith to God.

Roth's Response to Critiques

No statement, theological or otherwise, should be made that would not be credible in the presence of burning children.
—Irving Greenberg, "Cloud of Smoke, Pillar of Fire: Judaism, Christianity, and Modernity after the Holocaust"[28]

. . . God is light and in him is no darkness at all.
—1 John 1:5

"Perhaps some day I shall know how to laugh again."[29] When those words were published in 1944, a Jewish carpenter named Jankiel Wiernik was unsure. Deported by the Nazis from Warsaw to Treblinka on August 23, 1942, Wiernik would escape in a death camp revolt. But prior to that time, he went through experiences that made him say: "My life is embittered. Phantoms of death haunt me, specters of children, little children, nothing but children. I sacrificed all those nearest and dearest to me. I myself took them to the execution site. I built their death chambers for them."[30]

Jankiel Wiernik is on my mind as I reflect on the insightful replies that Davis, Griffin, Hick, and Sontag have made to "A Theodicy of Protest." So is Irving Greenberg's statement about burning children. So is the New Testament. As I respond to some of the most important questions raised about my point of view, I also mull over William James' conviction that people do have different spiritual needs.

What makes religion vital? According to David Griffin, the vitality of religion entails "the desire to be in harmony with what is taken to be the Holy Reality." No doubt that desire is fundamental. At the same time, harmony with God ought to be problematic after Auschwitz, and it is. Hence religion's vitality may depend less on Griffin's desire alone and more on what is done with that desire when it cannot be easily satisfied.

Certainly Griffin is correct: vital religous life depends on God's goodness. Another of his concerns—"belief that God is not perfectly good will eventually undercut our own concern for moral goodness"—cannot be regarded lightly either. Thus, a theodicy of protest takes God's goodness as one of its starting points, and it persists in emphasizing that goodness until the end. To be for-God-against-God makes sense only in light of the good that God has done and still might do in the future. Specifically, that stance makes sense only in light of this good news: God "loves righteousness and justice" and "love never ends" (Ps. 33:5 and 1 Cor. 13:8).

Granted, this theodicy does find God's total goodness wanting. It therefore refuses simple harmony with God as well. Within this perspective, however, *disharmony* intensifies concern for moral goodness. Yearning for harmony with God is felt, and yet that yearning must not and cannot be satisfied unless things change for good. Men and women have to do everything they can in that direction. History makes that point plain. It also shows that God must make his goodness much more decisive than heretofore.

Elie Wiesel says that a Jew "defines himself more by what troubles him than by what reassures him."[31] Jewish or not, morally concerned and vitally religious persons can be defined in the same way. "In the long run?" asks David Griffin. We shall have to see, which is to say that Paul is also correct: "work out your own salvation with fear and trembling" (Phil. 2:12).

Is Scripture authoritative for a theodicy of protest? Davis quizzes all of us about the use of Scripture in this book's theodicies. His probing is fair, and it merits a response in relation to what I just said about vitality in religious life. Scripture is authoritative in my theodicy; therefore, tensions abound. They do so because Scripture can never be the only authority in a person's life. What one feels, sees, comes to understand in other ways, has authority, too. Thus, the issue of how to sift and sort biblical words looms large.

Virtually every Sunday I hear that God is love, that he "is light and in him is no darkness at all." How do I react to those claims? If I said that I believed them, I would be lying. If I said that I did *not* believe them, I would also be lying. The former feeling has roots in my experience. So does the latter. My position copes between "yes" and "no"; God is love . . . but not enough. God is light

... but not enough, at least not for now. Smoke and shadow have authority along with Word made flesh or written.

What is the point? Do not let the tension go. To let it go invites harmony that flirts with indifference. So, hear that God is love, that he is light without darkness, that with him all things are possible. And then look again at the world, at freedom, at all that wastes us away. How does God's word retain authority in such a world? One way includes quarreling with it. Refuse to let its messages go unheard and unheeded, but also refuse to let them be totally acceptable unless things change for the better.

Cannot all evil be redeemed? Once more the voice belongs to Stephen Davis, who shares with me a belief in God's omnipotence. This time Davis questions the consistency of my emphasis that "with God all things are possible" (Matt. 19:26). If God is limited only by his own will, then why can it not be true that God "will one day achieve such great goods that all past evils will pale into insignificance, even for the victims and sufferers?" Davis admits that the past cannot be retrieved. Jankiel Wiernik's experience cannot be undone, but could not an omnipotent God render Wiernik's pain insignificant in comparison to greater goods that lie beyond it?

No doubt God could render Wiernik's suffering insignificant. He may have done so already, but the issue is *how*. God could forget Jankiel Wiernik. Or God might erase Wiernik's memory, or even persuade him with overwhelming good. But if God does so, should the outcome be accepted completely, praised unequivocally? Or should it be reiterated that God's omnipotence is bound by his own will, the very will that permitted Treblinka and underwrote a not-so-new testament from the tortured Jewish hand of a surviving carpenter?

To redeem means to make amends. God can give back what was lost. We should hope that he does so. Time does heal some wounds, but short of loss of memory, losses remain losses, most of them as needless as they were painful. Should Jankiel Wiernik discover that *anything* pales his past into insignificance, I hope that he laughs ... madly.

How long has God had a "moral defect?" David Griffin raises this issue, and the defect in question is one that impugns God's total goodness, namely, his penchant for needless waste. Griffin answers his question well: presumably forever. But then he argues that this divine defect may be necessary and therefore beyond redemption altogether. Although Griffin may be right on that score, too, I demur. If God's power is bound only by his own unnecessitated will, as I believe, then God can change his ways. Moreover, if the biblical narratives can be trusted at all, God's activities do form changed ways from time to time.

Conviction that God acted in events such as the exodus and Easter stands in stark contrast to what would otherwise be inferred about the nature and destiny of human life: for example, that Jankiel Wiernik witnessed Jews exterminated and the matter ends there as far as their personal lives are concerned. Ironically, then, the "good news" of Christianity is one factor that makes God's moral defect stand out all the more, unless one is persuaded when Griffin says that it is "an extremely weak argument" to state that if God raised Jesus from the dead, he had the might to thwart a Holocaust.

Human beings could have prevented the Holocaust. They did not. God can raise the dead to life, which so far as I know is something that no human persons can do. If he could bring Jesus back from total lifelessness to life, I believe that God could have changed the minds of Nazi leaders, thereby preventing Auschwitz. The reason for my belief has to do with overwhelming power that could be used for good ends far more than it is. If God wants to be morally defective, or to claim that he is not even if someone disagrees, or if he just wants to be serenely indifferent to the whole affair, I judge that he can do so. For the sake of Jankiel Wiernik, though, I hope that God gets his act together a little . . . no, a lot better . . . and soon.

Does my theodicy legitimate evil? Another good question comes from David Griffin. This one is based on the charge that—my intentions to the contrary notwithstanding—God's unnecessary involvement in waste makes evil unavoidable and also insurmountable on earth. God's decisions do make some evil unavoidable. Moreover, evil's accumulated effects leave us now in a situation where the waste we must combat cannot be totally surmounted by human energies alone. Indeed hope that is contrary to that realistic outlook can be a dangerous trap. It may stimulate conviction that we really can take fate into our own hands and transform the world along the lines of some utopian vision. Either such beliefs lean toward totalitarian nightmares or they must become more sober in realizing that on earth not all good things are going to be. None of these points, however, legitimate (i.e., justify) evil. This theodicy rests on the conviction that waste is never necessary.

The waste looming before us ought not to be. In addition, *ought* implies *can*, at least in my vocabulary. People can do much to thwart evil but not everything, and thus God's responsibility stands out once more. The evil that Jankiel Wiernik witnessed ought not to have been, and if men and women would not or could not prevent it, God should have done so and he could have. His will keeps pressure on us. If he regards evil as legitimate, that option is his business. Ours is to be sure that we do not agree, and then it is to act accordingly. As we do so, our protest and defiance may testify that in being for-God-against-God "we live and move and have our being" (Acts 17:28).

Does forgiveness justify God fully? Frederick Sontag rightly identifies a basic Christian message: God forgives sin. No genuine Christian experience can exist without consciousness of sin *and* some sense of release from its clutches. "Having accepted the justification of himself before God which the Christian forgiveness of sin offers," Sontag goes on to argue, "he or she transfers this across to God and assumes that God is fully justified too." Forgiveness is tricky business. There can be no lasting friendship without it, and therefore forgiveness should be sought, urged, and practiced without ceasing by humanity and God alike. But once we ask "Who can forgive whom and for what?" the situation complicates.

One who is wronged can forgive that wrong, but not always in ways that set everything right, unless we are willing to settle for an unwarranted authority that overlooks too many victims. For example, God can forgive the wrong I do to him, which may involve his identification with persons harmed by my actions. But where forgiveness is concerned, God cannot rightly speak for Jankiel Wiernik. And no Christian can either. To think otherwise is to allow God or our own arrogance to usurp the victim's prerogative and responsibility. Likewise, if God shares responsibility for the world's needless pain, then any one of us may forgive God for the evil from which he or she goes undelivered, but it is no one's place to speak for victims other than oneself. To do so, and especially for anyone to forgive God for *all* that has gone wrong at his hands, is to speak out of turn. It makes suffering insignificant through indifference.

God's integrity should not be mocked. Therefore, he should tolerate no cheap forgiveness of his own sin any more than he should permit us to bathe contentedly in cheap grace. And yet forgiveness might reconcile us—God and humankind—if it follows John Hick's model of being a free response on all sides. Whether it can ever justify God fully, however, is another matter, one that memories may determine differently.

Does "A Theodicy of Protest" turn me and others anti-religious? Yes, suggests Sontag, unless I answer this question satisfactorily: "Why did God create a wasteful world that incites us to rebellion?" To duplicate a move made frequently by Sontag himself, whether the outcome of his "yes" is good or bad depends on how some terms are understood, in this case "religious" and "anti-religious." If being "religious" means that one does or must have some single, fixed answer to the question "Why?", then I am anti-religious. For I do not know any answer that should or can silence all the "Whys?" short of an act of will that says: "Here I stand." But "Here I stand" makes good sense only if it holds unsatisfiable "Whys?" in tension with commitment.

To stay honest, theodicy needs anti-theodicy. The result of such tension, however, need not be anti-religious. Quite to the contrary, the result may be profoundly religious, if religious experience is understood as quest, odyssey, pilgrimage. Such spiritual journeys combine awe and mystery with intensity that protests against God in refusing to despair. Therefore, they can also lead one to stand with God in affirming that "every perfect gift is from above, coming down from the Father of lights" (James 1:17).

Tension between the "religious" and the "anti-religious" is ancient and multi-faceted. In the case at hand, it lives within an individual Christian who believes that the health of Christianity and indeed of humankind requires that at least some men and women should be religiously anti-religious, which is to say: for God *and* against God. I hope that this struggle will not leave me alone.

Still, for what do I hope? This question is from Davis. Behind it stands another: in a theodicy of protest, is there really any ground for hope at all? My reply is written in December. Shortest light and longest night are not far off. And yet these winter days are also the season of Hanukkah, the Feast of Lights, which commemorates the rededication of a Temple and tells us that energy to keep lamps burning can be replenished. In cold darkness the Christian calendar marks Advent, a time of expectant waiting, and then Christmas, which celebrates a promise made good, at least in part.

We shall pass through December, but not completely. Advent remains because God's promises, good though they are, still keep us waiting. Acceptance of those promises, especially when they are perceived as coming from a God whose goodness is less than whole, is as risky as childbirth in a Bethlehem stable. Is the risk too great? Responses to that question depend on the content of hope and on the odds against it.

In the words of the Christian creed from Nicaea, I "look for the resurrection of the dead, and the life of the world to come." Thus, I hope that Jankiel Wiernik will laugh again—joyously, honestly, without his past paled into insignificance, and without derangement. As for life right now, I hope that waste, such as that which stole Wiernik's laughter, can be checked. In this world I expect no ultimate beating of swords into plowshares, but absence of strenuous effort in that direction will be more than a sin. It will move toward punishment itself, for indifference to our own existence may finish us all. If that realization does not foster protesting hope against despair, we are in deep trouble.

Healing and restoration are badly needed. They will not set everything right, however. Existence is permanently scarred. Still, my proposition is that life can be better. If the risks and odds are vast, as surely they must be for anyone who will look and see, then my hope entails the conviction that those very odds must themselves become reasons that provoke us to do battle against them. Davis says he will only trust a God who is wholly good. He seems to have located such a God, and I am glad for the trust that he can have. To me, however, Davis' God stays hidden, absent, even non-existent. That fact makes hope risky. But risky hope need not die, and it does not.

Does a theodicy of protest make worship impossible? The criticism implied here is that any God less than wholly good deserves no worship. But does authentic worship really depend so much on God's purity and innocence? Like Davis, I do not wish to honor a Caligula or a Stalin. The very notion is abhorrent. Having rejected that option, however, it does not follow that I can sing a doxology—"Praise God from whom all blessings flow"—only if I believe that expressions of thanksgiving and awe-filled love are sufficient worship-responses.

Worship cannot have vitality without praise and thanksgiving. But honesty is no less important to its life. In worship one professes and celebrates God's goodness to the extent that such goodness is experienced and thereby anticipated. Other things have been experienced, too, and they rightly produce lamentation and rage, heartbreak and melancholy. God, why did you create this world? Why did you invent suffering? Why did you form men and women in your image? Those questions belong in post-Holocaust sanctuaries. Responses to them do as well: love, freedom, soul-making—those motifs have a place—but the "Whys?" remain. All good worship ends by sending people forth to relieve suffering, to create joy, and to make friends out of enemies. Thus, by showing that it is our task to turn divine injustice into human justice and compassion, by giving voice to commitment for-God-against-God, a theodicy of protest is itself a fitting act of worship after Auschwitz.

Will protest sell in Peoria? Frederick Sontag is unsure; John Hick thinks it should, at least on occasion. Both replies ring true to me. That experience, in turn, leads me to comment on one of the most important things I have learned in working on this book: none of the views expressed in these pages, including my own, satisfy me completely. And yet all of them express something that appeals to me, something I would like to share.

I admire Davis' confidence, and if I cannot possess it, that outcome is no cause for celebration. All can be well in the end, says John Hick. That message is winsome. I need to hear such claims from time to time even if I do not embrace them fully. David Griffin's yearning for goodness, his hunger and thirst for righteousness, are unmistakable. I thank him for his fervor, even as I find him saying too much and too little. Frederick Sontag prods us all to re-evaluate assumptions and to struggle with crucial words whose meanings elude unanimous agreement. Like his willful God, who does things because he wants to, Sontag burdens and provokes us but not without love. Finally, my protest seems to have a place as well. It is a moment, a fragment of human effort to cope with God and with human life alike. To keep faith in ferment, protest should be heard in Peoria no less than in Claremont. Maybe it will be.

A problem remains. How, if at all, can these pieces fit together? One possibility may be shown, more than said, by the pages of this book. The words set down here have taken the writers on a journey. All of us—I hope—have been stretched, changed by being opened up. Where theodicy, or anti-theodicy, is concerned, perhaps that outcome is the point: do not sit tight. Question and move.

In his memoir, *Night,* Elie Wiesel recounts a boyhood conversation with his eccentric teacher, Moché the Beadle.

> "Man raises himself toward God by the questions he asks Him," he was fond of repeating. "That is the true dialogue. Man questions God and God answers. But we don't understand His answers. We can't understand them. Because they come from the depths of the soul, and they stay there until death. You will find the true answers, Eliezer, only within yourself!"

"And why do you pray, Moché?" I asked him.

"I pray to the God within me that He will give me the strength to ask Him the right questions."[32]

Jankiel Wiernik remains on my mind. So do burning children. So does the message that "God is light and in him is no darkness at all." Questions remain as well. I pray they are the right ones.

2 An Irenaean Theodicy

JOHN H. HICK

Can a world in which sadistic cruelty often has its way, in which selfish lovelessness is so rife, in which there are debilitating diseases, crippling accidents, bodily and mental decay, insanity, and all manner of natural disasters be regarded as the expression of infinite creative goodness? Certainly all this could never by itself lead anyone to believe in the existence of a limitlessly powerful God. And yet even in a world which contains these things innumerable men and women have believed and do believe in the reality of an infinite creative goodness, which they call God. The theodicy project starts at this point, with an already operating belief in God, embodied in human living, and attempts to show that this belief is not rendered irrational by the fact of evil. It attempts to explain how it is that the universe, assumed to be created and ultimately ruled by a limitlessly good and limitlessly powerful Being, is as it is, including all the pain and suffering and all the wickedness and folly that we find around us and within us. The theodicy project is thus an exercise in metaphysical construction, in the sense that it consists in the formation and criticism of large-scale hypotheses concerning the nature and process of the universe.

Since a theodicy both starts from and tests belief in the reality of God, it naturally takes different forms in relation to different concepts of God. In this paper I shall be discussing the project of a specifically Christian theodicy; I shall not be attempting the further and even more difficult work of comparative theodicy, leading in turn to the question of a global theodicy.

The two main demands upon a theodicy-hypothesis are (1) that it be internally coherent, and (2) that it be consistent with the data both of the religious tradition on which it is based, and of the world, in respect both of the latter's general character as revealed by scientific enquiry and of the specific facts of moral and natural evil. These two criteria demand, respectively, possibility and plausibility.

Traditionally, Christian theology has centered upon the concept of God as both limitlessly powerful and limitlessly good and loving; and it is this concept of deity that gives rise to the problem of evil as a threat to theistic faith. The threat was definitively expressed in Stendhal's bombshell, "The only excuse for God is that he does not exist!" The theodicy project is the attempt to offer a different view of the universe which is both possible and plausible and which does not ignite Stendhal's bombshell.

Christian thought has always included a certain range of variety, and in the area of theodicy it offers two broad types of approach. The Augustinian approach, representing until fairly recently the majority report of the Christian mind, hinges upon the idea of the fall, which has in turn brought about the disharmony of nature. This type of theodicy is developed today as "the free will defense." The Irenaean approach, representing in the past a minority report, hinges upon the creation of humankind through the evolutionary process as an immature creature living in a challenging and therefore person-making world. I shall indicate very briefly why I do not find the first type of theodicy satisfactory, and then spend the remainder of this paper in exploring the second type.

In recent years the philosophical discussion of the problem of evil has been dominated by the free-will defense. A major effort has been made by Alvin Plantinga and a number of other Christian philosophers to show that it is logically possible that a limitlessly powerful and limitlessly good God is responsible for the existence of this world. For all evil may ultimately be due to misuses of creaturely freedom. But it may nevertheless be better for God to have created free than unfree beings; and it is logically possible that any and all free beings whom God might create would, as a matter of contingent fact, misuse their freedom by falling into sin. In that case it would be logically impossible for God to have created a world containing free beings and yet not containing sin and the suffering which sin brings with it. Thus it is logically possible, despite the fact of evil, that the existing universe is the work of a limitlessly good creator.

These writers are in effect arguing that the traditional Augustinian type of theodicy, based upon the fall from grace of free finite creatures — first angels and then human beings — and a consequent going wrong of the physical world, is not logically impossible. I am in fact doubtful whether their argument is sound, and will return to the question later. But even if it should be sound, I suggest that their argument wins only a Pyrrhic victory, since the logical possibility that it would establish is one which, for very many people today, is fatally lacking in plausibility. For most educated inhabitants of the modern world regard the biblical story of Adam and Eve, and their temptation by the devil, as myth rather than as history; and they believe that so far from having been created finitely perfect and then falling, humanity evolved out of lower forms of life, emerging in a morally, spiritually, and culturally primitive state. Further, they reject as incredible the idea that earthquake and flood, disease, decay, and death are consequences either of a human fall, or of a prior fall of angelic beings who are now exerting an evil influence upon the earth. They see all this as part of a pre-scientific world view, along with the stories of the world having been created in six days and of the sun standing still for twenty-four hours at Joshua's command. One cannot, strictly speaking, disprove any of these ancient biblical myths and sagas, or refute their confident elaboration in the medieval Christian picture of the universe. But those of us for whom the resulting theodicy, even if logically possible, is radically implausible, must look elsewhere for light on the problem of evil.

I believe that we find the light that we need in the main alternative strand of Christian thinking, which goes back to important constructive suggestions by the early Hellenistic Fathers of the Church, particularly St. Irenaeus (A.D. 120-202). Irenaeus himself did not develop a theodicy, but he did — together with other Greek-speaking Christian writers of that period, such as Clement of Alexandria — build a framework of thought within which a theodicy became possible which does not depend upon the idea of the fall, and which is consonant with modern knowledge concerning the origins of the human race. This theodicy cannot, as such, be attributed to Irenaeus. We should rather speak of a type of theodicy, presented in varying ways by different subsequent thinkers (the greatest of whom has been Friedrich Schleiermacher), of which Irenaeus can properly be regarded as the patron saint.

The central theme out of which this Irenaean type of theodicy has arisen is the two-stage conception of the creation of humankind, first in the "image" and then in the "likeness" of God. Re-expressing this in modern terms, the first stage was the gradual production of *homo sapiens*, through the long evolutionary process, as intelligent ethical and religious animals. The human being is an animal, one of the varied forms of earthly life and continuous as such with the whole realm of animal existence. But the human being is uniquely intelligent, having evolved a large and immensely complex brain. Further, the human being is ethical — that is, a gregarious as well as an intelligent animal, able to realize and respond to the complex demands of social life. And the human being is a religious animal, with an innate tendency to experience the world in terms of the presence and activity of supernatural beings and powers. This then is early *homo sapien*, the intelligent social animal capable of awareness of the divine. But early *homo sapien* is not the Adam and Eve of Augustinian theology, living in perfect harmony with self, with nature, and with God. On the contrary, the life of this being must have been a constant struggle against a hostile environment, and capable of savage violence against one's fellow human beings, particularly outside one's own immediate group; and this being's concepts of the divine were primitive and often blood-thirsty. Thus existence "in the image of God" was a potentiality for knowledge of and relationship with one's Maker rather than such knowledge and relationship as a fully realized state. In other words, people were created as spiritually and morally immature creatures, at the beginning of a long process of further growth and development, which constitutes the second stage of God's creative work. In this second stage, of which we are a part, the intelligent, ethical, and religious animal is being brought through one's own free responses into what Irenaeus called the divine "likeness." The human animal is being created into a child of God. Irenaeus' own terminology (*eikon, homoiosis; imago, similitudo*) has no particular merit, based as it is on a misunderstanding of the Hebrew parallelism in Genesis 1:26; but his conception of a two-stage creation of the human, with perfection lying in the future rather than in the past, is of fundamental importance. The notion of the fall was not basic to this picture, although it was to become basic to the great drama of salvation depicted by St. Augustine and accepted within western Christendom, including the churches stemming from the Reformation, until well into the nineteenth century. Irenaeus himself however could not, in the historical knowledge of his time, question the fact of the fall; though he treated it as a relatively minor lapse, a youthful error, rather than as the infinite crime and cosmic disaster which has ruined the whole creation. But today we can acknowledge that there is no evidence at all of a period in the distant past when humankind was in the ideal state of a fully realized "child of God." We can accept that, so far as actual events in time are concerned, there never was a fall from an original righteousness and grace. If we want to continue to use the term fall, because of its hallowed place in the Christian tradition, we must use it to refer to the immense gap between what we actually are and what in the divine intention is eventually to be. But we must not blur our awareness that the ideal state is not something already enjoyed and lost, but is a future and as yet unrealized goal. The reality is not a perfect creation which has gone tragically wrong, but a still continuing creative process whose completion lies in the eschaton.

Let us now try to formulate a contemporary version of the Irenaean type of theodicy, based on this suggestion of the initial creation of humankind, not as a finitely perfect, but as an immature creature at the beginning of a long process of further growth and development. We may begin by asking why one should have been created as an imperfect and developing creature rather than as the perfect being whom God is presumably intending to create? The answer, I think, consists in two considerations which converge in their practical implications, one concerned with the human's relationship to God and the other with the relationship to other human beings. As to the first, we could have the picture of God creating finite beings, whether angels or persons, directly in his own presence, so that in being conscious of that which is other than one's self the creature is automatically conscious of God, the limitless divine reality and power, goodness and love, knowledge and wisdom, towering above one's self. In such a situation the disproportion between Creator and creatures would be so great that the latter would have no freedom in relation to God; they would indeed not exist as independent autonomous persons. For what freedom could finite beings have in an immediate consciousness of the presence of the one who has created them, who knows them through and through, who is limitlessly powerful as well as limitlessly loving and good, and who claims their total obedience? In order to be a person, exercising some measure of genuine freedom, the creature must be brought into existence, not in the immediate divine presence, but at a "distance" from God. This "distance" cannot of course be spatial; for God is omnipresent. It must be an epistemic distance, a distance in the cognitive dimension. And the Irenaean hypothesis is that this "distance" consists, in the case of humans, in their existence within and as part of a world which functions as an autonomous system and from within which God is not overwhelmingly evident. It is a world, in Bonhoeffer's phrase, *etsi deus non daretur*, as if there were no God. Or rather, it is religiously ambiguous, capable both of being seen as a purely natural phenomenon and of being seen as God's creation and experienced as mediating his presence. In such a world one can exist as a person over against the Creator. One has space to exist as a finite being, a space created by the epistemic distance from God and protected by one's basic cognitive freedom, one's freedom to open or close oneself to the dawning awareness of God which is experienced naturally by a religious animal. This Irenaean picture corresponds, I suggest, to our actual human situation. Emerging within the evolutionary process as part of the continuum of animal life, in a universe which functions in accordance with its own laws and whose workings can be investigated and described without reference to a creator, the human being has a genuine, even awesome, freedom in relation to one's Maker. The human being is free to acknowledge and worship God; and is free – particularly since the emergence of human individuality and the beginnings of critical consciousness during the first millennium BC – to doubt the reality of God.

Within such a situation there is the possibility of the human being coming freely to know and love one's Maker. Indeed, if the end-state which God is seeking to bring about is one in which finite persons have come in their own freedom to know and love him, this requires creating them initially in a state which is not that of their already knowing and loving him. For it is logically impossible to create beings already in a state of having come into that state by their own free choices.

The other consideration, which converges with this in pointing to something like the human situation as we experience it, concerns our human moral nature. We can approach it by asking why humans should not have been created at this epistemic distance from God, and yet at the same time as morally perfect beings? That persons could have been created morally perfect and yet free, so that they would always in fact choose rightly, has been argued by such critics of the free-will defense in theodicy as Antony Flew and J.L. Mackie, and argued against by Alvin Plantinga and other upholders of that form of theodicy. On the specific issue defined in the debate between them, it appears to me that the criticism of the freewill defense stands. It appears to me that a perfectly good being, although formally free to sin, would in fact never do so. If we imagine such a being in a morally frictionless environment, involving no stresses or temptation, then we must assume that one would exemplify the ethical equivalent of Newton's first law of motion, which states that a moving body will continue in uniform motion until interfered with by some outside force. By analogy, a perfectly good being would continue in the same moral course forever, there being nothing in the environment to throw one off it. But even if we suppose the morally perfect being to exist in an imperfect world, in which one is subject to temptations, it still follows that, in virtue of moral perfection, one will always overcome those temptations – as in the case, according to orthodox Christian belief, of Jesus Christ. It is, to be sure, logically possible, as Plantinga and others argue, that a free being, simply as such, may at any time contingently decide to sin. However, a responsible free being does not act randomly, but on the basis of moral nature. And a free being whose nature is wholly and unqualifiedly good will accordingly never in fact sin.

But if God could, without logical contradiction, have created humans as wholly good free beings, why did he not do so? Why was humanity not initially created in possession of all the virtues, instead of having to acquire them through the long hard struggle of life as we know it? The answer, I suggest, appeals to the principle that virtues which have been formed within the agent as a hard won deposit of his own right decisions in situations of challenge and temptation, are intrinsically more valuable than virtues created within him ready made and without any effort on his own part. This principle expresses a basic value-judgment, which cannot be established by argument but which one can only present, in the hope that it will be as morally plausible, and indeed compelling, to others as to oneself. It is, to repeat, the judgement that a moral goodness which exists as the agent's initial given nature, without ever having been chosen by him in the face of temptations to the contrary, is intrinsically less valuable than a moral goodness which has been built up through the agent's own responsible choices through time in the face of alternative possibilities.

If, then, God's purpose was to create finite persons embodying the most valuable kind of moral goodness, he would have to create them, not as already perfect beings but rather as imperfect creatures who can then attain to the more valuable kind of goodness through their own free choices as in the course of their personal and social history new responses prompt new insights, opening up new moral possibilities, and providing a milieu in which the most valuable kind of moral nature can be developed.

We have thus far, then, the hypothesis that one is created at an epistemic distance from God in order to come freely to know and love the Maker; and that one is at the same time created as a morally immature and imperfect being in order to attain through freedom the most valuable quality of goodness. The end sought, according to this hypothesis, is the full realization of the human potentialities in a unitary spiritual and moral perfection in the divine kingdom. And the question we have to ask is whether humans as we know them, and the world as we know it, are compatible with this hypothesis.

Clearly we cannot expect to be able to deduce our actual world in its concrete character, and our actual human nature as part of it, from the general concept of spiritually and morally immature creatures developing ethically in an appropriate environment. No doubt there is an immense range of possible worlds, any one of which, if actualized, would exemplify this concept. All that we can hope to do is to show that our actual world is one of these. And when we look at our human situation as part of the evolving life of this planet we can, I think, see that it fits this specification. As animal organisms, integral to the whole ecology of life, we are programmed for survival. In pursuit of survival, primitives not only killed other animals for food but fought other human beings when their vital interests conflicted. The life of prehistoric persons must indeed have been a constant struggle to stay alive, prolonging an existence which was, in Hobbes' phrase, "poor, nasty, brutish and short." And in his basic animal self-regardingness humankind was, and is, morally imperfect. In saying this I am assuming that the essence of moral evil is selfishness, the sacrificing of others to one's own interests. It consists, in Kantian terminology, in treating others, not as ends in themselves, but as means to one's own ends. This is what the survival instinct demands. And yet we are also capable of love, of self-giving in a common cause, of a conscience which responds to others in their needs and dangers. And with the development of civilization we see the growth of moral insight, the glimpsing and gradual assimilation of higher ideals, and tension between our animality and our ethical values. But that the human being has a lower as well as a higher nature, that one is an animal as well as a potential child of God, and that one's moral goodness is won from a struggle with one's own innate selfishness, is inevitable given one's continuity with the other forms of animal life. Further, the human animal is not responsible for having come into existence as an animal. The ultimate responsibility for humankind's existence, as a morally imperfect creature, can only rest with the Creator. The human does not, in one's own degree of freedom and responsibility, choose one's origin, but rather one's destiny.

This then, in brief outline, is the answer of the Irenaean type of theodicy to the question of the origin of moral evil: the general fact of humankind's basic self-regarding animality is an aspect of creation as part of the realm of organic life; and this basic self-regardingness has been expressed over the centuries both in sins of individual selfishness and in the much more massive sins of corporate selfishness, institutionalized in slavery and exploitation and all the many and complex forms of social injustice.

But nevertheless our sinful nature in a sinful world is the matrix within which God is gradually creating children for himself out of human animals. For it is as men and women freely respond to the claim of God upon their lives, transmuting their animality into the structure of divine worship, that the creation of humanity is taking place. And in its concrete character this response consists in every form of moral goodness, from unselfish love in individual personal relationships to the dedicated and selfless striving to end exploitation and to create justice within and between societies.

But one cannot discuss moral evil without at the same time discussing the non-moral evil of pain and suffering. (I propose to mean by "pain" physical pain, including the pains of hunger and thirst; and by "suffering" the mental and emotional pain of loneliness, anxiety, remorse, lack of love, fear, grief, envy, etc.). For what constitutes moral evil as evil is the fact that it causes pain and suffering. It is impossible to conceive of an instance of moral evil, or sin, which is not productive of pain or suffering to anyone at any time. But in addition to moral evil there is another source of pain and suffering in the structure of the physical world, which produces storms, earthquakes, and floods and which afflicts the human body with diseases – cholera, epilepsy, cancer, malaria, arthritis, rickets, meningitis, etc. – as well as with broken bones and other outcomes of physical accident. It is true that a great deal both of pain and of suffering is humanly caused, not only by the inhumanity of man to man but also by the stresses of our individual and corporate life-styles, causing many disorders – not only lung cancer and cirrhosis of the liver but many cases of heart disease, stomach and other ulcers, strokes, etc. – as well as accidents. But there remain nevertheless, in the natural world itself, permanent causes of human pain and suffering. And we have to ask why an unlimitedly good and unlimitedly powerful God should have created so dangerous a world, both as regards its purely natural hazards of earthquake and flood etc., and as regards the liability of the human body to so many ills, both psychosomatic and purely somatic.

The answer offered by the Irenaean type of theodicy follows from and is indeed integrally bound up with its account of the origin of moral evil. We have the hypothesis of humankind being brought into being within the evolutionary process as a spiritually and morally immature creature, and then growing and developing through the exercise of freedom in this religiously ambiguous world. We can now ask what sort of a world would constitute an appropriate environment for this second stage of creation? The development of human personality – moral, spiritual, and intellectual – is a product of challenge and response. It does not occur in a static situation demanding no exertion and no choices. So far as intellectual development is concerned, this is a well-established principle which underlies the whole modern educational process, from pre-school nurseries designed to provide a rich and stimulating environment, to all forms of higher education designed to challenge the intellect. At a basic level the essential part played in learning by the learner's own active response to environment was strikingly demonstrated by the Held and Heim experiment with kittens.[1] Of two litter-mate kittens in the same artificial environment one was free to exercise its own freedom and intelligence in exploring the environment, whilst the other was suspended in a kind of "gondola" which moved whenever and wherever the free kitten moved. Thus the second kitten had a similar succession of visual experiences as the first, but did not exert itself or make any choices in obtaining them. And whereas the first kitten learned in the normal way to conduct itself safely within its environment, the second did not. With no interaction with a challenging environment there was no development in its behavioral patterns. And I think we can safely say that the intellectual development of humanity has been due to interaction with an objective environment functioning in accordance with its own laws, an environment which we have had actively to explore and to co-operate with in order to escape its perils and exploit its benefits. In a world devoid both of dangers to be avoided and rewards to be won we may assume that there would have been virtually no development of the human intellect and imagination, and hence of either the sciences or the arts, and hence of human civilization or culture.

The fact of an objective world within which one has to learn to live, on penalty of pain or death, is also basic to the development of one's moral nature. For it is because the world is one in which men and women can suffer harm — by violence, disease, accident, starvation, etc., — that our actions affecting one another have moral significance. A morally wrong act is, basically, one which harms some part of the human community; whilst a morally right action is, on the contrary, one which prevents or neutralizes harm or which preserves or increases human well being. Now we can imagine a paradise in which no one can ever come to any harm. It could be a world which, instead of having its own fixed structure, would be plastic to human wishes. Or it could be a world with a fixed structure, and hence the possibility of damage and pain, but whose structure is suspended or adjusted by special divine action whenever necessary to avoid human pain. Thus, for example, in such a miraculously pain-free world one who falls accidentally off a high building would presumably float unharmed to the ground; bullets would become insubstantial when fired at a human body; poisons would cease to poison; water to drown, and so on. We can at least begin to imagine such a world. And a good deal of the older discussion of the problem of evil — for example in Part xi of Hume's *Dialogues Concerning Natural Religion* — assumed that it must be the intention of a limitlessly good and powerful Creator to make for human creatures a pain-free environment; so that the very existence of pain is evidence against the existence of God. But such an assumption overlooks the fact that a world in which there can be no pain or suffering would also be one in which there can be no moral choices and hence no possibility of moral growth and development. For in a situation in which no one can ever suffer injury or be liable to pain or suffering there would be no distinction between right and wrong action. No action would be morally wrong, because no action could have harmful consequences; and likewise no action would be morally right in contrast to wrong. Whatever the values of such a world, it clearly could not serve a purpose of the development of its inhabitants from self-regarding animality to self-giving love.

Thus the hypothesis of a divine purpose in which finite persons are created at an epistemic distance from God, in order that they may gradually become children of God through their own moral and spiritual choices, requires that their environment, instead of being a pain-free and stress-free paradise, be broadly the kind of world of which we find ourselves to be a part. It requires that it be such as to provoke the theological problem of evil. For it requires that it be an environment which offers challenges to be met, problems to be solved, dangers to be faced, and which accordingly involves real possibilities of hardship, disaster, failure, defeat, and misery as well as of delight and happiness, success, triumph and achievement. For it is by grappling with the real problems of a real environment, in which a person is one form of life among many, and which is not designed to minister exclusively to one's well-being, that one can develop in intelligence and in such qualities as courage and determination. And it is in the relationships of human beings with one another, in the context of this struggle to survive and flourish, that they can develop the higher values of mutual love and care, of self-sacrifice for others, and of commitment to a common good.

To summarize thus far:

(1) The divine intention in relation to humankind, according to our hypothesis, is to create perfect finite personal beings in filial relationship with their Maker.

(2) It is logically impossible for humans to be created already in this perfect state, because in its spiritual aspect it involves coming freely to an uncoerced consciousness of God from a situation of epistemic distance, and in its moral aspect, freely choosing the good in preference to evil.

(3) Accordingly the human being was initially created through the evolutionary process, as a spiritually and morally immature creature, and as part of a world which is both religiously ambiguous and ethically demanding.

(4) Thus that one is morally imperfect (i.e., that there is moral evil), and that the world is a challenging and even dangerous environment (i.e., that there is natural evil), are necessary aspects of the present stage of the process through which God is gradually creating perfected finite persons.

In terms of this hypothesis, as we have developed it thus far, then, both the basic moral evil in the human heart and the natural evils of the world are compatible with the existence of a Creator who is unlimited in both goodness and power. But is the hypothesis plausible as well as possible? The principal threat to its plausibility comes, I think, from the sheer amount and intensity of both moral and natural evil. One can accept the principle that in order to arrive at a freely chosen goodness one must start out in a state of moral immaturity and imperfection. But is it necessary that there should be the depths of demonic malice and cruelty which each generation has experienced, and which we have seen above all in recent history in the Nazi attempt to exterminate the Jewish population of Europe? Can any future fulfillment be worth such horrors? This was Dostoevski's haunting question: "Imagine that you are creating a fabric of human destiny with the object of making men happy in the end, giving them peace and rest at last, but that it was essential and inevitable to torture to death only one tiny creature — that baby beating its breast with its fist, for instance — and to found that edifice on its unavenged tears, would you consent to be the architect on those conditions?"[2] The theistic answer is one which may be true but which takes so large a view that it baffles the imagination. Intellectually one may be able to see, but emotionally one cannot be expected to feel, its truth; and in that sense it cannot satisfy us. For the theistic answer is that if we take with full seriousness the value of human freedom and responsibility, as essential to the eventual creation of perfected children of God, then we cannot consistently want God to revoke that freedom when its wrong exercise becomes intolerable to us. From our vantage point within the historical process we may indeed cry out to God to revoke his gift of freedom, or to overrule it by some secret or open intervention. Such a cry must have come from millions caught in the Jewish Holocaust, or in the yet more recent laying waste of Korea and Vietnam, or from the victims of racism in many parts of the world. And the thought that humankind's moral freedom is indivisible, and can lead eventually to a consummation of limitless value which could never be attained without that freedom, and which is worth any finite suffering in the course of its creation, can be of no comfort to those who are now in the midst of that suffering. But whilst fully acknowledging this, I nevertheless want to insist that this eschatological answer may well be true. Expressed in religious language it tells us to trust in God even in the midst of deep suffering, for in the end we shall participate in his glorious kingdom.

Again, we may grant that a world which is to be a person-making environment cannot be a pain-free paradise but must contain challenges and dangers, with real possibilities of many kinds of accident and disaster, and the pain and suffering which they bring. But need it contain the worst forms of disease and catastrophe? And need misfortune fall upon us with such heartbreaking indiscriminateness? Once again there are answers, which may well be true, and yet once again the truth in this area may offer little in the way of pastoral balm. Concerning the intensity of natural evil, the truth is probably that our judgments of intensity are relative. We might identify some form of natural evil as the worst that there is — say the agony that can be caused by death from cancer — and claim that a loving God would not have allowed this to exist. But in a world in which there was no cancer, something else would then rank as the worst form of natural evil. If we then eliminate this, something else; and so on. And the process would continue until the world was free of all natural evil. For whatever form of evil for the time being remained would be intolerable to the inhabitants of that world. But in removing all occasions of pain and suffering, and hence all challenge and all need for mutual care, we should have converted the world from a person-making into a static environment, which could not elicit moral growth. In short, having accepted that a person-making world must have its dangers and therefore also its tragedies, we must accept that whatever form these take will be intolerable to the inhabitants of that world. There could not be a person-making world devoid of what we call evil; and evils are never tolerable – except for the sake of greater goods which may come out of them.

But accepting that a person-making environment must contain causes of pain and suffering, and that no pain or suffering is going to be acceptable, one of the most daunting and even terrifying features of the world is that calamity strikes indiscriminately. There is no justice in the incidence of disease, accident, disaster and tragedy. The righteous as well as the unrighteous are struck down by illness and afflicted by misfortune. There is no security in goodness, but the good are as likely as the wicked to suffer ''the slings and arrows of outrageous fortune.'' From the time of Job this fact has set a glaring question mark against the goodness of God. But let us suppose that things were otherwise. Let us suppose that misfortune came upon humankind, not haphazardly and therefore unjustly, but justly and therefore not haphazardly. Let us suppose that instead of coming without regard to moral considerations, it was proportioned to desert, so that the sinner was punished and the virtuous rewarded. Would such a dispensation serve a person-making purpose? Surely not. For it would be evident that wrong deeds bring disaster upon the agent whilst good deeds bring health and prosperity; and in such a world truly moral action, action done because it is right, would be impossible. The fact that natural evil is not morally directed, but is a hazard which comes by chance, is thus an intrinsic feature of a person-making world.

In other words, the very mystery of natural evil, the very fact that disasters afflict human beings in contingent, undirected and haphazard ways, is itself a necessary feature of a world that calls forth mutual aid and builds up mutual caring and love. Thus on the one hand it would be completely wrong to say that God sends misfortune upon individuals, so that their death, maiming, starvation or ruin is God's will for them. But on the other hand God has set us in a world containing unpredictable contingencies and dangers, in which unexpected and undeserved calamities may occur to anyone; because only in such a world can mutual caring and love be elicited. As an abstract philosophical hypothesis this may offer little comfort. But translated into religious language it tells us that God's good purpose enfolds the entire process of this world, with all its good and bad contingencies, and that even amidst tragic calamity and suffering we are still within the sphere of his love and are moving towards his kingdom.

But there is one further all-important aspect of the Irenaean type of theodicy, without which all the foregoing would lose its plausibility. This is the eschatological aspect. Our hypothesis depicts persons as still in course of creation towards an end-state of perfected personal community in the divine kingdom. This end-state is conceived of as one in which individual egoity has been transcended in communal unity before God. And in the present phase of that creative process the naturally self-centered human animal has the opportunity freely to respond to God's non-coercive self-disclosures, through the work of prophets and saints, through the resulting religious traditions, and through the individual's religious experience. Such response always has an ethical aspect; for the growing awareness of God is at the same time a growing awareness of the moral claim which God's presence makes upon the way in which we live.

But it is very evident that this person-making process, leading eventually to perfect human community, is not completed on this earth. It is not completed in the life of the individual – or at best only in the few who have attained to sanctification, or moksha, or nirvana on this earth. Clearly the enormous majority of men and women die without having attained to this. As Eric Fromm has said, "The tragedy in the life of most of us is that we die before we are fully born."[3] And therefore if we are ever to reach the full realization of the potentialities of our human nature, this can only be in a continuation of our lives in another sphere of existence after bodily death. And it is equally evident that the perfect all-embracing human community, in which self-regarding concern has been transcended in mutual love, not only has not been realized in this world, but never can be, since hundreds of generations of human beings have already lived and died and accordingly could not be part of any ideal community established at some future moment of earthly history. Thus if the unity of humankind in God's presence is ever to be realized it will have to be in some sphere of existence other than our earth. In short, the fulfillment of the divine purpose, as it is postulated in the Irenaean type of theodicy, presupposes each person's survival, in some form of bodily death, and further living and growing towards that end-state. Without such an eschatological fulfillment, this theodicy would collapse.

A theodicy which presupposes and requires an eschatology will thereby be rendered implausible in the minds of many today. I nevertheless do not see how any coherent theodicy can avoid dependence upon an eschatology. Indeed I would go further and say that the belief in the reality of a limitlessly loving and powerful deity must incorporate some kind of eschatology according to which God holds in being the creatures whom he has made for fellowship with himself, beyond bodily death, and brings them into the eternal fellowship which he has intended for them. I have tried elsewhere to argue that such an eschatology is a necessary corollary of ethical monotheism; to argue for the realistic possibility of an after-life or lives, despite the philosophical and empirical arguments against this; and even to spell out some of the general features which human life after death may possibly have.[4] Since all this is a very large task, which would far exceed the bounds of this paper, I shall not attempt to repeat it here but must refer the reader to my existing discussion of it. It is that extended discussion that constitutes my answer to the question whether an Irenaean theodicy, with its eschatology, may not be as implausible as an Augustinian theodicy, with its human or angelic fall. (If it is, then the latter is doubly implausible; for it also involves an eschatology!)

There is however one particular aspect of eschatology which must receive some treatment here, however brief and inadequate. This is the issue of "universal salvation" versus "heaven and hell" (or perhaps annihilation instead of hell). If the justification of evil within the creative process lies in the limitless and eternal good of the end-state to which it leads, then the completeness of the justification must depend upon the completeness, or universality, of the salvation achieved. Only if it includes the entire human race can it justify the sins and sufferings of the entire human race throughout all history. But, having given human beings cognitive freedom, which in turn makes possible moral freedom, can the Creator bring it about that in the end all his human creatures freely turn to him in love and trust? The issue is a very difficult one; but I believe that it is in fact possible to reconcile a full affirmation of human freedom with a belief in the ultimate universal success of God's creative work. We have to accept that creaturely freedom always occurs within the limits of a basic nature that we did not ourselves choose; for this is entailed by the fact of having been created. If then a real though limited freedom does not preclude our being endowed with a certain nature, it does not preclude our being endowed with a basic Godward bias, so that, quoting from another side of St. Augustine's thought, "our hearts are restless until they find their rest in Thee."[5] If this is so, it can be predicted that sooner or later, in our own time and in our own way, we shall all freely come to God; and universal salvation can be affirmed, not as a logical necessity but as the contingent but predictable outcome of the process of the universe, interpreted theistically. Once again, I have tried to present this argument more fully elsewhere, and to consider various objections to it.[6]

On this view the human, endowed with a real though limited freedom, is basically formed for relationship with God and destined ultimately to find the fulfillment of his or her nature in that relationship. This does not seem to me excessively paradoxical. On the contrary, given the theistic postulate, it seems to me to offer a very probable account of our human situation. If so, it is a situation in which we can rejoice; for it gives meaning to our temporal existence as the long process through which we are being created, by our own free responses to life's mixture of good and evil, into "children of God" who "inherit eternal life."

Critiques

Critique by David R. Griffin

Hick and I agree that theodicy involves the construction of a metaphysical hypothesis, and that to be successful this hypothesis must be *plausible*, not just logically *possible*. However, he also agrees with the other three authors that God must be conceived to be "limitlessly powerful," by which he means that no other actualities can be thought to have inherent power to limit the actualization of God's will. Any power actualized by other actualities is due entirely to the voluntary decision by God to grant them power; hence any limitation on God's power is a *self*-limitation (which could be revoked at any time). Since Hick, unlike Roth and Sontag, also thinks that God is limitlessly good, he must try to show that all the apparent evils in the world are necessary for the greatest possible good: "evils are never tolerable – except for the sake of greater goods which may come out of them." The question is whether Hick has made plausible the conviction that this inherently omnipotent God is perfectly good. I think not.

Hick seeks to justify the existence of every type of apparent evil in terms of its utility for soul-making – in other words, for the development of moral and religious virtues in beings capable of those virtues, which in effect means *human* beings. An obvious question is, why is the pain evidently suffered by *sub*-human beings necessary? If Hick replies that this pain can produce compassion and helpfulness in us, we can restrict the question to the hundreds of millions of years of life that preceded the advent of human beings. If Hick replies that a natural environment is necessary for our "epistemic distance" from God, we can ask why this natural environment had to be created through a long, slow, pain-filled evolutionary process. Hick's God, being essentially omnipotent, could have created the needed environment in the "twinkling of an eye." Hick claims that the "Irenaean" theodicy is superior to the "Augustinian" one in being more adequate to the modern knowledge of the evolutionary process. But Hick provides no reason why God should have wasted over four billion years setting the stage for the only thing thought to be intrinsically valuable, the moral and spiritual development of human beings. And the high probability that hundreds of millions of years of that preparation involved unnecessary and unuseful pain counts against Hick's defense of the omnipotent God's total goodness.

Hick's free-will defense is of a hybrid nature. That is, he says that freedom is a contingent aspect of the actual world, given to it by God's voluntary choice. This means that God could suspend or interrupt this freedom at any time. God could have converted Hitler from his hatred for Jews; God could overrule someone about to beat and rape a child; God could stop every human act that would result in suffering. Accordingly, Hick must defend God's decision to allow every instance of moral evil that has occurred. Furthermore, if Hick holds that part of the creation is unfree, then he must defend God's decision to *cause* every instance of natural evil. While one may be able to make a somewhat plausible case for God's goodness when discussing moral and natural evil in the abstract, when we are confronted with concrete, horrendous instances of evil, this abstract justification loses its convincing power.

Hick does seek to provide an answer to this question as to why God does not prevent the most horrendous forms of evil, but I find it inadequate. Surely an all-wise, omnipotent being could have found some happier middle ground between our present, all-too-destructive world, and the "hedonistic paradise" Hick fears would make us morally and spiritually flabby.

However, there is an even more basic question to raise about freedom: if there could be an actual world smilar to ours except devoid of real freedom and the evils it brings, why did God give us real freedom in the first place?

Hick claims that freedom is a necessary condition for the emergence of that which is most valuable. And what is most valuable, according to Hick, is moral and religious virtue. On the face of it, the argument appears sound, since there can be no authentic virtue unless there is genuine freedom to be non-virtuous. But when we look more closely, a problem arises. For whom is it important that the virtue be authentic? If it were for the human beings, there would be no problem: God would be justified in granting real freedom to humans, since this would be necessary for them to experience the greatest intrinsic value open to creatures. But it is *not* necessary from the human viewpoint: all that we human beings would need, in order to enjoy the feeling of being authentically virtuous, would be the *belief* that we were genuinely free. Hick's God could have created us such that we were absolutely convinced that we were free, even though we only did what God willed for us to do. In such a world, there would be no genuine evils, since God could program everything to work out for the best; no pains would occur except those absolutely needed for the desired human experiences. And yet we would not know the difference; we would think that freedom was real, that the possibility and even the actuality of genuine evil were real, that temptation was real, and that real victories were being won. Only God would know the difference.

And precisely this turns out to be the reason that Hick's God put real freedom into the world — it is for God's own sake, not ours. God makes humans genuinely free so that *God* can have the knowledge that the creatures have come to love God freely. (The analogy between God and a hypnotist in Hick's *Evil and the God of Love* makes this clear.) Is a creator who has the power to create a completely different type of world and yet who deliberately builds earthquakes, tornadoes, and cancer into the structure of the world, who creates us so that moral evil is necessary — moral evil that can produce Hiroshimas and Auschwitzes — is a deity who would do all this, solely for the sake of knowing that some of its creatures came to love their creator freely, "limitlessly good?" Again, Hick has not made this plausible.

Furthermore, such a deity, given a reasonable amount of circumspection, would surely know that it was not worthy of love; hence it could not derive much satisfaction from knowing that some of the creatures loved it anyway – except perhaps the satisfaction of having put one over on them.

Surely Sontag and Roth are correct: the hybrid free-will defense cannot save the total goodness of an omnipotent creator.

There is yet another problem of plausibility. Hick's theodicy absolutely requires belief in a life after bodily death. He himself points out that this makes his theodicy implausible for many today. And yet the problem is more serious than his admission suggests. For, the major problem, as he sets it up, is that our lives are simply too short for the soul-making process to reach completion, at least for most people. Accordingly, he projects a further life, or perhaps many lives, in which God will gradually, through persuasion, win us over. The important point is that the future life or lives will not differ qualitatively from this one in terms of the relation between God and the soul; it will only differ quantitatively, i.e., it will be much longer. But this raises the question as to why God did not simply make our earthly life-spans much longer, so that we could reach the goal on earth, or at least get much closer to it. This would have been very easy for an omnipotent God and would have made Hick's theodicy much more plausible. Hick's answer to this, I suppose, will be that God does not want faith to be an easy matter – God wants true faith, which is in things unseen. But this raises the distinction between faith and foolish credulity. If Hick's theodicy is truly as implausible as it seems to me, would acceptance of it, and faith in its God, really be a virtue?

Critique by Frederick Sontag

Hick asks if a world which contains sadistic cruelty can be regarded as the expression of "infinite creative goodness?" But the prior, and the more urgent, questions are: (1) What does "goodness" mean in God's case, and might it encompass cruelty?; and (2) Should we agree to regard the world as an expression of goodness in the first place? Hick acknowledges that there are different concepts of God, but he states that he will discuss a "specifically Christian" theodicy, as if somehow that solved the question of how to define God's nature. To work within a Christian framework certainly narrows the range, but our central and primary concern is still how to conceive of God. For instance, Hick states that Christian theology has centered on the concept of God as "limitlessly good and loving." That simplifies the argument if it is true, but what is the evidence that Christianity has accepted any such crucial assumption? Or more accurately, what is the evidence that we all agree on what "limitlessly good and loving'' means and that our problems do not stem from our differences here?

Hick opts for a view which makes the world a training ground for persons to grow in God's likeness. This is an edifying thought, as Kierkegaard would say, but then why does the world look so unlike that to so many people? And surely only a few piously religious treat it that way – even granting that such a minority could be right. It is true that Hick opts for an "epistemic distance" from God, so that we are not overwhelmed in our growth by an overpowering divine presence. This is a plausible way to look at the God-human relationship, but what it does not explain is why so many, perhaps a majority, were put so far away that they do not even see this world as a divine training ground. Would Hick argue that we are at "just the right" distance to achieve optimum growth? Our world hardly looks that way.

If God wants finite persons to come to know and love him in their own freedom, why did he create so many obstacles in our way? Those children who die young, as so many do in so many lands, hardly have a chance to get a start on God's race track. The sport of horse racing seems to have worked out a better and a more rational system of handicaps than God imposed on us. If he wants us to freely love him, most humanity simply responds: give us half a chance! Hard won virtues are better than virtues created ready-made. We can agree with Hick. But is that what the problem of evil is all about, or is it not rather that wanton destruction too frequently breaks out? In placing us at a distance from him to learn to love him, did God go too far and shove too many into outer darkness? Do we really all seem to exist at "just the right" distance from God? If so, why are we in such continual confusion about even the right direction to look for him? God is too good, or else he is unfair, at playing hide and seek.

Hick is content if he can show that our actual world is at least one of those which might exemplify God's plan, but we need to know more than that. If we are not to think God poor in his choices, we need to know why we inhabit this particular world, which is not optimal for Hick's purposes, rather than some other one designed to give more of humanity an even break. God has arranged stages of creation through which we must go, Hick thinks, but does our world look like a training gym, now equipped with universal machines in the twentieth century, designed to hone our bodies and spirits to perfection? Only a few beautiful bodies survive out of billions, and spirits are broken every day. If God designed this training program, we need a new coach. We would not be able to develop without danger, it is true, but my problem is why the dangers were designed so that they actually break and destroy so many?

Hick argues that growing toward God beginning from a distance requires moral choices in a pain and stress environment in "broadly the kind of world of which we find ourselves to be a part." Here is the heart of the issue, but "broadly" is too vague. Unless we are to think God clumsy or imprecise in his choices, we must either argue that our world is optimum for these purposes or admit that God's pressure on us goes beyond all bounds justified by these gentle aims. Our world has the pain and stress needed for spiritual growth, but enough is enough, and it would appear God turned the pressure up so as to destroy some while educating only a few. If he is "gradually creating perfected finite persons," we must accuse God of poor engineering and suggest a refresher course at M.I.T. Hick admits that the threat to his argument comes from the "sheer amount and intensity" of evil, but recognizing this he still does not alter his argument in any way as a result.

Hick asks us: we do not want God to take away freedom, do we? But this is like the college administrator arguing against a proposed new curriculum by saying, we don't want lower salaries, do we? The issue with our administrator is whether curriculum changes really necessitate lower salaries, and the issue with God is whether freedom is possible only in this way, or whether we could have freedom *and* more desirable circumstances in which to exercise it. "All's well that ends well," Hick's countryman agrees with him, but even if God has some "glorious kingdom" in store for us, this in no way proves that our world was the only way to get there, or that every horror in it was somehow necessitated or justified. People at their best seem more flexible and capable in improving design than this, which I suppose is why so many in the modern age have rejected treating evil as theodicy and have opted for anthropodicy (evil as solely the creation of human beings and thus of no religious concern).

Our judgments about the intensity of evil required may be "relative," but surely they are good enough to know that evil in our world is destructive beyond any necessity, whether or not we can specify the exact perfect balance. In fact, there may be no simple balance point, which if true should cause us to rethink what "perfection" in God means. The fact that some people find any evil intolerable no matter how small does not prove that all the evils of our world are necessitated. Hick admits that the evil in nature is a bit of a mystery. He calls for us to build up mutual caring and love. That is well and good, but it also lets God dodge the argument of explaining why he chose the degree of destruction he decided to unleash on the world. Hick's own children would not let him get away with answering "do your best" when they ask why he places excessive demands on them, and we should let neither Hick nor God slip out of accountability so easily. We may be within the sphere of God's love and moving toward the kingdom, but that explains very little about why God chose a route through so dark a jungle.

Hick again delays his answer to "some sphere of existence other than this earth." There may be a heaven in store, but to say that isn't a theodicy, is it? Our task in theodicy is to explain God's ways to humanity, which means to account for why evil was allowed to have the decisive place it has. To say "we'll have a nice time in heaven" even if true does not touch this question. If John Hick "gets there before I do," I hope he will thank God for the nice heaven, but then ask him why on earth he chose the avenue to it he did. If Hick will not, I will, granted St. Peter has not imposed marshal law in order to silence all unfriendly questions from philosophers. However, like so many who are religiously or politically silenced, I ask only because I care for those lost on earth, and because I think the answer is our key to understand God.

Critique by Stephen T. Davis

Everyone who is interested in the philosophy of religion must by now be familiar with Hick's "Irenaean Theodicy." It has been chewed over considerably in the journals, and since I have no wish to go over ground that has already been covered, I will try to look at things here from a fresh perspective. Of the theodicies presented in this book (besides my own, of course) Hick's is the one with which I am in most sympathy. The main reason for this is that Hick (like me and unlike the others) tries to retain rational belief in "a limitlessly good and limitlessly powerful being."

In addition, I agree with Hick on several other important points: that there is a sense in which God is ultimately responsible for the state of the world and a sense in which human beings are responsible for their own evil deeds; that human beings were created as free, morally neutral creatures in a religiously ambiguous world; that eschatology is crucial to theodicy; that moral values (and thus moral growth) could not exist without pain and suffering; and that in the midst of life's ambiguities and suffering people must trust in God.

However, I do have several reservations about Hick's theodicy, some of which are more important than others. Let me mention four.

First, while no theodicy is free of difficulties, I believe Hick's is not entirely convincing in its handling of the amount of evil that exists in the world. I notice, for example, that while Hick stresses the need for plausibility and not just logical possibility in theodicy, when he turns to the question of the plausibility of the Irenaean theodicy, he finds himself twice saying only that it "may well be true." I agree that it may well be true, but *is* it true? Well, what gives me pause is Hick's argument that since no amount of evil, however small, would be tolerable to us (if God subtracted, say, cancer from our world something else would then rank as our most feared disease), the amount of evil that actually exists in the world does not tell against the Irenaean theodicy. But the problem with this argument is that it appears to cut the other way too: it seems to imply that human suffering could get infinitely worse than it now is and still be compatible with the existence of a perfectly good and omnipotent God. And this, at the very least, seems to me implausible.

Second, I am dubious about Hick's hope of a gradual spiritual evolution till human beings reach a full state of God-consciousness. Since I see no convincing evidence that the human race is improving morally or spiritually, I prefer to hope for a sudden spiritual revolution in the eschaton. Now I am not accusing Hick of 19th century theological optimism; he knows that God's "person-making" process "is not completed on this earth." Most people only attain it after death, he says. But if people are as morally and spiritually free after death as they are now – as Hick claims – then the evidence of how people behave here and now does not give me much hope that the human race will gradually improve till all are the God-conscious "persons" God intended. My own view is that at a decisive point in history God will seize the initiative and will give those who say yes to him a new "heart made of flesh" (Ezek. 11:19-20). He will, in short, suddenly transform us into "new persons."

Third, I believe Hick also faces what I call the "cost-effective" criticism of the free will defense (see my main essay), and I am curious how he would answer it. It may be true, as he claims, that virtues which are freely learned on one's own are intrinsically more valuable than virtues bestowed as a gift of God. But is this excess virtue worth the price we pay for it, i.e., the great evils in the world human freedom has produced? It may also be true, given the physical and psychological laws at work in the world, that free kittens and persons develop adaptive behavior patterns in our inimical world much more readily than unfree ones. But surely an omnipotent being is not bound by these laws. Surely he could have made us grow and learn in a much less painful, harsh, and destructive world.

My final and most serious criticism of Hick concerns his commitment to universalism. By way of introduction I would like to call attention to Hick's requirement that in order to be acceptable a theodicy must be "consistent with the data . . . of the religious tradition on which it is based." I strongly agree with this. My complaint is that I do not believe universalism is consistent with the data of the Christian tradition. But before speaking further about universalism, let me briefly move to a related general question which I, as a theologically conservative Christian, would like to address not only to Hick but to the other contributors to this book as well. My question is this: if fidelity to the teachings of the Bible and to the Christian religious tradition no longer plays the normative role it once did in developing theological propositions that are acceptable to Christians, what will?

It seems clear, both from what they officially say and from what they clearly presuppose, that none of my fellow contributors feels any strong need to be guided in theology by Scripture or Christian tradition. They do not feel particularly bound in any normative sense to do theology either on the basis of the Protestant methodological principle of *sola scriptura* or the Catholic principle of "Scripture and tradition." How then do we determine what is allowable and what is not in Christian theology? I mean this as a serious question. Can a person come up with *any* thesis, however bizarre, and push it on Christians? What if some future theologian says that the devil created God or that Jesus Christ was an astronaut from Tralfalmadore or even that God wants all red-headed people to move to Borneo? In an age of religious charlatans like Jim Jones (who reportedly told his people, "I'm the nearest thing to God you'll ever see") I would have thought we needed far more, not less, adherence to the Bible and to the Christian religious tradition. This, I believe, is our only epistemological protection against religious figures and theologians who stray from the truth.

Let me say a word about universalism and the Bible. The Bible does teach that it is God's will that everyone be saved (Rom. 11:32; 1 Tim. 2:4; 2 Peter 3:9) and that the work of God's grace in Christ was designed for the salvation of everyone (Titus 2:11; Heb. 2:9; 1 John 2:2). Pauline thought also includes the notion of God's ultimate total victory and of the eventual reconciliation of everything to him (Rom. 8:19-21; 1 Cor. 15:22-28; 2 Cor. 5:19; Eph. 1:10, 20-23; Col. 1:19-20). But none of this implies universalism. There are also a few texts which universalists say explicitly predict the salvation of everyone (John 12:32; Rom. 5:18; Phil. 2:9-11). But on the assumption — which I am prepared to make — that Paul and the author of the Fourth Gospel do not blatantly contradict themselves, we can see that universalists fail to interpret these texts correctly. For these same biblical authors can also make the statements found in John 3:17-18; Romans 5:18-19; and 1 Timothy 4:10 (assuming 1 Timothy is Pauline). The first shows, contrary to the universalist's interpretation of the "all" passages in the Fourth Gospel, that the Son's being the savior of the world, whatever precisely it means, is quite consistent with some people being condemned. The second shows that Paul's doctrine that "all men" are acquitted and have life, whatever precisely it means, does not entail universalism, for it can equally well be stated (as if in Hebrew parallelism) in terms of "many" men. And the third shows that the sense in which God is the savior of "all men" is not the same sense in which he is the savior of "those who believe." He is the savior of all, but he is *especially* the savior of those who believe.

Let me confess that I would like universalism to be true. I would find it comforting to believe that all people will be saved, and Hick may be correct that the problem of evil is a bit less intractable for the universalist than for the non-universalist. But as a matter of theological method, we cannot affirm a doctrine just because we would like it to be true. The plain teaching of Scripture, I believe, is that some will be condemned to eternal separation from God. See, for example, Matthew 7:13; 12:32; 25:41; 2 Cor. 5:10; and 2 Thessalonians 1:8-9. And the reality of hell seems inextricably tied to such major themes in New Testament theology as God, sin, judgment, atonement, and reconciliation. That is enough for me; that is why I cannot affirm universalism.

But how can a just and good God condemn someone to eternal torment? In the first place, I do not believe hell is a place of torment. New Testament metaphors that seem to suggest this are merely metaphors. Second, I believe the citizens of hell are there because they freely choose to be there. Unless one bows to God and makes his will one's own, heaven is too much to bear and one chooses hell. Thus it is not only just but loving that God allows them to live forever in hell. Third, hell may have the effect on many of hardening their resolve never to repent; sin may voluntarily continue; and if it is right for evil-doers to be punished for the evil deeds they do here and now, this will be true of the evil deeds they do after death. Fourth, Christians believe their salvation is a matter of sheer grace; we deserve to be condemned, but out of love rather than sheer justice God forgives us and reconciles us to him. If hell is inconsistent with God's love, then our salvation is not a matter of grace: it becomes a matter of our justly being freed from a penalty we don't really deserve.

Critique by John K. Roth

Three features of Hick's theodicy attract me. I concur with his emphasis on God's omnipotence. I share his belief that theodicies are doomed unless they include an eschatological dimension that points to personal life beyond death. I also agree that demonstrations of logical possibility take us hardly anywhere. Far more decisive is the degree to which a theodicy is plausible.

By Hick's reckoning, a theodicy's plausibility rises or falls to the extent that the theory fits facts. Unfortunately, even if one accepts that qualification, what is plausible to one person may be a snare and a delusion to another. No doubt John Hick has a possible theodicy. However, because I find it falling short by its own criterion, his perspective is not one that I can accept. In a word, Hick's theodicy is just too good to be true.

Hick rightly calls the Holocaust an instance of "demonic malice and cruelty." His theodicy requires him to reconcile that event with other crucial claims. They include these affirmations: (1) God is not only "limitlessly powerful" but also "limitlessly good and loving." (2) This God has created human life in an evolutionary setting where progress toward person-making is the aim and where achievement of person-perfecting is the end. Hick's theodicy is implausible to me because I am convinced that his claims about God's goodness cannot stand the onslaught of what he calls the principal threat to his own perspective: "the sheer amount and intensity of both moral and natural evil."

Hick's theory tends to keep the most wanton qualities of evil at arm's length. Some hardship and pain may make persons stronger and better, but Hick, I think, sees the world too much as a schoolroom when it is actually more like a dangerous alley. How is the Holocaust compatible with the plan of person-perfecting that he describes? How does Auschwitz fit the claim that there is divine intent ensuring evolutionary progress where human character is concerned? In the Holocaust persons were ruined and destroyed more than they were made or perfected. Auschwitz is waste, the very antithesis of providential design and purpose in God's economy.

Of course, an Irenaean theodicy banks on life after death to redeem waste and to justify God's limitless love and goodness. Presumably God's heavenly persuasion will reconcile everything and everybody; all experience will figure into our ultimate perfection. Still, how will that process work in relation to waste that cannot be undone any more than it did not have to be? Much explanation — from Hick, if not from God — is needed if it is going to be plausible that our lives have always been surrounded by a limitless love and goodness that never let us go and that make all things well. The arguments may not be God's, but Hick does offer examples of how that explanation might unfold. They are plausible if one wants to legitimate evil.

John Hick is critical of some free-will defenses for God. Yet his own theodicy belongs in that genre. According to Hick, persons-in-the-making must be free. Indeed they must be free to do all manner of evil. In addition, if men and women are to grow into a genuinely loving relationship with God, human freedom will entail both an "epistemic distance" from God and a pilgrimage through moral dilemmas and natural difficulties in which failure, pain, and untimely death are live options.

The general outline may be correct: if we are fully to become God's children, our environment may have to be "broadly the kind of world of which we find ourselves to be a part." Its breadth, however, makes that claim insufficient. It will not do for Hick to take what may be a wiser course and to admit that some facts cannot be reconciled with God's limitless goodness and love. But so long as he stays with his general approach, the effect is precisely to leave unjustified the grisly details and the structures that produce them. When he does move to consider those details, however, his theory fares no better. The reason is that Hick must defend evil, and he cannot do so without condoning — even if only inadvertently or unintentionally — what happened to its victims.

For instance, Hick notes that there is "intolerable" evil. He mentions this reality, however, not to reveal its sheer waste but to mitigate evil by relativizing it. In a world of person-making freedom, Hick implies, people can always find something to fault no matter how good things are. There will always be some evil, something that is "worst" and therefore intolerable. Since we must have some "intolerable" evil in order to become the perfected persons we are destined to be, the further implication appears to be that we ought not to protest very much.

Such implications, unintended though they may be, lurk in Hick's apologies. Those implications do everyone a disservice. Most people will not protest hardship, or even pain, if they can clearly see a commensurate benefit. Moreover, it is not impossible that there could be a world with commensurability between hardship and benefit, even if this present one cannot qualify. On Hick's terms, though, moral value would be diminished in that case, for virtue would never be its own reward. In a theodicy so heavily dependent on an eschatological resolution for the problem of evil, it is questionable whether virtue will ever be its own reward in the final analysis, but however that dilemma comes out, Hick's apologies still seem to be offered at the expense of evil's victims.

Like Leibniz, Hick urges contentment with the metaphysical structure of our current world, if not with the details of our experience. Thus, he argues that if one lets reason prevail, we will not want God "to revoke ... freedom when its wrong exercise becomes intolerable to us." Hick makes this claim on the grounds that our taking "with full seriousness the value of human freedom and responsibility" will enable us to see that "humankind's moral freedom is indivisible, and can lead eventually to a consummation of limitless value which could never be attained without that freedom."

Is it clear, however, that moral freedom is or must be indivisible, or that such indivisibility is all that good? The moral fabric of human existence, for example, depends on intervention, on stopping people from doing certain things. On the other hand, Hick's vaunted indivisibility allows freedom to make all hell break loose. Apparently God will not intervene to stop this waste, but that fact does little to enhance the plausibility of his limitless love and goodness – unless "limitless" implies something very strange in this case. Rather the waste of permissiveness, God's and ours, in allowing freedom to be indivisible augurs against God's benevolence. True, if some "limitless value" (whatever that might be) results from indivisible liberty, we can be more tranquil. The problem, though, is to imagine how evil's waste will fit. If our epistemic distance from God were less, we might understand more, but Hick also suggests that if we knew too much now, the risk factors in our lives would be curtailed and the grandeur of our character might be diminished. Such excuses, I fear, defend evil too much.

If Hick is correct, my fear is groundless. Waste will waste away. Evil will be transcended, rendered inconsequential, forgotten so that neither God nor humanity is in any way permanently soiled. There shall be pie in the sky by and by – a whole one, not just a slice. This theodicy is nice. Its plausibility, however, must be judged in terms of how nice life seems to be. John Hick finds it nice enough to justify calling God's love and goodness limitless. The sheer amount and intensity of evil's waste make me demur.

Hick's Response to Critiques

Much depends, in the formation and criticism of theodicies, upon whether one starts from the pressing fact of evil in its many forms, and proceeds from this to develop a conception of God; or starts from a conviction as to the reality and goodness of God, derived from the stream of religious experience of which one is a part, and then asks whether the grim reality of evil is compatible with this. The first path leads to the conclusion that there may be a good but finite, or an infinite but partly evil, deity. This is the path followed by Griffin, Roth, and Sontag. I can see how it is that having set their feet on this path they are led to that destination.

However, others of us start elsewhere: from a powerful sense of the reality and love of God, as known particularly through the life and teaching of Jesus and the religious tradition which has flowed from him. The "Godness" of God entails that he is creator of and sovereign over the universe of which we are part. Further, "God is love" (1 John 4:8), known as our heavenly Father. He gives and forgives; and his ultimate gift is eternal life. He is sovereign, but leaves one free both for good and for evil. He could, for example, have intervened to rescue Jesus from death, but it was not in accordance with his purpose to do so (Matt. 26: 53-4). He allows people a genuine freedom, and accordingly "makes his sun rise on the evil and on the good, and sends rain on the just and on the unjust" (Matt. 5:45). God is known in Christian experience as the creative love in whose hands we are, who calls us to give ourselves to him in return amidst all the ambiguities of human history, and who is leading us through further stages of self-giving to that fulfillment of being, beyond the scope of our imaginations, which is eternal life.

Given this faith in the love and sovereignty of God, how are we to understand the oppressive realities of human wickedness, and of pain and suffering, in ourselves and others? This is the form of the theodicy question to which the Irenaean type of theology offers an answer. It can offer a general but not a detailed understanding of our human situation in its relation to God. A vast surrounding mystery remains — much greater than in the case of theodicies which reject the problem by denying either God's limitless goodness and love or his limitless power. Thus we cannot show that the "epistemic distance" from God at which humankind has been brought into being, in order to endow one with cognitive freedom in relation to the maker, is the precisely optimum "distance"; or that the level of natural and moral evil in the world is precisely the right level — neither more nor less — for this stage of the creation of human animals into children of God; nor can we spell out the exact nature of the life to come and its ultimate eschatological fulfillment; nor, again, can we prove that the product of God's long creative process will be worth its cost — unless the abstract principle be accepted that an infinite gain must be worth a finite loss. But on the other hand this acknowledgement of mystery is not a mere evasion, but follows from the basic Irenaean theodicy principle. For the world, considered as an environment for the first phase of a long process of spiritual creation, is not a deterministic system but a living realm involving important elements of freedom and contingency. Its successive events, both good and evil, have not been individually "sent" by God, nor planned as a divinely prearranged obstacle course. What is divinely created is a world, functioning in accordance with its own laws, in which human freedom is to be exercised with real consequences in response to real problems and challenges. That life's contingencies, including both its blessings and its calamities, affect us indiscriminately, and not in proportion to our desert, is a precondition of the moral life and hence of the moral growth of the person. For if bad things happened always and only to evil people, and good things only to good people, we should inevitably be seeking rewards and avoiding penalties rather than making genuine moral choices.

Accordingly I do not accept Griffin's demand that "Hick must defend God's decision to allow every instance of moral evil that has occurred." What has to be defended, surely, or at least accepted, is God's decision to create us as free beings who are to come to our eventual perfection through the exercise of our own freedom. For if we accept the precious gift of freedom, we accept that we and others may misuse that freedom without God intervening to revoke it. (I find it hard to take seriously Griffin's suggestion that God's purpose in creation might be satisfied by giving us the mere illusion rather than the reality of freedom. The kind of God he is talking about must be morally and intellectually limited as well as limited in power). Nor can I accept Sontag's insistence that it is not sufficient "that our actual world is at least one of those which might exemplify God's plan" but that we "need to know why we inhabit this particular world." If knowing why we inhabit this particular world means knowing why the world is just as it is – why, for example, it contains this and that specific danger and challenge, why God did not bar this and that particular disease and peril, why his creative work proceeds on this rather than a different time-scale, – then we cannot know this. All that we can do is to see that our world, with its ambiguities and mysteries, its evils as well as the good within it, may be a phase in the outworking of a creative divine purpose which is leading us to limitless good. And if our awareness of God as good and loving is strong enough to bear the weight, we are, I believe, entitled to opt for this interpretation of human existence.

To a great extent the defense of this view has to consist in correcting misunderstandings and repudiating misleading caricatures. The eschatological aspect of the Irenaean type of theodicy is particularly vulnerable to these. Thus it is a common misunderstanding to characterize its eschatology in some such terms as the hope that "We'll have a nice time in heaven." The Irenaean theme, however, is not compensation, but the fulfillment of our nature in relation to God. There is also misunderstanding involved in Griffin's view that "the future life or lives will not differ qualitatively from this one in terms of the relation between God and the soul; it will differ only quantitatively, i.e., it will be much longer." In discussing possible conceptions of life after death (in *Death and Eternal Life*) I have argued for a very different view from this. One cannot go beyond hypotheses. But the hypothesis that seems to me somewhat probable is that any continuation of the person-making process beyond death will consist in a series of lives, each with its own beginning and end; for it is the boundaries of life that provide the pressure that constitutes it a person-making history. I conceive of these as embodied lives in a real environment. But the transition from one life to the next will, according to this hypothesis, be via a temporary *bardo* phase in which the disembodied consciousness, creating its own mind-dependent world, and finding its real desires reflected in that world, comes to a greater self-knowledge. This is a kind of psycho-analytic experience, preparing the individual for a relative new beginning. Thus the further lives are not mere quantitative continuations of the present life, but part of a spiritual progress towards the ultimate state which lies beyond the series of finite lives.

It is another misunderstanding of the Irenaean hypothesis — in this case on Davis' part — to suppose that it postulates "a gradual spiritual evolution" such as would be contradicted by a lack of signs "that the human race is improving morally or spiritually." It is hard to determine whether the human race is improving, ethically or religiously, along the plane of earthly history. But the hypothesis of an ascent towards God through many lives in many worlds does not entail that successive generations *in this world* should show a moral or spiritual advance. Rather, the postulated movement towards human perfection should occur in the personal histories and interactions of individuals through the successive par-eschatological worlds.

This hypothesis of a development brought about by free human responses, from self-centered human animal to self-transcending child of God, seems to me more probable than Davis' theory that God will suddenly transform us into "new persons." For the implication that it is consistent with the divine method of creation for God suddenly to transform us into perfect beings, seems to undermine the significance of our present life. If God can transform us at death (which comes for some in old age but for others in youth or even within moments after birth) into the perfect beings whom he desires to exist, he could presumably do this at any point in our lives, and so the long hard business of person-making through interactions with others in a harsh and challenging environment would be unnecessary. It therefore seems to me preferable to postulate a continued process of person-making in other environments beyond this world.

Still in the realm of eschatology, Davis argues that the idea of universal salvation, which the Irenaean type of theodicy requires, is not "consistent with the data of the Christian tradition." The reason why universalism is required in an Irenaean type of theodicy is that a justification of suffering and wickedness as part of the process through which finite spiritual life is being brought to perfection, requires that the process shall eventually succeed. If it fails, the sin and pain that it has involved remain unjustified. A person's sin and suffering can be redeemed, retrospectively, by becoming part of the history by which that person arrives at the fulfillment of God's purpose. But if only some arrive at that fulfillment, whilst others are eternally lost, then the depravity and suffering of human history will only have been partially redeemed. It is thus a memorable understatement of Davis' that "the problem of evil is a bit less intractable for the universalist than for the non-universalist." If part of humankind is in the end condemned to hell, this will itself constitute an infinite, because unending, aspect of the problem of evil. God's good purpose will have been eternally frustrated, leaving the eternal evils both of sin and of punishment.

Davis is able to say that "The plain teaching of Scripture . . . is that some will be condemned to eternal separation from God" because he apparently treats the many different documents comprising the New Testament as though they were a single writing by a single author, who must be assumed to be consistent, so that one must interpret the universalist passages in terms of the non-universalist passages. But would it not be more realistic to acknowledge that there are both universalist and non-universalist strands within the diverse literature of the New Testament? And within this diversity is it not striking that the teachings of the historical Jesus, so far as they are recorded in the Synoptic Gospels, contain only one passage (Matt. 25:41) – or two if we include the mysterious saying about the sin against the Holy Spirit – in which eternal punishment is threatened; and this despite the fact that the idea was widespread within the popular Judaism of his time?

But how can we affirm an eventual universal salvation if men and women are genuinely free to respond or fail to respond to God's love? This traditional dilemma is created by leaving out of account the doctrine of God's initial creation of humankind "in his own image," for relationship with himself. In Augustine's words, "Thou hast made us for thyself, and our hearts are restless till they rest in thee." Here we have the idea of a basic bias of human nature towards its creator, a bias which will sooner or later lead all people to him. And so instead of the image of the irresistable force (God) confronting the immovable post (human freedom), a less misleading analogy might be that of the relationship between a psychiatrist and a patient who is so inwardly mixed up that he or she cannot enact his or her own deepest desires. In so influencing the patient as to achieve change, the psychiatrist is not forcing the patient against the will but is on the contrary releasing him or her from an inner "bind" and making him or her more free to be and do what the patient really wants to be and do. We can conceive that God, in the infinite resourcefulness of infinite love, acts in many ways, through many worlds, to bring his creatures to himself by their own free insights and choices, thereby fulfilling their own deepest nature as beings made in his image.

Sontag rightly raises the question of pain in the sub-human sentient world. If God is all-good and all-powerful, why has he created "nature, red in tooth and claw"? Here one might be tempted to turn to the traditional doctrine of the perversion of the natural order as a consequence of the fall. But unfortunately that doctrine is totally implausible: we know that life preyed on life, and that animals suffered from painful diseases (there is evidence, for example, of arthritis in the bones of some pre-historic animals) long before humankind had come into existence. A Christian theodicy has therefore to look elsewhere. The right question to ask is not, I would suggest, why do animals feel pain? The pain mechanism is necessary to the survival of organisms inhabiting a world with a fixed structure. It is by means of this mechanism that we, and the other animals, learn to conduct ourselves successfully within a common environment. (It should however be added that the lower animals, living wholly in the present moment of experience, are entirely or almost entirely exempt from the kinds of suffering we know at the self-conscious human level, involving memory of the past and anticipation of the future. We should not project upon them our own form of consciousness, capable of unhappy memories, remorse, guilt, jealousy, anxiety, fear of the future and awareness of death.) The question, then, is not why animals feel the kinds of pain that they feel, but why there should be a realm of animal life at all. A theologian is not obliged to claim to know the answer to every question. There is a place for trust in the goodness of God beyond our understanding. But it may nevertheless be possible to see some gleam of light on this particular question. Perhaps we should learn to see all life as forming a unitary process. Hindu and Buddhist thinkers have seen spiritual life developing through successive animal embodiments until it reaches self-consciousness in humans, and they accordingly treat all life as related, inter-linked, and indeed as ultimately one. We do not have to adopt the distinctive eastern theory of reincarnation through animal into human life to accept the basic conception of animal and human existence as forming one continuous ongoing complex of organic life, which is the process whereby ''children of God'' are gradually being created out of human animals, themselves created out of lower forms of life, which was in turn created out of inorganic matter. One effect of our embeddedness within this larger stream of life is to make possible our cognitive freedom in relation to the infinite Creator.

I must end by stressing again the limits of a Christian theodicy of the Irenaean type. As I emphasized in my main essay, it offers an understanding of our human situation; but this is not the same as offering practical help and comfort to those in the midst of acute pain or deep suffering. Further, because of the central part played in it by humankind's free response to God's non-coercive modes of revelation, and by human trust in God as thus known by faith, such a theodicy does not expect to be able to see in detail how ''all things work together for good'' for God's creatures, or how it can be that by wrestling with evil we are ultimately being created through it. We believe that the history of the universe is God's creative action; that the formation of spiritualized personality is a long, hard and painful process; and that its justification lies in the limitless good to which, beyond this world, it finally leads. But from our present standpoint in the midst of this process of creation we still have to live in faith and trust.

3 Free Will and Evil
STEPHEN T. DAVIS

Let me begin by exposing the main assumptions that control what I will say in this chapter. I approach the problem of evil – as I approach all philosophical and theological problems – wearing, as it were, two hats. I am both an analytic philosopher and an evangelical Christian. As an analytic philosopher, trained in logic and twentieth century linguistic philosophy, I am interested in the rigor and soundness of the arguments I encounter. My controlling presuppositions are that people ought to believe what it is rational for them to believe and that human reason is a normative guide to all belief and action.[1]

As an evangelical Christian, I accept orthodox Christian claims about God, Christ, human beings, and human history. I believe that all truth is from God and is consistent with the existence, goodness, and omnipotence of God. Evangelicals are not the theological obscurantists they are sometimes made out to be, but it is quite correct that they are loath to give up crucial Christian claims. This includes the following claims:

(1) Evil exists;

(2) God is omnipotent;

and

(3) God is perfectly good.

So as I approach the problem of evil my aim is to find a solution that is both philosophically defensible and consistent with these (and other) central Christian affirmations.

Thus I will not be interested in any "solution" which denies that evil exists – e.g., which claims that evil is "an illusion of the material sense," or some other sort of metaphysically unreal thing. Nor will I be interested in any "solution" which denies God's omnipotence – e.g., which says that God is very powerful but is simply not able to prevent evil. Nor will I be interested in any "solution" which denies that God is wholly good – e.g., which says that he has an evil or demonic side which sometimes expresses itself in malevolent acts.

Let me distinguish between two aspects of the problem of evil, what I will call the logical problem of evil (LPE) and the emotive problem of evil (EPE). I will introduce the EPE later, but let us call the LPE the problem of reconciling (1), (2), and (3), i.e., the problem of showing that these three statements are logically consistent. That this is one serious aspect of the problem of evil is clear. Many critics of theism state the problem of evil in such a way as to suggest that (1), (2), and (3) form an inconsistent set of statements. That is, they claim that it cannot be the case that (1), (2), and (3) are all true; the truth of any two of these statements, they say, implies the falsity of the third.[2] Thus the rational theist must give up (1), (2), or (3). If God is omnipotent it seems he is *able* to prevent evil; if God is perfectly good it seems he is *willing* to prevent evil; why then (they ask) does evil exist?

What I want to argue, then, is that (1), (2), and (3) are quite consistent and can all be accepted by a rational person. Many theists have tried to argue to this conclusion, but the reasoning of most seems (to me, at least) weak and quite unable to solve the problem of evil. The one line of argument I have always found promising is the so-called free will defense (or FWD, as I will call it). It was first presented with great vigor by St. Augustine (354-430 A.D.) and has recently been skillfully defended by Alvin Plantinga (among others). Let me now sketch out the FWD as a solution to the LPE.

What were God's aims in creating the universe? According to the FWD, he wanted two things. First, he wanted to create the best universe he could, i.e., the best possible balance of moral and natural good over moral and natural evil. And second, he wanted to create a world in which created rational agents (e.g., human beings) would decide *freely* to love and obey him. Accordingly he created a world in which there originally existed no moral or natural evil, and he created human beings with the facility of free moral choice.

Let us say that people are *free moral agents* if and only if in the case of the decisions they make

(4) *their choice is not coerced or causally determined.*

and

(5) *they have genuine alternatives, i.e., it is actually in their power, under the same antecedent conditions, to do one thing or another.*

Obviously, in making humans free God ran the risk that they would choose evil rather than good. The possibility of freely doing evil is the inevitable companion of the possibility of freely doing good. Unfortunately this is just what human beings did: they chose to go wrong; they fell into sin. So God is not to be blamed for the existence of evil in the world — we are. Of course God is *indirectly* responsible for evil in the sense that he created the conditions given which evil would come into existence (i.e., he gave us free choice), and he foreknew the evil choices we would make. But even given these conditions, it was not inevitable that evil exist. The non-existence of evil was quite possible; humans could have chosen to obey God. Sadly, they didn't.

Why then did God create free moral agents in the first place? Does it not look as if his plan went wrong, as if his righteous desires were thwarted? Not so, says the FWD. God's policy decision to make us free was wise, for it will turn out better in the long run that we act freely, even if we sometimes err, than it would have turned out had we been created innocent automata, programmed always to do the good. God's decision will turn out to be wise because the good that will in the end result from his decision will outweigh the evil that will in the end result from it.[3] In the eschaton it will be seen that God chose the best course and that the favorable balance of good over evil that will then exist was obtainable by God in no other way.

In response to the problem of evil, some theists have argued that this is "the best of all possible worlds." Must the FWD make this claim? I believe not. In the first place, it is not clear that the notion *the best of all possible worlds* is coherent. Take the notion *tallest conceivable man*. This notion is incoherent because no matter how tall we conceive a tall man to be we can always conceptually add another inch and thus prove that he was not, after all, the tallest conceivable man. Just so, it may be argued, the notion *the best of all possible worlds* is incoherent. For any possible world, no matter how much pleasure and happiness it contains, we can think of a better one, i.e., one with slightly more pleasure and happiness.[4] Accordingly, there logically *cannot* exist such a world, and the FWD need not claim that this world is the best of all possible worlds.

But even if this argument is incorrect, even if the notion is coherent, the FWD still need not claim that this is the best of all possible worlds. Better worlds than this world are quite conceivable, in my opinion. For example, so far as I am able to tell, this world would have been morally better (would have contained less moral evil) had Hitler not hated Jews. The death of six million Jews in the Holocaust, I believe, was based on decisions made by free and morally responsible human agents, Hitler and others. So the FWD must in a sense say that the amount of good and evil that exists in the world is partially up to us and not entirely up to God. If so, it then becomes easy to imagine worlds better than this one – e.g., a world otherwise as much as possible like this one except that no Jews are ever murdered. Thus this is not the best of all possible worlds.

What the FWD must insist on is, first, that the amount of evil that in the end will exist will be outweighed by the good that will then exist; and second, that this favorable balance of good over evil was obtainable by God in no other way. (The free will defender need not claim, incidentally, to be able to explain how or why each evil event that occurs in history helps lead to a greater good. As regards the Holocaust, for example, I confess I am quite unable to do so.)

But let us return to propositions (1), (2), and (3), which the LPE critic says form an inconsistent set. Is this true? How does the FWD answer this charge? Let me restructure the problem slightly. It will be less cumbersome to work with two rather than three propositions, so let us now ask whether

(3) Evil exists

is consistent with the conjunction of (1) and (2), which we can call

(6) God is omnipotent and God is good.

Those who push the LPE will claim that (3) and (6) are inconsistent — if one is true the other must be false. Is this true?

Well, Alvin Plantinga has used in this connection a recognized procedure for proving that two propositions are logically consistent.[5] Let us see if it is usable here. We can prove that (3) and (6) are consistent if the FWD can provide us with a third proposition (I will call it [7]), which has three properties. First, it must be possibly true. Second, it must be consistent with (6). And third, in conjunction with (6) it must entail (3).

Now what is the proposition that the free will defender can use to show that (3) and (6) are consistent? Let me suggest the following:

> *(7) All the evil that exists in the world is due to the choices of free moral agents whom God created, and no other world which God could have created would have had a better balance of good over evil than the actual world will have.*

What this says is that God's policy decision to create free moral agents will turn out to be wise and that it was not within God's power to have created a better world. Now (7) certainly seems *possibly true* (the question of its truth will come up later); I can detect no contradiction or incoherence in (7). And (7) seems consistent with (6) — I see no reason to call them inconsistent, at any rate. And the conjunction of (6) and (7) does indeed entail (3). Thus (3) and (6) are consistent and the LPE is apparently solved. A rational person can believe that God is omnipotent, that God is good, and that evil exists. It is apparently false to claim that the LPE shows that Christianity and other forms of theism are contradictory.

However, there are three serious objections that must be dealt with before we can consider the LPE solved. The first can be stated as follows: "If the whole creation was originally perfectly morally good, then human beings, as originally created, were perfectly morally good. But then how do we explain the fact that people sin? A fall into sin seems logically impossible for a perfectly morally good being; a being sins only if it has a moral flaw. Since humans do sin, it follows that they were not originally created perfectly morally good, and thus God is directly responsible for moral evil."[6]

Several things here are true. I agree that a perfectly morally good being will never sin. I agree that there was no evil in God's original creation. And it is also true that Genesis 1:31 says of God's entire creation (which obviously includes human beings) that "it was very good." But despite this, the answer to the above objection is that the FWD is not committed to the view that humans were created perfectly morally good. The biblical expression *very good* quite obviously does not mean *perfectly morally good* – how could created things like the moon or Mount Baldy or the eucalyptus tree outside my office be perfectly morally good? Clearly they cannot, and so *very good* must mean something else. I would suggest God judged his creation to be very good in that it was a harmonious, beautiful, smoothly working cosmos rather than the ugly, churning chaos over which the Holy Spirit had moved (Gen. 1:2). Human beings too were created good in *this* sense, but not perfectly morally good. Since God wanted them to be free moral agents, he must have created them as spiritually immature, morally neutral creatures, capable of choosing either good or evil. And this is just what the FWD says he did.

The second objection asks why an omnipotent being couldn't have created free beings who always freely choose the good. If this is logically possible, a good creator who was able to do so would certainly have done so. Since he obviously did not do so, at least some of the claims theists make about God must be false. Thus J.L. Mackie argues as follows:

> If God has made men such that in their free choices they sometimes prefer what is good and sometimes what is evil, why could he not have made men such that they always freely choose the good? If there is no logical impossibility in a man's freely choosing the good on one, or on several occasions, there cannot be a logical impossibility in his freely choosing the good on every occasion. God was not, then, faced with a choice between making innocent automata and making beings who, in acting freely, could sometimes go wrong: there was open to him the obviously better possibility of making beings who would act freely but always go right. Clearly, his failure to avail himself of this possibility is inconsistent with his being both omnipotent and wholly good.[7]

Mackie appears to be making two claims here – first, that there is no logical impossibility in a free moral agent always freely choosing the good; and second, that God can create free moral agents such that they will always freely choose the good. Now if these claims are true, they constitute a refutation of the FWD. For their effect is to falsify a crucial assumption of the FWD, viz., that it is impossible for God to create moral agents such that they are both free and will always choose the good, that the possibility of doing evil is the inevitable companion of the possibility of freely doing good.

I have no wish to dispute Mackie's first claim. Though it seems highly improbable, it does seem *logically possible* that all free moral agents always freely choose the good. "Jones is a free moral agent and Jones never sins," is not necessarily false. Of course, given the definition of "free" stated earlier, it follows that had this possibility been actualized, i.e., had the moral agents whom God created never sinned, it would have been what might be called a "pleasant

accident." God would not have brought it about, nor would he be responsible for
it. For if the agents were really free no one could have caused or coerced them
to behave as they did.

Thus Mackie's second claim – that it is logically possible for God to create
free moral agents such that they always freely choose the good – is false. "Jones
is a free moral agent whom God creates in such a way that Jones never sins," is
necessarily false. There is a logical tension between an agent's being free vis-a-
vis certain acts and that agent's somehow being influenced by God always to
behave in a certain way regarding those acts. Again we see that given God's
decision to create free moral agents, it follows that it is in part up to those agents
and not entirely up to God what the world will be like. There are some logically
possible worlds that God cannot create. If there is a given free moral agent, say
Jones, who in a given situation will freely decide to sin, it is not in God's power
to create a world in which Jones is free, the situation is exactly the same, and
Jones does not sin.[8]

The third objection has to do with the distinction between moral and natural
evil. Now the FWD, as I have formulated it, relies on (7), which begins with the
claim that "*All* the evil that exists in the world is due to the choices of free moral
agents whom God created." But this seems clearly false (so this objection would
run). If the FWD works at all it is perhaps a solution only to *part* of the LPE,
viz., that part that concerns moral evil. But how can such natural evils as
earthquakes, disease, and famine be attributed to moral agents? This seems
absurd, which is precisely why we call such evils *natural* rather than moral in the
first place. Thus (7) is clearly false, and the FWD fails.

For years I would have been inclined to agree with the substance of this
objection. I was of the opinion that the FWD solved the problem of moral evil
but not the problem of natural evil. I felt that other arguments beside the FWD
had to be appealed to when dealing with natural evil, although I confess none of
these arguments seemed particularly convincing to me. But in recent years Alvin
Plantinga has suggested that the FWD can indeed solve the problem of natural
evil. He appeals to an often neglected aspect of Christian tradition, which was
also used by Augustine in his writings on the problem of evil, viz, the notion of
Satan or Lucifer as the cause of natural evil. Augustine, Plantinga says,

> attributes much of the evil we find to Satan or to Satan and his cohorts. Satan,
> so the traditional doctrine goes, is a mighty nonhuman spirit who, along with
> many other angels, was created long before God created man. Unlike most
> of his colleagues, Satan rebelled against God and has been wreaking what-
> ever havoc he can. The result is natural evil. So the natural evil we find is
> due to the free actions of nonhuman spirits.[9]

What is to be said about this? Plantinga admits many people find belief
in the devil preposterous, let alone Augustine's idea that the devil is responsible

for whatever natural evil we find. But this does not amount to much of an argument against Augustine's thesis, Plantinga insists. Truth is not decided by majority vote. However, Plantinga's main point against those who object to his luciferous defense is to insist that to do the job of solving what I am calling the LPE, proposition (7) (which, as we have seen, claims that *all* evil is due to the choices of created free moral agents) need only be *possibly true*. And this seems quite correct. As we saw, in order to solve the LPE, (7) need only be consistent with (6), capable of entailing (3) when conjoined with (6), and possibly true. As far as the LPE is concerned, Plantinga seems to be quite correct, and I confess he has convinced me. It certainly does seem *possible* that natural evil is due to the choices of Satan. Thus the luciferous defense can solve the LPE as concerns natural evil.

All three objections to the FWD as a solution to the LPE apparently fail. Those who push the LPE argue that Christians and other theists contradict themselves by believing in the omnipotence and goodness of God and the existence of evil. We can now see that this is not true. The FWD successfully rebuts this charge.

But even if it is true that theism is logically consistent, there is another difficulty that remains, viz., what I call the EPE. This difficulty too concerns this proposition that is believed by theists:

> *(8) God is omnipotent and God is good and evil exists.*

Now against (8), someone might say something like this:[10]

> I admit there is no logical inconsistency in (8), but the problem of evil, when grasped in its full depth, is deeper than a mere logical exercise. A cold logical approach that merely shows the consistency of (8) fails to touch the problem at its deepest nerve. To show, as a sheer logical exercise, that (8) is consistent does nothing to convince people to believe (8). To show that (8) is *possibly true* does not show that it is *true* or even *probably true*, i.e., it does nothing to show that people should believe in God's omnipotence and goodness.

There is much that must be sorted out in these words. What exactly does the EPE come to? This is not altogether clear in the above lines, and perhaps it might help to suggest some possible interpretations.

Words such as those above are sometimes expressed with deep emotion. Perhaps the EPE means something like this: the existence of evil in the world somehow *makes us deeply feel* that

> *(6) God is omnipotent and God is good*

is false. That is, the existence of evil in the world makes us deeply feel that (2) and/or (3) must be rejected or modified. Because of evil, we find (6) *hard to believe*. Now there are obviously people about whom this could truly be said. Albert Camus comes to mind. So does Elie Wiesel. But despite this, it is hard to detect any real difficulty for theism here. By itself, this seems no more serious an objection to theism than, say, the following comment: "You theists believe in God but somehow I can't."

But perhaps the EPE means something more than this. Perhaps the claim is that the existence of evil makes (6) *improbable* or *implausible*, that the existence of evil constitutes *strong evidence against* (6). But the problem with this is that it is difficult to see how any probabalistic judgments can be made here. And this is for the obvious reason that we do not seem to be in a position to make a probability judgment about the truth of the FWD. As I have claimed, the FWD claims that (8) is consistent because the following proposition is possibly true:

> (7) *All the evil that exists in the world is due to the choices of free moral agents whom God created, and no other world which God could have created would have had a better balance of good over evil than the actual world will have.*

If we knew that (7) was false or improbable we might have good reason to deny (6). But in fact we do not know that (7) is false or improbable (at least I am aware of no good argument or evidence that falsifies [7]), and so we do not seem to be in a position to say that (6) is false or improbable.

There seems to be no way for us to argue analogically either. We might be able to do so if the following proposition were known to be true:

> (9) *There are ninety universes in which evil exists but no good, omnipotent God and only ten universes in which evil and a good, omnipotent God both exist.*

If (9) were known to be true we might be able to make a probability estimate – someone might claim, at any rate, that (9) renders the probability that (6) is true.1. But in fact (9) is not only not known to be true – it does not even appear to make good sense. Since the term *universe* is all-inclusive (nothing except perhaps God lies outside "the universe"), there are no "other universes" than ours with which we can compare it.[11]

But perhaps there is another way of stating the "probability" interpretation of the EPE. "If you were the Christian God – the omnipotent and good creator of the world – what sort of world would you create? One thing is certain: you wouldn't create this sort of world. You wouldn't create a world containing cancer, atomic bombs, child abuse, and famine. You would create a world without these evils. Thus it appears highly improbable that the world was created by the Christian God."[12]

I will say some things later that are relevant to this objection, but for now I wish simply to insist that I have not the vaguest idea what sort of world I would create given the stated conditions, nor do I believe anyone else does. Of course, my general aim would be to create a world with the best possible balance of good over evil. Would eliminating cancer or free moral agents achieve this end? I just don't know, and I do not believe anyone else does either. Of course it is *possible* that if I knew all relevant facts I would create a world much different than this one. But it is also *possible* that I would create a world as much like this one as I could. I just don't know enough to say, and neither does anyone else, in my opinion. And I fail to see any argument here that renders the first more probable than the second. Perhaps, somehow, the existence of evil in the world (or the existence of a large amount of evil in the world) does render (6) improbable. But I am unable to see how it does or even can. At best, we must await the skeptic's explanation precisely how the existence of evil renders (6) improbable. It is not clear at this point that it does.

Possibly there are other interpretations of the EPE that are more threatening to theism than these. I cannot think of any, however, and so I conclude that the EPE poses no philosophical difficulty for theism. If the theist's problem when confronted with the LPE is the apologetic task of responding to the critic's charge that theism is inconsistent, then if the LPE can be solved (by the FWD or any other argument) I see no added philosophical problem for theism in the EPE. I believe I have shown that (8) is consistent, and so believe that this defensive apologetic task has been accomplished.

But perhaps there is still a residual feeling that the problem of evil has not been completely disposed of. *I* confess to having such a feeling, and perhaps other theists will too. But I believe this residual feeling that somehow still not all is well is based on no philosophical difficulty but rather on what might be called the *evangelistic difficulty* that the problem of evil poses for theists. This difficulty is not the negative apologetic task of responding to a philosophical criticism, but rather the positive evangelistic task of *convincing people to believe* (6).

I have been using the term *philosophical difficulty*. There exists what I call a philosophical difficulty for a belief if there is some reason to consider it either logically inconsistent or disconfirmed by the preponderance of available evidence. Thus all philosophical difficulties are also "evangelistic difficulties," for it is usually hard to convince someone to accept an apparently inconsistent or apparently ill-founded belief. But some evangelistic difficulties are clearly not philosophical — e.g., the difficulty we might have trying to convince a patient in a mental hospital to accept the belief that he is not Napoleon.

Now trying to convince people to believe
> *(6) God is omnipotent and God is good*
may indeed be a serious difficulty. But evangelism is not philosophy. If philosophers have successfully defended theism against the charge that
> *(8) God is omnipotent and God is good and evil exists*
is inconsistent or improbable, it is difficult to see what else they can or must do. They may not be able to convert a person who says, "I'm sorry, but because evil exists I just can't see how a good, omnipotent God can exist." But they can point out that this person's inability to believe does not in itself constitute a good reason for the theist to give up belief. Thus, I conclude the EPE may pose difficulties for theism, but not philosophical difficulties.

One obvious weakness of many theodicies is that they cannot account for the huge *amount* of evil that apparently exists in the world. For example, some theodicists claim that pain and adversity are really good because they help people rise to new moral and spiritual heights in overcoming them. No doubt this is true in some cases – the athlete who improves performance because of a rigorous and painful training regime, the novelist whose works are more deeply insightful into human nature because of early struggles, say, with poverty and rejection notices from unappreciative publishers. But this theodicy simply cannot account for the amount of suffering that we see in the world. How can the murder of six million Jews in World War II lead people to new and otherwise unobtainable heights? The very thought seems absurd, almost obscene.

At first glance, the FWD seems less embarassed than other theodicies by the amount of evil that exists in the world; the free will defender will simply say of all evil events that they are due not to God (or at least not directly to God) but rather to created free moral agents who choose to do evil. But at a deeper level, the FWD still seems open to this objection. For when we consider people like Hitler and events like the Holocaust we are bound to wonder whether the facility of free moral choice, which the FWD says God gave human beings, has turned out to be worth the price. Even if we grant that it is a *prima facie* good that God created us free moral agents rather than causally determined automata, we can still wonder, to put it in economic terms, whether this freedom has turned out to be cost-effective. Surely some will say (perhaps one of the millions of surviving Jews who lost family and friends in the Holocaust), ''I wish God had created a world of more determinism and less murder.''

The notion of our being *less free* than the FWD claims that we are seems to make perfectly good sense. For example, I am not now free to destroy the planet Saturn: apparently God has not given me that ability. But then why couldn't God have created me with an analogous inability to commit murder? Why didn't God, for example, place us in an environment that provided fewer opportunities or temptations to go wrong than he in fact did? Or why didn't he create us with a stronger psychological endowment – say, a stronger desire to do good or a weaker desire to do evil?

There are two points I wish to make about this. First, we do not know whether freedom is cost-effective. Let us be clear what it is we are evaluating: it is the policy decision God made (according to the FWD) to allow human beings moral freedom, i.e., freedom to do right or wrong without interference. Obviously, a correct decision on whether or not a given policy is cost-effective cannot be made till the results of the policy are in and can be evaluated. But how can we now correctly decide whether freedom will turn out to be cost-effective when we have no idea how human history will turn out? Perhaps it is true, as Christians believe, that the eschaton holds in store for us such great goods that all pre-eschaton evils will be outweighed. We do not know whether this claim is true, and so we do not know whether God's policy will turn out to be cost-effective.

Of course decisions often have to be made on the basis of inconclusive evidence. Perhaps it is true that each person, here and now, must decide whether to believe that freedom is cost-effective, just in the sense that each person must decide, here and now, whether to believe in a good, omnipotent God despite the presence of evil in the world. And such a decision can obviously be made only on the basis of evidence that is presently available (although some people believe there is evidence that the Christian eschaton is coming). But even if, for pragmatic reasons, such a decision must be made here and now, it can still be seen that it is ultimately unfair to try to make (at this time and with the evidence we now have) a correct judgment about the cost-effectiveness of God's policy. If there turns out to be no Christian eschaton, or if history ends in a violent bang or a desperate whimper, then perhaps we will see that freedom is not cost-effective. But we cannot see that now.

The second point is that only God knows whether freedom will turn out to be cost-effective. Only he knows how human history turns out, what our destiny is. Furthermore, only God is in a position to weigh huge goods and evils against each other in order to make correct judgments whether, say, World War II was, on balance, a morally good or morally evil event. Thus only God is in a position to judge whether moral freedom will turn out to be worth the price.

Of course it may be difficult for Christians and other theists to *convince people* that freedom is cost-effective. But this reduces to the evangelistic difficulty, which, as I said, is not a philosophical difficulty. Questions about the cost-effectiveness of freedom do not succeed in showing that theism is inconsistent, nor do they give the theist any good reason to doubt that freedom is cost-effective. Thus, so far as I can see, they raise no philosophical difficulties for theism.

Let me now return to the question of the truth and not just the logical possibility of the Augustinian answer to the problem of natural evil. Here we face the following difficult question: are the general claims made in the context of the FWD *true* and not just *possibly true*? I believe they are, but can I convince someone else? Can the evangelistic difficulty be solved? Of course, in answering the LPE all I needed was possibly true, i.e., logically consistent, statements. But if I am able to solve the evangelistic difficulty of the EPE I must show that they are true. For if I can show people that they are true I have done about all I can do to evangelize them, i.e., convince them to believe that God is omnipotent and good. The rest is up to them. But, sadly, I do not believe I can do so.

To solve the evangelistic aspect of the EPE would in general require two convincing arguments — first, that natural evil *is* caused by the choices of free moral agents such as Satan, and second, that God's policy decision to create free moral agents is wise because freedom *will* turn out to be cost-effective. All

Christians believe the second and many Christians believe the first. But the difficulty is that these propositions are only known by revelation; they are objects of faith, not knowledge. Private evidence would typically be appealed to by Christians in explaining why they believe them. I do not see how they can be substantiated by means of public evidence.

This same result appears when we consider a fourth objection to the FWD. It comes in several forms, but since all forms question the compatibility of the FWD with the doctrine of divine foreknowledge, I will call it the "foreknowledge objection." To facilitate matters, let me speak of several possible categories of free human agents. First, there is the set of all free human agents who are morally perfect, i.e., who never sin. Then there is the set of all free human agents who are morally imperfect, i.e., who sometimes err. Then there is the subset of morally imperfect agents called the Blessed, i.e., those who will spend eternity with God in heaven. Next there is the subset of morally imperfect human agents called the Damned, i.e., those who will spend eternity apart from God in hell. Finally, there is the subset of the Damned who are by all accounts moral monsters who cause great human suffering, e.g., people like Hitler.

We can now pose the various forms of the foreknowledge objection as a series of questions: first, why didn't God foresee which persons, if created, would be morally perfect and which would be morally imperfect and then choose to create only those who would belong in the first group? Second, if there is some reason why morally imperfect people must exist, why didn't God at least foresee which morally imperfect persons would be blessed and which would be damned and then choose to create only those who would be blessed? Third, if there is some reason why some members of the set of the Damned must exist, why didn't God at least foresee which of the Damned would be moral monsters and then refrain from creating them? These, then, are the various forms of the fore-knowledge objection. Let me attempt to deal with them in turn.

In response to the first question, I have already admitted that it is logically possible for free moral agents never to sin — I only insisted that if this happened it would be a sort of happy accident from God's perspective, not attributable to him. Now in response to this first form of the foreknowledge objection, Plantinga raises the possibility of what he calls "transworld depravity."[13] This is the property of any being which does at least one morally wrong action in every possible world which God could have actualized. Plantinga says that it is logically possible that every free human agent whom God could have created suffers from transworld depravity. This seems to me quite correct — it is possible and does indeed help show that the LPE can be solved.

But in the context of the EPE, we must ask whether the claim that all possible free human agents suffer from transworld depravity is not just possible but true. And I believe the answer is that it is not. There are, in my opinion, possible worlds in which even Hitler never sins, e.g., those in which he dies at the age of two days. However, there is a weakened kind of transworld depravity from which I believe all free human agents do indeed suffer. I believe in transworld depravity for all free human agents, first, who live long enough to make a significant number of moral choices, and, second, who live in worlds relevantly similar to the actual world. And the main relevant similarity I have in mind here is that the world be one which God has designed with the same purpose in mind that I claimed earlier he in fact has for the actual world. I believe it is highly probable that any free human agent who must make a significant number of moral choices in a world like ours will eventually go wrong.

So the answer to the first question is: given God's aims and desires in creation, i.e., his aim to create a world in which free human agents would freely say yes to him, it may well be that the category of morally perfect human agents is an empty set (with the exception of Jesus Christ). Given the pervasive influence of evil in the actual world, I seriously doubt that any free human agent who reaches an age of moral and spiritual responsibility (whatever it is) will remain morally innocent for long. Of course God could have ensured that evil would have no pervasive influence in the world, but given his aims in creation he ran the risk that evil would run rampant, and unfortunately it did.

The second question asks why God didn't create only those whom he could foresee would be blessed and not those whom he could see would be damned. As is well known, some believers answer this objection by denying that there are any damned: we can be sure, they say, that all people will eventually be saved. Much as I would like to follow this line, I do not believe any biblical Christian can do so. Universalism is far too clearly inconsistent with Scripture to constitute a viable option to those like me who have a high regard for its authority.

The quick answer to the second question is: I don't know. I do not know why God created those whom he knew would be damned and not just those whom he knew would be blessed. But fortunately this is not all that can be said. For one thing, I believe there are serious problems of personal indentity here. Perhaps these problems can be solved; but my point can be made in this way: suppose that John Jones, Sr. is in the actual world part of the Damned and that his son, John Jones, Jr., is in the actual world part of the Blessed. Now the second form of the foreknowledge objection can be seen as asking why God, foreseeing this, didn't choose to create John Jones, Jr. but not John Jones, Sr., his father. But the problem here is that John Jones, Jr. just *is* John Jones, Sr.'s son. Could John Jones, Jr. *be* John Jones, Jr. without being John Jones, Sr.'s son? The answer to this, I believe, depends on the answer to two further questions: do souls as coherent individuals preexist their embodied lives? and can souls at birth be packaged, so to speak, in any number of ways? Those who, like me, strongly suspect that the answer to both questions is no will be inclined to deny that God could have created John Jones, Jr. without having created John Jones, Sr. To ask God to do so is to ask him to do the logically impossible.

But the main point I wish to make in response to the second form of the foreknowledge objection is that the existence of hell is quite compatible with the existence of a good God, once we rid ourselves of common misconceptions about it. I do indeed believe that there is a place called hell but I do not believe it is a place where, a la Dante, protesting people are led against their will to be tortured vengefully. I believe the people who will end up separated from God freely choose hell and would be unhappy in God's presence. Having lived their lives apart from God, they will choose to go on doing so. Furthermore, I do not believe hell is a place of suffering or torture. Biblical metaphors that seem to suggest so point, I believe, to the deep regret the citizens of hell will feel that they are not able to live in the presence of God, the source of all life, light, and love in the universe. Though they freely choose hell and could not be happy in paradise, I believe they will clearly understand what they have chosen to miss.

The third question asks why God didn't avoid creating those free human agents whom he foresaw would be moral monsters. Again I must say here that I do not know. It is similar to what I said earlier about particularly heinous events in world history: Christians need not feel that they can explain why God allowed them to occur. Ultimately it comes down to trust. Some people trust in God and some do not; the ones who do trust in God choose not to question him inordinately (Isa. 45:9-11). They believe he has the answers to many questions that now appear to us unanswerable. Christians, then, believe, though they cannot prove, that God had a good reason for allowing evil people to exist and evil events to occur. Christians do not claim to know what that reason is, but trust in God.

Thus, again, we see that there is an aspect of the emotive problem of evil that remains a problem: the difficulty the believer has in convincing the nonbeliever to believe in God's goodness and omnipotence. This leads me to conclude as follows about the problem of evil: on a philosophical level, the LPE can be solved but the evangelistic aspect of the EPE cannot. That is, I have no *philosophical* tools for convincing people who because of evil deny God's omnipotence and/or goodness instead to affirm God's omnipotence and goodness. Perhaps there are other tools at my disposal; perhaps I can *preach* to them. But it is at this point that Christian philosophy comes to the end of its tether and can do no more for faith.

Let me conclude by indicating briefly why I find the FWD, or at least this version of it, attractive. The first and most obvious is that the FWD is a theodicy which does not require that theists give up any of their crucial beliefs. If sound, the FWD shows that a rational person can indeed believe in the existence both of evil and of a good, omnipotent God. Second, the FWD is a theodicy which grows out of the witness of the Christian Scriptures. It is not the arbitrary invention of some philosopher or theologian; rather, it emerges from two great biblical stories – the story of the moral freedom of God's creatures and of the contingent entry of evil into the world in Genesis 2 and 3, and the story of God's final triumph over all the forces of sin, disorder, and death in the book of Revelation and in the theology of Paul. Finally, the FWD is a theodicy which recognizes its limits. There are such things as mysteries; not all theological questions can be answered. There is a level at which faith as trust in God is necessary. Free will defenders are quite prepared to admit that there are questions they cannot now answer, or at least not very well. They only trust that some day they will know the answers, as God now knows them. "For now we see in a mirror dimly, but then face to face. Now I know in part; then I shall understand fully" (1 Cor. 13:12).

Critiques

Critique by Frederick Sontag

The main question which Davis must answer before we can decide about the adequacy of his theodicy is how he distinguishes what he cannot know about God from what he can. His proposition number seven admits that the core of the question is whether God could or could not have created a better world. But he backs away from answering this by claiming he just doesn't know and doesn't believe anyone else does either. He wants to postpone any decision about whether God's plan for the world is "cost-effective" until the end of time. However, I can easily conceive of better worlds than the one we occupy, and I find it quite clear that our present system is wasteful in achieving good results for everyone (if we accept this as God's intent). Davis knows a great deal about God in other respects. Why does he wrap himself in pious mystery at this crucial point? No one has asked for a final divine pronouncement. But according to Davis' best present judgment, couldn't the world have been better, and couldn't good have been achieved more efficiently, if that is God's intent?

Davis believes that God is "perfectly good," but the whole issue hangs on the meaning of "good," which is far from obvious. Need "goodness" exclude "evil"? There is no a priori reason that it should, unless we agree to define it in that way. We begin neither with the meaning of "good" clear nor the nature of God obvious, and everything depends on how we work these terms out, given the number of choices in front of us. Davis asserts (somewhat peevishly?) that he will be uninterested in any solution which "denies that God is wholly good." But the issue is not to shout "yes" or "no," but to ask what does "wholly good" mean? I think God is wholly good, but I also think that God is freely the source of some of the evil that plagues human existence. Obviously Davis and I do not mean the same thing by "wholly good," but let's set the issue there, and not assume goodness to be one thing or defined in some obvious way.

In Davis' FWD defense he assumes that God wanted "to create the best universe he could." But why should we assume this, when it begs the whole question? Little in the world we experience justifies such an assumption. Hume is right on naturalist grounds, and I believe it is a questionable assumption even on religious grounds. God didn't just run the risk so that people might choose evil. Given our world, it is more than "quite possible" that evil will appear. It is unavoidable, and any God with intelligence must have known this. Davis offers us only two alternatives, that the good will turn out to outweigh the evil, and this option is opposed to our being denied free will. But did God have only two options? From what we know of possibility, God had a whole scale of alternatives varying in degree. Such neat, simple options are for children not for Gods or responsible people. The "best possible world" notion is not like the tallest conceivable man, and in neither case is it a matter of pressing the increase to infinity. It is a question of why God stopped where he did on the sliding scale. Davis' options are too neat, too cut and dried; they are an offense to a subtle God.

If the balance of good over evil, which Davis expects to obtain in the end, could be obtained by God "in no other way," God is not free. He is bound by Davis' restrictions. What we know of life and the world before us denies that our options are so fixed, so I see no reason not to open God's options at least as widely as ours. This means that God could have achieved his ends in a variety of ways. Our argument and his dilemma concern why he chose the option he did when he did not have to. Davis confesses that he cannot explain how a Holocaust will turn out to be good, so why either restrict God to a plan which ends with a favorable balance of good or prevent him from choosing among a variety of options? Davis again restricts God's power when he says God could not have created a better world than ours. This postulates a weak deity since humans, given the same power, might have.

The possibility of doing evil may be an inevitable companion to the possibility of freely doing good, but again the issue is one of the degree and the alternative plans which might have given us more favorable odds. We may not live in the best of all possible worlds, but certainly we do not live in the world which offers us the best possible odds for human success. Too many have no chance at all for that to be true. The world is not a Marine Corps survival course. Some of us are poorly equipped and ill-trained for what we must face. A few succeed and learn, if that is what God wanted, but those who survive are not too many, given the mass of humanity. Davis makes a quick reference to Satan as the cause of evil, but that needs more explanation before it can be taken seriously. Davis claims not to know what kind of world he would have created that would have been any better, and he doesn't think anyone else does either. I can only reply: "Speak for yourself, Stephen." I can think of 101 improvements we could make that would improve our odds and not take away the element of struggle or free choice, and so can many other men and women who work to improve human conditions.

Can there be an "evangelistic difficulty" in convincing people to believe, if there is no remaining philosophical difficulty concerning evil, as Davis suggests? That does not quite make sense, for then the religious option should be so logical and obvious that believing would be the easiest option. If there is an evangelistic difficulty, it must be because our philosophical options are wide and our choices not obvious. Davis offers a neat definition of "philosophical difficulty" according to which there are none regarding evil. But the problem is that philosophers for centuries have not accepted such neat definitions and insisted on opening up every issue again, as I do. Davis admits he cannot account for the "amount" of evil in the world, but that is the core of the problem. Like the warmth of the porridge the three bears tasted, if we thought that evil was "just right," it would not be the painful issue it is.

Davis creates a friendly, non-threatening God for himself when he shifts all the responsibility for evil over to "free moral agents," but surely we know that all the destruction in the world is not of human origin. We don't have to wait till the end of history to see if God's design is cost-effective. We have seen so much waste to date that neither a utopia on earth nor a heavenly existence later could justify it. Surely we have no reason, now that our optimism over "progress" is gone, to think that human history in the future will be any better? Or if it is, it will be thanks to humans and no thanks to God for having delayed improvements so long. Why is it "unfair" to make a judgment on the cost-effectiveness of God's policy? Every evil force destroying our world demands that we do so. And it is better to have tried, even if we are proven wrong, than to accept evil on some supposed grounds of piety.

If God knows the answer now, as Davis suggests, should he care if we second guess him? The theist has no good reason to doubt the cost-effectiveness of God's plan, Davis asserts. But if he cannot know that it is so, why doesn't it raise doubts in his mind? – that I cannot understand. And if I do not believe God's policy decisions will turn out to be cost-effective, Davis cannot assert that "all" Christians believe this. It would be nice if there were such unanimity in Christendom but there is not, not even about the statement of the issues or the definition of terms. Davis slips in an appeal to "revelation" to support his view, but I do not think we have had any revelations concerning these matters. At times Davis knows quite surely why God does certain things, but at other times he hides behind a claim to ignorance concerning God. We cannot decide about Davis' theodicy until we know how he distinguishes what he can know about God from what he cannot.

Critique by John H. Hick

Davis represents what is probably the most vigorous philosophical contribution to the theodicy discussion during the last decade, a contribution associated above all with the name of Alvin Plantinga. However I see two vulnerable points in Davis' version of this position.

The basic concern of a theodicy in this tradition — a tradition which goes back to St. Augustine — is to shift the blame for the occurrence of evil from the creator to the creatures. As Davis puts it, "So God is not to be blamed for the existence of evil in the world — we are." The first vulnerable point, as it seems to me, occurs in his account of the origin of moral evil. The traditional Augustinian doctrine, which Davis feels obliged to modify, was that the creation was originally perfect. It came directly from God's hand and was as God wanted it to be, lacking nothing and containing no flaw of any kind. But within this perfect creation — Augustine claimed — free creatures nevertheless rebelled and thus brought evil into being. This scheme has been criticized from the time of Schleiermacher on the ground that perfect creatures, although formally free to fall, would never in fact do so. Davis apparently accepts this criticism, and suggests that the free creatures were created, not as finitely perfect beings, but as "spiritually immature, morally neutral creatures." My question is whether he should not now go further in the direction of the Irenaean alternative to the Augustinian type of theodicy, and acknowledge that human kind was originally not only spiritually immature but also morally imperfect. For it seems to be a fact that humans emerged within the process of biological evolution as intelligent animals, programmed to seek their survival within a harsh environment, and thus with a basic self-regardingness which is the essence of "sin." Human beings also, however, emerged as spiritual beings, with a potentiality to transcend their natural egoism; and human life has been the story of the interplay of these two aspects of human nature.

As well as being faithful to the empirical facts as made known to us by biological and anthropological science, an acknowledgment that persons were brought into existence as morally and spiritually imperfect creatures at the beginning of a long further creative process would in my view also make possible a more realistic interpretation of the natural evil of the world. Davis has to attribute the occurrence of earthquakes, tornadoes, droughts, floods, epidemics etc., to the agency of morally responsible powers, namely devils or the Devil. Aware that such an attribution is today almost totally lacking in plausibility, he follows Plantinga into the logical vacuum of holding that this attribution need only be *possibly* true. And of course it is, uncontroversially, that. It is not only logically possible that a "mighty nonhuman spirit" has deliberately cracked the earth's crust so as to produce earthquakes, but equally possible that multitudes of nonhuman spirits are at this moment busily at work around the world causing accidents, diseases, toothaches, bad weather, blighted crops, and all the other natural ills that flesh is heir to. But such a logical possibility does not amount to a theodicy that most of us can be expected to take seriously.

However if we follow out the implications of the acknowledgment that human beings were created, through the evolutionary process, as morally and spiritually imperfect creatures, and ask what *sort* of a world would constitute an appropriate environment in which such beings might freely develop the potentialities of their spirit, we can I believe see that it will not be a painfree paradise but something like the kind of world in which we find ourselves. For moral and spiritual development comes by challenge and response, and in a paradise this would not occur.

Turning very briefly to the second half of Davis' chapter, I do not think that we can separate what he calls the "philosophical" and "emotive" problems as he wishes, restricting the philosophical task to the production of a bare logical possibility and relegating the plausibility of this possible metaphysical picture to the realm of the emotive. Surely the philosophical task is not merely to construct a logically possible hypothesis, but to construct one which also accounts for the data of human experience and is consistent with our existing knowledge. To attempt this is to respond to a philosophical and not merely an emotive problem.

I do, however, think that Davis is importantly right in holding that a Christian theodicy has to be eschatologically oriented. It has to maintain that "the eschaton holds in store for us such great goods that all pre-eschaton evils will be outweighed." On this fundamental issue I want to accept Davis' position.

Critique by David R. Griffin

Much of my response to Davis' essay was given in advance in the second section of my essay: he holds the positions I argue against in points 2, 3, 5, 7, 8 and in the conclusion.

Our most central difference is that Davis believes there to be explicit doctrines vouchsafed by "revelation," and that the task of the theodicist is to show that the revealed doctrines relevant to the problem of evil are not inconsistent with each other. Merely showing that they are not necessarily inconsistent completes the job; there is no need to present an account of the world that can be readily perceived by troubled minds to be more probable than other accounts of the world. Hence, Davis sets an easier task for himself than does Hick, who at least tries to make his view plausible.

Davis examines what the criterion of plausibility might mean and dismisses all the interpretations of it that occur to him. From this he concludes that the charge that orthodox Christian theism is implausible constitutes no difficulty for it. However, he does not consider what I would take to be the central meaning of the claim that the Christian view of reality should be plausible: it should be able to provide plausible answers to the various types of questions it arouses. When Davis does give answers, they have an *ad hoc* flavor. For example, after denying Hick's doctrine of universal salvation on the basis of the Bible's authority, he rejects the notion that hell is a place of suffering by saying that the biblical statements implying that it is are mere "metaphors." And he defends as highly probable the view that "any free human agent who must make a significant number of moral choices in a world like ours will eventually go wrong," but in the next paragraph he exempts Jesus from this universal claim. (Also, I am unclear why he thinks a "highly probable" judgment is possible on this issue, given what he said about probabilistic judgments earlier.)

But for the most part, Davis does not even attempt to give answers to the obvious questions raised by his position; he simply says, "I don't know," time and time again. For example, he feels no need to give even a hint as to why his God, who could have easily prevented the Nazi Holocaust, chose to allow it to occur.

Accordingly, although Davis begins his essay by saying that "people ought to believe what it is rational for them to believe," his notion of what is "rational" is much too limited for me. For him, being rational is consistent with simply trusting that God has all the answers and not even trying to discover them. If I had to choose, I would find Roth's attitude of protest much more compatible with the full use of our God-given powers to which I believe God calls us.

Davis thinks it is rational to wait until the end of history to see if there are answers to all the questions, and to assume in the meantime that there are. He considers the obvious objection, that we must formulate our beliefs on the basis of evidence that is presently available. But he argues that it would be "ultimately unfair to try to make . . . a correct judgment about the cost-effectiveness of God's policy." Unfair to whom – to God? This is to beg the question, which is whether Davis' kind of God exists. Furthermore, if it is unfair to make a negative judgment, then is it not equally unfair to make a positive judgment? Rather than the trust which Davis advocates, the rational position would seem to be (by his argument) to withhold judgment altogether.

There is even a prior problem in Davis' position. He begins by saying that he will not accept a theodicy that gives up (among other things) the claim that "evil exists." Yet he seems to do just that, if we are talking about *genuine* evil (anything without which the universe would have been better, all things considered). In seemingly denying that it is necessary to say that this is the best of all possible worlds, he illustrates by suggesting that the world would have been *morally* better without the Nazi Holocaust. But in the next paragraph and elsewhere he seems to say that the Holocaust was necessary for the world to have been *better overall* than it could have been without it. In other words, the *moral* evil was compensated for by the goodness (perhaps moral *and* non-moral) to which it contributed. But this is simply to say that the moral evil was not *genuinely* evil, once its instrumental value is taken into account. And in his seventh proposition Davis seems to affirm explicitly that this is at least *one* of the best possible worlds, since he says that "no other world which God could have created would have had a better balance of good over evil than the actual world will have." If "genuine evil" is that which prevents this from being one of the best possible worlds, then Davis is making his three propositions consistent by simply denying one of them. If he does not accept this definition of (genuine) evil, then he is surely giving some definition to the term that would make it puzzling why the "problem of evil" had ever arisen: no one would be disturbed by the doctrine that God is omnipotent and perfectly good if they believed that nothing ever happens that prevents the world from being as good overall as it could have been.

Furthermore, as I suggested in the fifth point in the second part of my essay, the notion that genuine evil occurs is one of those "common notions" which we all accept in practice. It is because we *know* that genuine evil occurs that the twin claims about God's omnipotence and perfect goodness are troubling. Accordingly, from my point of view, Davis has "solved" the logical problem of evil by denying the one premise of the three that we all know to be true. This provides another sense in which I cannot accept his view as rational. And this for me also counts against its being fully Christian, since I believe the Christian God calls us to full rationality.

As a footnote, one can wonder whether Davis, by following Plantinga, has not denied God's omnipotence, as defined by Davis. He says it would be a denial of omnipotence to say that God "is simply not able to prevent evil." But in endorsing Plantinga's notion of transworld depravity, he is saying in effect that, since every possible world contains moral evil in it, God simply cannot create an actual world devoid of moral evil. I wonder why a limitation placed on what God can do by other *actualities* (my position) is unacceptable to Davis, while a limitation placed on God by *possibilities* is not.

Critique by John K. Roth

Stephen Davis has the office next to mine. Usually we are not very far apart on philosophical issues either, but for a long time our views on the problem of evil have been at odds. Since Davis has rightly linked me with what he calls "the emotive problem of evil" (EPE), a position to which he takes strong exception, I shall concentrate on the portion of his essay that deals with it.

Speaking philosophically, Davis implies that it is not only necessary but also sufficient for him to accomplish a "defensive apologetic task." Committed to the proposition that God is both omnipotent and perfectly good in spite of a world full of evil, he claims first that there is no logical inconsistency in that belief.

Because the logical possibility of a theory tells us so little about its soundness, especially where theodicy is concerned, I am willing to let Davis' logical analysis stand uncontested. His position, though, has a second dimension that is much more problematic.

This second dimension involves Davis' demonstration that his own position is not "disconfirmed by the preponderance of available evidence." If that case can be made, he believes, all philosophical difficulties are set aside. The only remaining problems are evangelistic. To make his case, Davis resorts to what I shall call the "I Just Don't Know Defense." (Though tempted to do so, I refrain from labeling it the IJDKD.) I find this defense untenable, and thus Davis' theodicy fails to persuade me.

According to Davis, God wanted to create "the best possible balance of moral and natural good over moral and natural evil." Although humanity's sinful abuse of freedom bollixed original perfection, an outcome that Davis repeatedly calls sad and unfortunate, nonetheless "good . . . will outweigh the evil." Of course, it will not do just to have some arbitrary outweighing of good over evil, say 50.1% of good vs. 49.9% of evil, unless that is the best that God can do. Either of those outcomes would cause inconvenient questions to come to the fore. For example, could not God have arranged things so that a more favorable percentage of good prevailed? Indeed should he not have done so, given that the ideal situation would have been one in which beings created free to sin never did? If God really wants the best possible balance of good over evil, is it not evident that his choices backfired? And is it not clear that they did so precisely because of the nature of freedom that God created originally and because of his refusal to take decisive steps to reduce its wasteful propensities as time passed?

The Holocaust, Davis asserts, occurred because human freedom was badly used. At the same time, Davis confesses that Auschwitz is quite beyond him when it comes to offering an account for that event's presence in God's presumably cost-effective economy. Ordinarily, inability to render such an account would serve as evidence against God's perfect goodness, but Davis aims to turn the tables. By enlarging the confession, ignorance becomes his ally. To the question, for instance, of whether cancer's immediate elimination would enhance the best possible balance of good over evil – or I assume we could think of the non-occurrence of the Holocaust in this same regard – Davis says, "I just don't know."

Appearances to the contrary notwithstanding, "we do not know whether freedom is cost-effective." The conclusion, unintended though it may be, is obvious; ignorance is bliss. But there is even more. Not only does Davis argue that these defensive appeals to ignorance are supposedly justified because the final results have not yet appeared. He even believes that "it is *ultimately unfair* to try to make (at this time and with the evidence we now have) a correct judgment about the cost-effectiveness of God's policy" (my italics). In response to this curious reasoning I can only ask: ultimately unfair to whom?

The appeal of ignorance eludes me, but not because emotion has carried me away. On the contrary, Davis' defense-based-on-ignorance simply fails to take seriously enough how much *evidence* there really is that an optimal balance of good over evil could be much enhanced by the elimination of cancer now, or by God's direct intervention to check the freedom that can unleash a Holocaust. Otherwise how are we to understand the huge amounts of money, time, and energy spent annually in trying to rid human life of cancer's waste. From a human point of view, these efforts are made just because people are convinced beyond any reasonable doubt that cancer ought not to be. Other persons work equally hard to forestall repetitions of Auschwitz. Why? Is it not because the preponderance of available evidence is so plain? Mass murder wastes and destroys too much, so much in fact that many people find reasons good and sufficient enough to deny that evil can be outweighed by a perfectly good God. A perfectly good God – in any justifiable sense that we can give to those terms – would never have permitted such murder in the first place.

Davis, it seems to me, has the problem exactly backwards. He would make it the skeptic's responsibility to show how cancer and the Holocaust render improbable the claim that "God is omnipotent and God is good." But let us not forget that the latter part of that quoted statement must read "perfectly good" – unless Davis has changed his mind – and that qualification makes all the difference. Sufficient evidence is available for anyone who will see it. It consists of millions who have suffered without justification and died without peace. If God is omnipotent, his "perfect" goodness becomes less perfect every day.

Perhaps, then, the fundamental issue raised by Davis' essay is simply this: what shall count as *evidence*? Davis' persuasive powers may be considerable, but I doubt that he can accomplish the evangelistic task of getting me to assent to his creed. The reason he will not be able to do so is because I see evidence in terms of waste that makes it abundantly clear to me that there is no credible sense of "perfectly good" that I could attach to God. Davis admits that waste poses a problem, but ignorance is his defense, and from that fortress he calls upon the skeptics to show him his error. Of course, if one has already concluded that there cannot be sufficient damning evidence because we do not know enough to judge, there is an impasse indeed. Short of testimony that heaven alone can give, we should ask Davis, is there anything that could possibly count as sufficient evidence that his propositions about God's omnipotence and perfect goodness are mistaken? I suspect that he must say, "I just don't know," or else pronounce an inconsistent "absolutely not." Meanwhile Auschwitz can be visited, cancer wards can be observed, racked and ruined lives cry out in anguish on every hand. How ignorant can we be? How ignorant *should* we be?

In conclusion Davis tells us that his theodicy has three advantages. It does not require one to give up the belief that God is omnipotent and perfectly good. Maintaining that belief, however, would be an advantage only if the belief makes good sense and where God's perfect goodness is concerned, I am unable to follow Davis' lead. I know, too, that I am far from alone. Evidence gives me company. Second, Davis says, his theodicy grows out of Christian Scripture. But so do many others; Scripture does not contain some single theodicy alone. In fact, that outcome is itself one facet of the problem of evil. It may also imply God's intention that there should be multiple theories about him — and us — no one of which will or can be adequate for everybody. Third, Davis notes that his theodicy recognizes its limits. Here I agree and disagree. Granted, Davis rightly recognizes that there is much that we cannot explain or understand, but at the same time a problem remains: is there not a point where an appeal to ignorance legitimates evil too much?

According to Davis, all Christians believe that "freedom *will* turn out to be cost-effective." As a Christian, I dissent, especially if we are to interpret "cost-effective" in terms of God's perfect goodness and omnipotence. This theodicy also holds that those who trust God do not question him. To urge that view, however, is to ignore selectively the scriptural tradition that Davis claims to take so seriously. Apparently Jeremiah, Job, and even Jesus himself will have to be censored in order for trust to be ensured. Like John Hick, Stephen Davis has a whole pie in the sky by and by, at least for some of us. But if it turns out to be pie for the ignorant, for those who never saw "any good reason to doubt that freedom is cost-effective," will you, should you, want any?

Davis' Response to Critiques

Since many of the objections raised by my critics converge around certain major themes, I will defend my theodicy topically rather than person-by-person.

(1) *Revelation and the Christian Tradition.* It is clear that I approach the problem of evil in a different way than at least most of the other contributors to this book. The main differences — which control many other differences — are that I accept the notion that the Bible is religiously authoritative and believe what the Christian tradition says about God, the world, and human destiny. Thus I approach the problem of evil with certain beliefs already intact, e.g., that a perfectly good and omnipotent God exists. This does not mean, as Sontag and Griffin say, that I "beg the question," for the problem of evil for me consists in just this question: can I rationally retain my beliefs in the light of the evil that exists in the world? I do not approach the problem trying to find God or discover what God is like; I am interested in whether it is rational for me to believe as I do. I am

aware that other people do not believe as I do, and I can also see that if my beliefs turn out to be irrational, I must begin a Sontag-like search for "an adequate notion of God." But naturally I will only do so if the problem of evil first convinces me that my beliefs *are* irrational.

(2) *Possibility and Plausibility.* My colleagues seem irritated with free will defenders like Plantinga and me for what they see as our obsessive concern with logical possibility. It is not enough, they say, to show that theism is possibly true; what the problem of evil obliges us to do is show its *plausibility*. I have three things to say to this. First, I could not agree more that our aim ought to be to show the plausibility of theism; merely to show that it is logically possible is quite insufficient. (Of course I find the free will defense and thus theism plausible; this is precisely the reason I accept them.) Second, free will defenders should not be blamed for the fact that they have found it theologically and philosophically important to argue that theism is coherent. In doing so, they have simply been replying to critics like Flew and Mackie who, as is well known, have forcefully argued that the problem of evil shows that theism is contradictory, i.e., not possibly true. We can be quite sure that had free will defenders and other theodicists not successfully replied to Flew and Mackie, their charges would still be the basis on which critics would attack theism. Third, it should not be overlooked that there is an important connection between possibility and plausibility via omnipotence: if it is *logically possible* that God can explain, redeem, or overcome evil, then for persons who believe that God is both *omnipotent* (can do anything which it is logically possible for him to do) and perfectly good, it is *plausible* to believe he *will do so*.

(3) *Revelation and Ignorance.* Sontag, Griffin, and Roth all say that I hide behind ignorance; I avoid answering certain critical questions raised by the problem of evil by the device of denying that I know God's answer to them. And Sontag thinks it crucial for me to explain how I distinguish between what I claim to know about God and what I do not. My reply to this is that ignorance is not an *ad hoc* expedient appealed to by me for apologetic purposes. Let me explain.

It is obvious that there are some things we know and some things we don't know. And if it is true that God has revealed himself to us (as I believe and as − so I suspect − all or at least most of the contributors to this book believe in *some* sense or another), then it makes sense to say the same thing about God and his plans − there are some things we know and some things we don't. What I claim to know in the area of theodicy, then, is (A) what I can figure out for myself (by what Aquinas would have called "human reason alone"), and (B) what the Christian tradition tells me God has revealed. All the rest is ignorance. Sontag wonders why I assume that God wanted to create the best universe he could. It is because I believe God has revealed that this was his intention. Griffin wonders why I offer not a hint as to why God allowed the Holocaust. It is because, so far as I can tell, God has not chosen to reveal this. Since I am unable to figure it out for myself based on other things I think I know or God has revealed, honesty dictates a confession of ignorance.

(4) *Cancer and Probability Judgments.* Sontag is correct that we human beings can think of innumerable ways of decreasing the world's suffering and waste. And Roth is equally correct when he says that one such way would be the elimination of cancer. The best judgment we can make is that cancer is an evil and should be fought against with all our power. My point was and is, however, that: (A) we do not know all the causal connections between things and so are not in a perfect position to discern good and evil (I remember my amazement when as a child my father told me that it was a good thing that flies existed); and (B) God, who according to the Christian tradition is omniscient and infinitely wise, *is* in such a position. Furthermore, we have all seen reversals of this sort happen in our lives, or at least I have. I recall an event which at the time it occurred I considered one of the greatest personal tragedies in my life; I now believe it was a good thing that it occurred.

Let me be quite clear on this. I am not saying that all evil is only apparent. I am sure there are some events which the world would have been better without. Nor am I saying that no probabalistic judgments can be made about the goodness or evilness of events. I am saying four things: (i) We are sometimes wrong in making such judgments. (ii) It is very difficult for us to make such judgments about huge, complex events like, say, World War II, and virtually impossible for us with the facts we know to make such judgments about the "omnievent" of the history of the universe (nothing can stand in a probabalizing relationship to the universe). (iii) Some events we now consider evil — perhaps even the Holocaust — may turn out good (though in the case of the Holocaust I again confess I do not see how). (iv) Even if some ineradicably evil events occur (because of the freedom God gives his creatures), these events while retaining their evilness will either be used by God to produce the eschaton or else will be overcome in it. This is why against Roth I would deny that it is evident that God's choices have backfired. It may appear that way to us here now; but the problem is that we are not yet able to see things from God's perspective.

In my main essay I said it was unfair to decide on the basis of the evidence we now have whether God's decision to create this sort of world was cost-effective. Sontag, Griffin, and Roth all now ask me: unfair to whom? Well, to God, obviously. It is unfair to the architect of any plan to judge the plan when the results are ambiguous and when we do not see the end. But Sontag and Griffin are wrong in suggesting I recommend waiting till the end of history before deciding. Obviously, we may not live that long; hence, as I pointed out, each of us must decide here and now on the question, i.e., we must decide on the basis of the incomplete evidence we now have. I agree with Roth and Sontag that it may be rational to deny that God's policy of creating this sort of world is cost-effective, and with Griffin that it may be rational to suspend judgment on the issue — *if the only evidence we consider is the present state of the world.* But it may also be rational to trust in God if one also allows the evidence of Christian revelation. I confess I would be quite prepared to follow the Roth-Sontag line in theodicy if I did not accept the Christian revelation of God's intentions and promises. Thus, against Sontag, I should point out that my optimism about the future of human life has nothing whatever to do with worldly "progress." It has to do with trust in God.

(5) *God and the Redemption of Evil.* My main claim in theodicy is that God will emerge victorious and in the end will redeem all evil. This does not mean he will make it such that the evil events we have seen in the world's history never occurred (it is too late for God or anyone else to do anything about that) or even that precisely all of them will turn out to be causally necessary to produce God's victory (though some will be). Like Sontag, I too can conceive of worlds which so far as I can tell are better than this one. Unnecessary evil does exist as a by-product of our moral freedom. The Holocaust, so far as I can tell, was an evil event that did not have to occur. Thus, in response to something Roth said in his original essay, I do not "legitimate" the Holocaust by saying there could be no adequate display of human virtue or heavenly glory without it. Nor, contrary to Griffin, do I say that the Holocaust was "necessary for the world to have been *better overall* than it could have been without." What I do say is (A) that God's giving us moral freedom was necessary to the goods that will exist in the eschaton; (B) that *some* of what now seems evil to us will be used by God to help produce the eschaton (though in the case of some evils I cannot now explain how he will do so); and (C) that *all* evil will be redeemed by God in the sense that the goods that will exist in the eschaton will outweigh all the evils that have ever existed and will make them pale into insignificance. Thus God's policy decision to create us with moral freedom will be shown to be wise; the end result will have been achievable through no other policy.

But what about these ineradicably evil events that I admit occur? Roth asks whether God could have achieved his end result without them or with fewer of them, e.g., by intervening to prevent them. Here I might appeal to a striking metaphor Peter Geach uses in another connection, viz., that of God as the supreme chess master.[14] God gives us freedom to commit genuinely evil deeds, just as opponents of the supreme chess master are free to make whatever moves they want to make. But whatever we do God will outsmart us and his ends will be achieved, just as the supreme chess master in the end will win the game no matter what moves the opponent elects to make. But could not the supreme chess master intervene to prevent opponents from making certain moves, i.e., could not God have intervened to prevent, say, the Holocaust? The answer is — so far as I can tell — yes. Then why didn't he? Here is where I must once again appeal to what Roth says he was tempted to call the IJDKD. For the truth is that I don't know, and neither (in my opinion) does anybody else. Perhaps in some way that

I don't now see the Holocaust serves God's good purposes. But perhaps it does not, too. IJDK.

(6) *Trust in God*. Roth says that a perfectly good God would never have permitted mass murder and that sufficient evidence therefore exists to rule out the possibility that God is both omnipotent and perfectly good. Sontag says that so much waste has occurred that "neither a utopia on earth nor a heavenly existence later could justify it." And Griffin criticizes what he sees as my pose of "simply trusting that God has all the answers and not even trying to discover them." Nevertheless, I remain convinced that faith as trust in God is allowable in theodicy. I would also like to note in passing that the biblical figures Roth names (Jeremiah, Job, Jesus) against my recommendation of trust in God are in fact paragons of trust. Each in the face of disaster asks God tough questions (and so can we) but each ultimately rests his case and trusts (see Job 1:21; 13:15; Lam. 3:21-26; Luke 22:42; 23:46).

Contrary to Roth, a perfectly good and omnipotent being may well allow mass murder if he has good reason to do so. I am prepared to trust that God does have such reasons, though I too am sometimes plagued by the question Why? Contrary to Sontag, I do not see how Sontag knows that the waste that has existed and will exist cannot be justified. I believe it can and will be justified, as we will all see in the eschaton. And contrary to Griffin, I do not recommend not even trying for answers. Obviously, I would never have decided to write anything in the area of theodicy, including my contributions to this book, were that my stance. Of course, I have no illusions that my decision to trust that God has answers that we don't will satisfy my colleagues. This is why I said in my main essay that the evangelistic difficulty remains a difficulty. It is not easy to convince someone to trust in God – especially someone who sees no reason growing out of experience for doing so. Nevertheless, I believe it has not been shown that my beliefs, i.e., orthodox Christianity, are irrational. On the contrary, I still hold that while there are difficulties, there are no serious philosophical difficulties for theism. Sontag denies this, saying it would mean that theism is verified. But this is not so. A philosophical difficulty for a position is created by evidence against it or incoherence in it. I do not claim to have produced evidence *for* theism – only to have answered certain arguments against it.

(7) *Seven Animadversions*. First, Sontag is quite right that much in theodicy depends on the definitions we give to the terms we use. But given what Sontag says about God in his essay, it is hard for me to understand how he can affirm – as he says he does – that God is wholly good. I think most people who read his contributions to this book will rightly conclude that this is precisely what he *denies*. Second, Sontag says my reference to Satan as the cause of some of the world's evil cannot as it stands be taken seriously, and Hick says that it is "almost totally lacking in plausibility." But *why* is it implausible? I have never been able to grasp this point. I think it is quite plausible. Shouldn't I? Why not? What

precisely are the problems with my view? Both Sontag and Hick believe that *God* is responsible for much of the world's suffering; if so, why is it so hard to imagine that *devil* is responsible for some of it as well? Perhaps the heart of the problem is that these men do not believe in *the existence* of the devil. But let me add here a point I now see I should have included in my main theodicy. It is that the devil, while typically a contingent part of most versions of the free will defense, is logically dispensable to it. I make use of the figure of the devil (and I assume Augustine, Plantinga, and others do so for the same reason) not because the devil is essential to the free will defense but because the devil as the cause of much havoc in the world is part of the Christian tradition. Obviously, whether one speaks of the devil or not, it is *God* who is ultimately responsible for natural evil. He created the world in which natural evil occurs and, although God has the power to prevent natural evil (whether proximately caused by the devil or not), does not do so. Why does he not do so? Because for reasons he knows but I do not it will turn out best that he not do so. Third, Hick asks whether I should acknowledge not only that human beings are created spiritually immature but also morally imperfect. Well, it depends. If "morally imperfect" means just "not fully morally developed," I am happy to agree. But if it means sinful or culpable I do not agree. I agree with the Irenaean theodicy that we are all born with a basic "self-regardingness" in an inimical world of scarce resources and keen competition. Thus it is virtually inevitable that we sin. But I do not agree that this self-regarding tendency is the essence of sin. I would have thought that culpability is due to conscious acts rather than dispositions.

Fourth, Griffin says that since I adopt Plantinga's notion of transworld depravity, he wonders why I can countenance limitations placed on God by possibilities but not by actualities. But I do not accept Plantinga's notion of transworld depravity; the much weakened version of transworld depravity I do accept is spelled out in my main essay. And the answer to Griffin's question is that since the time of Aquinas omnipotence has been traditionally defined in terms of power to do the logically possible. That God cannot do something which it is logically impossible for him to do (e.g., make a square circle, bring it about that Jones sneezes a sneeze that was not caused by God) is no limitation on omnipotence. But it *is* a limitation on omnipotence to say that God cannot cure cancer or deflect a speeding automobile. Fifth, Sontag says that the notion of "the best of all possible worlds" is not, as I suspect it is, on a logical level with the incoherent notion, "the tallest conceivable man." But surely we will need an argument for this conclusion before we accept it. For reasons I specified in my main essay, I am still suspicious that the first notion is incoherent. And contrary to Griffin , if the notion of "the best of all possible worlds" is incoherent, then so is the notion of "*one of* the best of all possible worlds." Accordingly, my proposition (7) should not be taken as saying that this world is "one of the best of all possible worlds."

Sixth, Sontag argues that the God I believe in is both weak and unfree – weak, because I say that God could not have created a better world than this (but given the same power, Sontag says, any of us could improve the world considerably); unfree, because I deny that God could have obtained in any other way the favorable balance of good over evil that he will achieve in this world. But, as I said in my main essay, I do not think it at all clear that we could improve the world if we had divine power. Our well motivated but *ad hoc* interventions might well backfire and make God's eschatological aims unachievable. And I do not hold that God is unfree. The issue of divine benevolence is complicated, and I cannot explore it fully here. But my view of it is that God is free at any moment to do evil (and thus cease being perfectly morally good) but because of his free choices hasn't and won't. Seventh, Roth asks whether my beliefs about God are falsifiable. Although I do not consider this question any more damning to my views than to the views of any other contributor to this book, I nevertheless consider it a fair question. I do not have space to answer it in detail, as I have done elsewhere (see *International Journal of Philosophy of Religion,* Spring, 1975). The short answer is that there certainly are events which if they happened would make me cease trusting in God. What if intense human suffering became universal, prolonged, and destructive of personality? Perhaps some believers would cling to their faith ("God is testing us"), but I am quite sure I would eventually be forced to demur. I can hardly be blamed, however, for the fact that no such event has yet occurred.

(8) *An Analogy.* As a freshman in high school many years ago I turned out for the school's "B" football team. Having never before played organized football, I had no idea what to expect. My dominant impressions the first two weeks of practice were bewilderment and suppressed outrage at the constant suffering we were made to endure. The conditioning drills were exhausting, the blocking and tackling practice painful, the discipline rigid, the coaches hard, loud, and unbending. Every night I collapsed into bed, exhausted and aching. I reached the conclusion that the head coach was as monstrous a man as I had ever encountered. Only much later in the season did I realize that the suffering we endured was for a purpose, that we were being prepared to perform on the football field as well as we possibly could, and that the coach was not sadistic. In fact, after many years of participation in high school and college athletics, I now look back on him as the best and most compassionate coach I ever played under.

Yes, John and Fred, I know – life is not like a football season and God is not like a coach. I admit my analogy breaks down in an infinite number of ways. All I ask of it is that it illustrate the simple point that suffering which at a certain point in time we cannot understand or explain may possibly be explainable. I agree with my colleagues that there is evil in the world which we cannot now explain. I only want to insist it does not follow from this that it cannot be explained.

(9) *Postscript.* One might gather from what I have written so far that my views have remained inflexible throughout the writing of my contributions to this book. This would be a mistaken impression, and it would be best if I correct it. While obviously I still advocate the free will defense as the most promising response to the problem of evil, I confess I am much more conscious of its limitations and of the insights contained in other approaches than I was when work on this book began. I now see that the great divide in theodicy — and in this book — is between those who (like Hick and me) have a developed view of God and set out to try to show that belief in this God is *not irrational* and those who (like Roth, Sontag, and Griffin) try to use the problem of evil to discover what God is like and who accordingly accuse people like Hick and me of having failed to demonstrate the *rationality* of their belief. But to show that a given belief is not irrational in the light of a given problem is not the same thing as showing that it is rational. Nevertheless, I now see in ways that I did not see before that there is much to learn from other approaches beside my own and that the free will defense has rough edges and unanswered questions. So my participation in the writing of this book has not only helped me clarify my own views but has helped me see the value of avoiding tunnel vision in theodicy.

4 Creation Out of Chaos and the Problem of Evil

DAVID R. GRIFFIN

"In the beginning, God created the heavens and the earth." This is how Genesis 1:1 has traditionally been translated. Even the Revised Standard Version so renders it. However, the RSV in a footnote gives an alternative reading: "When God began to create the heavens and the earth, the earth was without form and void. ..." I understand that most Hebrew scholars believe this to be the more accurate translation. For many years I did not give much thought to the possible implications of the alternative reading. Recently I have come to see that the alternative reading suggests a radically different view of the God-world relation from that which has dominated traditional theology and has thereby had a decisive influence upon Jewish and Christian sensibilities. If accepted, this radically different view will influence every aspect of Christian thought; but its most obvious and central impact will be upon that problem which has increasingly been perceived as the Achilles' heel of traditional theology, the problem of evil. (This metaphor is overly generous to traditional theology: Achilles had only *one* vulnerable spot.)

The central issue between the two readings is whether creation was *ex nihilo*, i.e., whether God created the world out of absolutely nothing.[1] The traditional reading of Genesis 1:1 does not *say* that it was, but it suggests it more readily than does the alternative reading. And it has been used by traditional theologians to support the doctrine of *creatio ex nihilo*.

The alternative reading, while also not spelling out things with the precision desired by philosophical theologians, suggests that God's creation of our world did not involve the absolute beginning of finite existence but rather the achievement of order out of a pre-existing chaos. This interpretation of creation, which is reflected in many passages in the Old Testament, would make the Hebrew view structurally similar to that reflected in many other Near Eastern creation myths, and to that of Plato's *Timaeus*. In the *Timaeus* the "Demiurge" is a craftsman working with materials that are not completely malleable to his will. They confront him with elements of "necessity," and he works to create out of the chaos a world that is as good "as possible." The world achieved represents a victory of "persuasion" over necessity.

Traditional theologians have contrasted the "Christian" or "biblical" understanding of creation with this Platonic view. Creation really worthy of the name, they have said, is not the mere remolding of pre-existing materials, but is making things out of nothing. Most importantly, the Platonic view held that these pre-existing materials put limits on what God could do; since they were not created by him out of nothing, they were not totally subject to his will. This runs counter to clear biblical statements of divine omnipotence (e.g., Gen. 18:14: "Is anything too hard for the Lord?"; Matt. 19:26: "With God all things are possible"). And it is destructive of the hope that God will totally defeat the powers of evil and make all things new. Accordingly, the traditional Christian view of *creatio ex nihilo* was formed in direct opposition to the idea of creation out of chaos.

It is interesting to note that a doctrine so central to traditional theology has so little direct biblical support. The only clear statement is in II Maccabees (7:28), a book that Protestants and Jews do not include in their Bibles. The majority of passages in the Old Testament that speak to the issue one way or the other support the idea that creation involved bringing order out of pre-existing materials. Many contemporary theologians who think the notion of *creatio ex nihilo* is important agree that they have the weight of the biblical evidence against them, but argue that this is not decisive: the crucial question is, which view is more compatible with the essence of Christian faith? Some would add: and which view is, all things considered, most reasonable? These indeed are the grounds upon which the debate should rest, especially since the biblical evidence is so ambiguous. Of course, having argued that the number of explicit biblical passages is not decisive in regard to *creatio ex nihilo,* upholders of traditional theology should in fairness grant this in regard to the related issue of divine omnipotence, where they have the majority of explicit passages on their side.

The point to be stressed here is that the contrast between the two views is not a contrast between one view that is "biblical" and based on "revelation" and another that is a "departure from the biblical view" based on "dubious speculation." The biblical support is ambiguous. And *both views are speculative hypotheses.* The only question is which hypothesis has more to commend it.

Statement of the Problem of Evil

In order to compare different solutions to the problem of evil, we need to have a clear statement of what the problem is. The apparently simple statements found in most text-books are riddled with ambiguities. The usual 4-step statement is:

(1) If God is all-powerful, God could prevent all evil.

(2) If God is all-good, God would want to prevent all evil.

(3) Evil exists.

(4) Therefore God is either not all-powerful or all-good (or both).

The central ambiguity is that none of the premises indicate whether the evil to which they refer is *genuine* evil or merely *apparent* evil. This ambiguity has allowed many theologians to have a false confidence that the problem is quite easily solved. They reject premise 2 on the grounds that a good God would not want to prevent all evil, since much evil turns out to contribute to higher good. But, rather than being a rejection of premise 2, this move is really a rejection of premise 3, as these theologians are saying in effect that there is no *genuine* evil—all the evil is merely apparent evil since it contributes to a greater good.

For these and other reasons, I find the following 7-step statement to be most helpful in eliminating ambiguities, thereby allowing one to see just which premise is being rejected by the various theodicies.[2]

(1) To be God, a being must be omnipotent (with an "omnipotent being" defined as one whose power to bring about what it wills is essentially unlimited—except [perhaps] by logical impossibilities).

(2) An omnipotent being could unilaterally bring about a world devoid of genuine evil (with "genuine evil" defined as anything that makes the world worse than it could have otherwise been).

(3) To be God, a being must be morally perfect.

(4) A morally perfect being would want to bring about a world devoid of genuine evil.

(5) If there is a God, there would be no genuine evil in the world.

(6) But there is genuine evil in the world.

(7) Therefore there is no God.

I will comment upon some of the six premises, pointing out the ambiguities some of the terms are designed to eliminate.

In premise 1, the key term is "essentially." Some theologians believe in a divine self-limitation, in which God voluntarily gave up power. This would *not* be *essential* limitation. God's power is essentially limited only if this limitation is "in the nature of things," not being a product of God's will. This limitation could be due to another actuality or actualities having its or their own inherent power, or to some impediment to God's will in God's own nature (a "dark side" to God not totally controllable by the divine will), or to the possibilities open to God (perhaps the realm of "possible worlds" contains none that is devoid of evil). Regarding the last phrase of the premise: most theologians who have affirmed divine omnipotence have held that God cannot do that which is logically impossible, but they have not considered this to be a real limitation on God's power.

In premise 2 one of the key terms is "unilaterally." If that term is not inserted, the statement could mean: God could bring about a world devoid of genuine evil, *if* God is lucky, i.e., if the creatures decide to co-operate. But if that were all that were meant, premise 5 would not follow from premises 1-4, and the whole argument would be invalid. It is only if God could *unilaterally* bring about such a world that God can be blamed for not doing so. We do not blame parents for not raising perfect children, even though it is logically possible for them to do so, since we recognize that there are all sorts of limitations upon their influence—the main one being the power of self-determination possessed by the children by which they can resist their parents' wills.

I have already pointed out the importance of inserting the word "genuine" before "evil." With this insertion, we can be spared those lengthy explanations as to why a good God *would* allow evil for the sake of a higher good, since the statement already says that the only kind of evil in question is *genuine* evil, precisely that kind which does *not* make the world a better place, all things considered. Hence this insertion forces those who might otherwise attack premise 4 to *openly* reject premise 6—a move that is possible but which makes most sensitive people uncomfortable, especially in this post-Holocaust world.

Creation and Divine Power

I now turn to the solution I favor, to which the rejection of *creatio ex nihilo* is fundamental. In fact, the problem of evil is uniquely a problem for those theistic positions that hold the doctrine of omnipotence implied by the doctrine of creation out of nothing. For, the problem of evil can be stated as a syllogism validly entailing the non-existence of deity only if deity is defined as omnipotent in the sense of having no essential limitations upon the exercise of its will. And it is precisely omnipotence in this sense that the speculative hypothesis of *creatio ex nihilo* is designed to support.

Two issues are involved. First, if God in creating our world necessarily worked with some pre-existent actualities, these actualities might well have some power of their own with which they could partially thwart the divine will. Second, there might be some eternal, uncreated, necessary principles (beyond purely logical truths) about the way these actualities can be ordered which limit the sorts of situations that are really possible. But if God created this world out of absolutely nothing, then the beings of this world are *absolutely* dependent upon God. Any power they have is not at all inherent, but is totally a gift of God, and as such can be overridden (or, which amounts to the same thing, withdrawn) at any time. And if there has not always been a multiplicity of finite actualities, it does not make sense to think of any uncreated and hence necessary principles as to how the actualities of the world can be ordered. Any such principles would be purely contingent ones, created along with the actualities whose behavior they describe, and hence alterable at (divine) will.

My solution dissolves the problem of evil by denying the doctrine of omnipotence fundamental to it. Of the various ways of denying deity's essentially unlimited power to effect its will, mine is to hypothesize that there has always been a plurality of actualities having some power of their own. This power is two-fold: the power to determine themselves (partially), and the power to influence others.

Traditional theism has always held that energy or power is eternal. But it hypothesized that this power all essentially belonged to God alone, and was at some point all embodied in God. I share the view of those who hold instead that power has always existed in non-divine actualities as well as in the divine actuality. No special philosophical problems are raised by this view: if it is intelligible to hold that the existence of God requires no explanation, since *something* must exist necessarily and "of itself," then it is not unintelligible to hold that that which exists necessarily is God *and* a realm of non-divine actualities. Nor is this a denial that our world is contingent and created by God. My view is that the beings making up our world, including the most primitive ones (such as quarks and electrons) are contingent, having been brought about and sustained through the creative providential activity of God. All that is necessary to the hypothesis is that power has always been and necessarily is *shared* power, that God has never had and could never have a monopoly on power, and that the power possessed by the non-divine actualities is inherent to them and hence cannot be cancelled out or overridden by God.

This last point is the most essential one. Some theologians might agree that we have power, even power in relation to God, and yet say that God could overpower us and hence totally determine our activities, including our willing and desiring. But that is excluded by what I mean by saying that we have inherent power in relation to God. The claim is precisely that our self-determining activity, and the consequent influence we have on others, *cannot* be totally controlled by God. Hence God cannot control but can only persuade what we become and how we affect others.

My position is that this inherent power did not arise at some point in the past, such as with the creation of human beings. All creatures have at least some iota of this two-fold power. And there have, by hypothesis, always been such creatures. Hence God never had a monopoly on power, and has always created by persuading creatures that have had some power of their own by which they could resist the divine creating activity.

Our present view that the creation of our world occurred through a long evolutionary process jives with the notion of creation out of chaos and its correlative assumption that divine creative power is necessarily persuasive. The out-dated view that all the present species were created instantaneously in their present forms jived with the doctrine of *creatio ex nihilo* and its correlative idea of divine omnipotence. Contemporary theologians who accept the evolutionary hypothesis and yet hold to the hypothesis of divine omnipotence have a lot of explaining to do. Most centrally, they must explain why a God whose power is essentially unlimited would use such a long, pain-filled method, with all its blind-alleys, to create a world. The need for explanation is further aggravated when they hold that human beings are the only creatures that are really important to God, and that the rest of the creation exists only for the sake of the divine-human drama. If that is so, why did God take so long getting to the main act? Of course, theologians can claim that they need not answer these questions. But the hypothesis of divine omnipotence must, like any hypothesis, commend itself by its explanatory power. Each unanswered question reveals deficiencies in that power.

Necessary Correlations Between Power and Value

The fact that our world arose through an evolutionary process has further theological relevance beyond the support it gives for the idea that God's power is necessarily persuasive. It also gives support to the idea that there are certain necessary principles correlating *power* and *value*. These correlations form the second major part of my theodicy (the first being that all individuals have inherent power so that God's power is necessarily persuasive). My thesis here is that there is a positive correlation among the following four variables, so that as one rises in degree the others necessarily rise proportionately:

> *(1) The capacity to enjoy intrinsic goodness (or value).*
> *(2) The capacity to suffer intrinsic evil (or dis-value).*
> *(3) The power of self-determination.*
> *(4) The power to influence others (for good or ill).*

By "intrinsic value" I mean the value that something has for itself, apart from any value it may have for others. Intrinsic value can be possessed only by individuals that experience, although this experience need not be self-reflexive or even conscious. According to the non-dualistic position which I accept but cannot defend here, there are no non-experiencing individuals which are mere objects. All individuals experience, which means that all individuals have some capacity, however minimal, to enjoy and to suffer, i.e., to experience intrinsic goodness and intrinsic evil. This does not entail the extreme and totally unwarranted hypothesis that *everything* experiences. *Aggregates* of individuals do not experience (e.g., when there is a crowd of people, the crowd itself has no experience over and above the experiences of the individual people). Rocks, chairs, planets, typewriters, automobiles and probably plants are aggregates which as such have no experience; the only experiences contained in them are those of the individuals making them up. Examples of *genuine individuals* would be electrons, atoms, molecules, cells, and animal (including human) souls or psyches.

This means that there is a hierarchy of individuals: less complex ones are compounded into more complex ones. For example, electrons and other sub-atomic individuals are contained in an atom; atoms are contained in molecules; molecules in cells; and cells in living animals dominated by a central experience called the soul. (The major difference between plants and animals is that the former do not seem to have one member that dominates over and coordinates the rest.)

The direction of the evolutionary process toward increasing complexity raises the question as to whether this directionality is explainable as a reflection of the creative purpose of God. This would be the case if complexity could be correlated with something that a loving God would be interested in promoting. And this is precisely what we find: increased complexity of the organism seems to be the condition for increased richness of experience, hence of increased intrinsic goodness. Whatever experience is possessed by electrons, atoms and molecules must be extremely slight; hence any intrinsic good they can enjoy must be extremely slight (so we are justified in not considering their "rights" in our ethical deliberations). But when we come to living cells, we are probably at the stage where significant degrees of enjoyment can first be experienced. With animal souls, especially those supported by a central nervous system, we have another quantum jump in the capacity to experience value. Finally, the human soul is capable of enjoying all sorts of values not open to the souls of the lower animals.

However, every increase in complexity in this hierarchy is Janus-faced: each increase in the capacity to enjoy intrinsic goodness is likewise an increase in the capacity to suffer. It probably does not make sense to speak of the capacity for pain below the level of the cell. And—to jump to the top—the human being is susceptible to all sorts of sufferings to which the lower animals are virtually oblivious.

My thesis is that *this correlation between the capacity to enjoy and the capacity to suffer is a necessary, metaphysical correlation, inherent in the nature of things*. This thesis provides an answer to one of the central questions involved in the problem of evil, namely, "Why did God create us so that we are so susceptible to physical pain and psychological suffering?" The answer, according to this thesis, is that God could do no other. That is, not without foregoing beings capable of the kinds of values we can experience. To have the good is necessarily to risk the chance of the bad.

Of course, there is nothing certain about this thesis. It is a speculative hypothesis. But—and this is often overlooked—the *denial* of the thesis is *equally speculative*. No one *knows* for certain that such a positive correlation does not necessarily exist. In fact, to deny that the correlation is necessary i.e., that it would have to obtain in any world, is even *more* speculative. For, we know from our experience of *this* world that worlds in which the correlation obtains are really possible. But we have no experiential basis for knowing that a world in which the correlation would not obtain is even possible. (And hopefully no one will maintain that this philosophical knowledge has been vouchsafed us by revelation.)

My hypothesis is that the other variables rise proportionately with the first two, and with equal necessity. Individuals with greater capacity for the enjoyment of values necessarily have more power of self-determination, i.e., more freedom. One of the other questions most often asked is, "Why didn't God create rational saints?"—by which is meant, "Why didn't God create beings who would be like us in every respect (having the capacity for rationality and all the values this allows), except that they would never sin?" The answer provided by my theodicy is, "Because God couldn't." That is, God couldn't do it *unilaterally*—recall the insertion of this word into the formal statement of the problem. The idea of a being capable of rational thought who would always use this capacity to make the right decision is not a logically contradictory idea. Hence there is nothing contradictory in the idea that God could produce such a being. What is contradictory—given the hypothesis that all individuals have some power of self-determination—is that God could *unilaterally* produce such a being.

However, someone might well grant that answer and still press the question, refining it to this form: "Granted that God cannot completely control any individuals, since they all have *some* power of self-determination by which they can resist the divine persuasion, why did God give human beings such an *inordinate degree* of this power? Electrons, atoms, and molecules have, according to the hypothesis, some degree of self-determinancy, and yet they seem to do pretty much what they are supposed to. Why aren't human beings kept on a shorter leash?" It is to this refined form of the question that the correlation between the first and third variables supplies an answer. To have creatures who can enjoy much more intrinsic good than can electrons, atoms, and molecules is necessarily to have creatures with much more power of self-determination with which to deviate from the divine will. Greater freedom is a necessary corollary of the possibility of higher value experiences.

The correlation between this third variable and the second one (the capacity to suffer) helps illumine the reason for the extent and depth of human suffering. It is precisely we creatures who have by far the greatest capacity for suffering who likewise have by far the greatest power to deviate from God's will for our lives. Combining these two factors gives us an extraordinary capacity to make ourselves miserable. God did not, according to my hypothesis, make us this way because of some mysterious reason totally beyond our ken, nor because of a desire to "toughen us up," nor because of some sadistic strain in the divine nature. God did it because there was no choice—except the choice of calling off the evolutionary advance before beings of our complexity had emerged.

The fourth variable explains the need for an evolutionary process in order to attain the kind of world we now have. This fourth variable says that those individuals with more intrinsic value (for themselves) also have more instrumental value (to contribute to others). For example, electrons and protons do not have as much intrinsic value as molecules. Accordingly they do not have sufficient data to contribute to support a living cell; the cell could not emerge prior to the requisite atoms and molecules. Likewise an animal soul could not be supported by the data that can be derived from a large aggregate of atoms; a large aggregate of cells was required before the animal soul could emerge.

From the perspective of my theological position, the fact that our world was evidently formed through a long, step-by-step process constitutes no refutation, even partially, of the hypothesis of divine creation. Nor does it present theology with a probable fact that can only be handled by some *ad hoc* hypothesis. Rather, it suggests a way of understanding God's creative activity that does not present theology with an insuperable problem of evil. And it fits in perfectly with a set of principles that commend themselves on other grounds.

The fourth variable also illuminates even further the reason this world is such a dangerous place, especially since human beings have arrived in it. Those beings with the greatest power of self-determination, and hence the greatest power to deviate from the divine will for the good of the whole, necessarily have the greatest power to influence others—for good or ill. The capacity to create and the capacity to destroy go hand in hand.

Again, this feature of our world was not ordained by God for some reason that God only knows. Rather, by hypothesis this is a feature that would necessarily obtain in *any* world; the principles correlating value and power are uncreated. (Incidentally, they need not be conceived as metaphysical principles external to God. Rather, they can be thought of as belonging to the divine essence. Like divine omniscience and love, they can be considered principles that are neither the product of the divine will, nor contrary to it.)

The Goodness of God

What then is the upshot of my theodicy, my attempt to "justify the ways of God"? It is not to maintain that God is not responsible for any of the evil in the world. For, in a very real sense, God *is* ultimately responsible for all of those things that we normally think of when we refer to the problem of evil. For, if God had not persuaded the world to bring forth living cells and then animal life, there would be no significant suffering in the world. If God had not continued to draw the creation upward until creatures with the capacity for rational thought were evoked, there would be no moral evil, or sin, i.e., deliberate disobedience of the divine will; nor would the most awful forms of suffering exist—there would be no Holocausts.

The question then is, "Can God be thus responsible without being indictable, i.e., blameworthy?" I would say "Yes." In the first place, although God is ultimately responsible for the world's having reached a state in which significant evils can occur, God is never totally responsible for the evils that do occur. Each situation contains seeds for good and evil. God (by hypothesis) seeks to lure the creatures to realize the greatest good that is possible in that particular situation. When the creatures actualize a lesser possibility, this failure is due to their exercise of power, not God's.

In the second place the aim of a "morally good being" is more accurately stated positively than negatively. That is, the aim is first of all to produce good, not to avoid suffering. If the moral aim could be adequately expressed as the intention to avoid suffering, then moral adults would never have children—that would be the way to guarantee that they would never have children who would suffer or cause suffering. Analogously, a perfectly moral God would simply avoid bringing forth a world with any creatures capable of any significant degree of suffering. But—by hypothesis—this would mean that there would be *no world with any significant value in it*. Surely that cannot be our idea of what a perfectly moral being would do! The aim must be to create the conditions that allow for the greatest good while minimizing the evils.

In other words, suffering and sinful intentions resulting in suffering are not the only forms of evil. Any absence of good that could have been realized is evil even if no suffering is involved. Recall that the definition of genuine evil offered earlier was "anything which makes the world worse than it could have otherwise been." Any absence of good that makes the world worse than it could have been, all things considered, is an evil. Hence, for God to have failed to bring forth beings capable of experiencing significant value when this was possible would have made God indictable.

Unless, of course, the evils that were thereby made possible are so great that the goods that could be achieved are not worth the risk. That is a question that each of us can only answer for ourselves. Those of us who are among the most fortunate people who have ever lived on the face of the earth must of course be aware of our biased perspectives, and must be sensitive to the response that may come from the less fortunate. But, even when trying to take into account my biased perspective, I cannot imagine that I would ever conclude that the evils of life have been so great that it would have been better had life never emerged, or that the evils of human life, as horrendous as they have been (and quite possibly the worst is still to come!), are such that it would have been better had human life never been created.

There is one other theological conviction that reinforces my judgment on this matter. This is the conviction that God shares all our sufferings (analogously to the way that I share the pains of my bodily members). Accordingly, while every advance in the creative process has been a risk, since greater sufferings were thereby made possible as well as greater goods, this has never been a risk which God has urged us creatures to run alone. It has always been a risk for God too. In fact God is the *only* being who has experienced every single evil that has occurred in the creation. This means that God is the one being in position to judge whether the goods achievable have been worth the price.

Natural Evil

Thus far, insofar as I have discussed the *cause* of evil, I have focused attention primarily on *moral* evil, as I have sought to explain why human beings can cause so much evil. But the theological position being outlined here is equally capable of explaining so-called "natural evil," that which is caused by non-moral agents. And it is this form of evil that most theodicies find most problematical. For, they employ what I call a "hybrid free-will defense" to account for the evil caused by human beings. I call it a *hybrid* free-will defense because it does not say that freedom is inherent in the world as such, but instead says that God voluntarily bestows freedom upon the creation—and usually only to a select portion of creation, i.e., to human beings alone, or to them and other rational creatures (angels).

Accordingly, this hybrid free-will defense has a difficult time with evils apparently caused by sub-human nature, since the beings constituting this realm by hypothesis have no power with which to deviate from God's will. One way out is to say with Augustine that no genuine evil ever results from sub-human causes. But in the face of the enormous and non-rationalizable distribution of sufferings caused by tornadoes, earthquakes, droughts, germs, and cancer cells, this is a difficult assertion to make. Another way out is to affirm that all such evils are caused by a fallen angel (Satan). This is, of course, not readily falsifiable, but it does strain credulity (for me, at least, much more than the hypothesis that all creatures have some power of their own). Also it raises the question as to why God allows Satan to do things that make the universe worse than it could have been; hence it calls God's goodness or wisdom into question.[3]

According to my theodicy, all creatures great and small have some power with which to deviate from the divine will for them. This means that there never has been a time at which we could say that the creation was necessarily "perfect" in the sense of having actualized the best possibilities that were open to it. Granted, very low-grade actualities cannot be thought to deviate *very much* from the divine aims for them. But over a period of billions of years very slight deviations occurring in each moment can add up to a state of the world that is very far removed from the state that would have resulted had the divine aims been actualized all the way along. Accordingly, if God has always worked with materials that were not necessarily in a perfect state, and which have some inherent power to deviate from God's aims and to influence their successors forevermore, there is no reason to infer that cancer, polio, tornadoes, and earth-quakes exist because God wanted our world to have them.

Why God Does Not "Prevent" Some Evils

I will conclude with a discussion intended to drive home more clearly why God (according to my hypothesis) simply cannot prevent the major types of evils that usually lead people to question God's goodness or even reality. These questions can be phrased in the form: "Why didn't God prevent such and such?" For example, why didn't God prevent that bullet from striking my son? Why didn't God prevent that mine shaft from caving in? Why did God allow all the pain that occurred in the evolutionary process? Why didn't God prevent Hitler from murdering six million Jews?

The answer to questions of this type will be more evident to us if we think in terms of the way God can affect the following three types of entities: (1) low-grade enduring individuals; (2) high-grade enduring individuals; (3) aggregates of individuals. (For the sake of simplicity I have left out the whole spectrum of medium-grade individuals, from the lowest animals through the non-human primates.) These three types of entities differ from each other in having (1) very little power of self-determination, (2) very great power of self-determination, and (3) no power of self-determination, respectively.

(1) God acts in the world, by hypothesis, by seeking to persuade individuals to actualize the best possibilities that are *real* possibilities for them. (E.g., it is not a real possibility for a chipmunk to write a symphony.) Low-grade enduring individuals, such as electrons, atoms, molecules, having very little power of self-determination, and not having many real possibilities open to them, cannot change their behavior very quickly. Individuals at this level are largely the products of their inheritance and their environment. They essentially repeat the same patterns of behavior, century after century. Even as we move into the medium-grade level, with living cells, the capacity for novel self-determining behavior is very limited, compared with that of human beings.

The theological significance of this discussion is this: on the one hand, these low-grade individuals cannot deviate very much from the divine aims for them. On the other hand, the divine aims for them, since they can only be for possi-bilities that are *real* possibilities for these low-grade creatures, cannot be aims for very radical changes in behavior. Insofar as God can move these individuals to change their ways, it must be over a very long period of time. (This is why evolutionary change occurred so gradually until relatively recently on our earth.)

Accordingly, if the behavior of one or more of these individuals is causing destruction in its environment, God cannot do much quickly to change things. For example, if you have been exposed to radio-active materials, God cannot divert the alpha, beta, and gamma particles out of your body before they have done irreversible damage. If cancerous cells have developed in your body, God cannot lure them to leave voluntarily.

(2) By "high-grade enduring individuals" I am referring here exclusively to human beings. These individuals have much power of self-determination, and have many more real possibilities open to them than do the lower creatures. Hence, very rapid changes of behavior can occur with them. What is God's power to affect them? On the one hand, God can present quite novel aims to them, one after another. And God can seek to persuade them to change their behavior quite rapidly—for example to stop one's journey to help the victim of a crime. But on the other hand, these creatures have tremendous power with which to deviate from the divine aims for them, and they can deviate much more widely than can lower individuals. In a relatively short time after they learned to write, these individuals could discover that $E = mc^2$; and they can use this knowledge to destroy the world even more quickly.

Thus far I have been speaking of individuals. Most of these are *compound* individuals in which a number of individuals are ordered hierarchically, with one dominant member giving a unity of experience and activity to the whole society. The atom, the molecule, and the cell all have a unity of activity due to this hierarchical organization. Likewise the animal, by virtue of the dominating influence of its soul, has a unity of response to its environment.

(3) But some of the entities of this world seem to have no such unity. They are mere *aggregates*. Non-living things such as rocks, bodies of water, planets, automobiles, and timbers are obvious examples. Plants also probably have no dominant member, no soul. In any case, those things which are aggregates cannot, *as* aggregates, be directly affected by God. Since God acts by seeking to persuade individuals, and there is by definition no individual dominating the other members of an aggregate, God cannot directly get an aggregate to do anything. God can move a living human body by persuading the soul to move; if the soul decides to cross the street, the rest of the body has little choice but to go along (assuming a healthy body). But there is no corresponding means by which God can directly move a rock—or get it to stop moving down the bank towards the highway. There is no way for God to stop that bullet speeding toward the heart of a man "too young to die." There is no way for God to stop the overburdened timbers in a mine shaft from caving in. There is no way God can stop the automobile with a sleeping driver from crashing into the oncoming cars. There is no way God can prevent that aggregate of molecules called a hurricane from devastating the towns in its paths.

In the earlier part of the paper I stressed what God has been doing in the world, by way of creating the conditions for good. With more space, I would describe some of the ways in which God seeks to overcome evil in the world. But I thought it best in these last few pages to stress the limitations on God's prevention of evil, since God's "failure" to prevent evil is usually the chief source of complaint, by theists and non-theists alike. This brief analysis of these limitations leads to the following three-fold conclusion:

(1) Those things which cannot deviate much from the divine will also cannot be influenced by God very quickly.

(2) Those things which can be influenced by God quickly can deviate drastically from the divine will.

(3) Those things which can do nothing on their own cannot be directly influenced by God at all.

I could not, of course, in the brief space of this essay hope to justify the wide-ranging hypothesis outlined here. But I do hope that readers find the hypothesis potentially helpful enough to consider it worthy of further exploration. It (including variations on it) is the only hypothesis I have found that makes faith possible in the face of the horrendous evils that occur in our world.

Faith, Reason, and Theodicy

The foregoing completes the sketch of my substantive theodicy. However, a theodicy is only one part of a complete theology. The differences between theodicies are closely correlated with different understandings of the total theological task. In this final section I will briefly summarize my understanding of this task, especially the relation between "faith" (in "revelation") and "reason," and how this understanding is related to the theodicy sketched above.

The central theme running through the following points is that I reject all views according to which faith is somehow *opposed* to reason.

(1) I reject the view that we are called to believe any ideas, allegedly based on "revelation," that are self-contradictory. For example, some theologians admit it is contradictory to maintain both that (A) God determines all events and that (B) human beings are partly free and hence responsible for their actions; yet these theologicans claim that "faith" demands that we affirm both of these ideas. I reject the view that "faith" forces us to reject "reason" in the sense of logical consistency.

(2) Some theologians hold that logical consistency is the only requirement of "reason" to which our beliefs must conform. According to this view, reason's task of determining the *most probable* view of the world need not influence our religious beliefs. Hence the believer is said to be "rationally justified" in maintaining some theological belief that seems very improbable as long as no *logical* impossibility (inconsistency) is involved. Theologians, to defend the rationality of some doctrine, need only present some hypothesis, however improbable, that shows the doctrine *might* be true. I reject this view. The theological task as I see it is to present a view of reality that seems more probable than other available views.

(3) Implicit in the previous two points is the view that the Christian "revelation" does not provide us with a set of clearly formulated statements

which can then be compared with another set of statements produced by "reason." All Christian doctrines are human attempts to formulate the significance of experiences taken to be revelatory. For example, it was never shouted down from heaven, or even whispered, that God is triune, or that the world was created out of nothing, or that God is omnipotent, or that God is perfect love. Each of these doctrines arose in the past as fallible human beings, guided but not controlled by the divine spirit, tried to express their understanding of God in the most adequate way possible, given their contexts, including their questions, their knowledge of the world, and the conceptual tools available to them. *Our theological task today is not to try to hold on to their formulations at any price,* but to re-think the implications of the Christian revelatory events in the light of *our* contexts—our questions, our knowledge, and our conceptual tools. Accordingly, one theologian cannot dismiss another's position as "unchristian" simply by showing that it does not accept some ancient dogma, especially some previous attempt to state quite precisely the meaning of some fundamental Christian idea. For example, the idea that we and the world in which we find ourselves owe our existence to God is one I consider central to Christian faith; but I see no warrant for the insistence that this idea must be expressed in terms of "creation out of nothing," especially if that means that there was a time when God existed all alone, without any realm of finitude whatsoever.

(4) The idea that "faith" and "reason" confront each other as two sets of possibly conflicting statements not only reflects an unacceptable view of revelation; it also reflects a misunderstanding of reason. There is no such thing as a world-view that is based upon "pure reason," unaffected by some "faith." Every world-view is based upon a pre-rational acceptance of some "insight" or "hunch" or "clue" as to the nature of reality. Some dimension of experience or part of reality is taken as the essential clue to the nature of the whole. One's reasoning is guided by this pre-rational acceptance of a starting-point. Faith in the Christian revelation gives Christian theologians a starting-point for their reasoning that is analogous to the starting-points accepted on faith by theologians of other persuasions. (These theologians are usually called "philosophers" when their acceptance of some "faith" as a starting-point is not acknowledged.) The Christian starting-point justifies itself rationally insofar as it provides the basis for a more probable (i.e., more consistent, adequate, and illuminating) account of this mysterious world in which we find ourselves than those views which begin with some other "revelation."

(5) In the preceding sentence, one of the criteria for a "more probable" account was that it had to be "more adequate." This means, "more adequate to the facts." What are the "facts" to which an account must be adequate? This is, of course, often precisely the point at issue among various theological and philosophical systems. One system is seeking to account for facts that the other system dismisses as "myth" or "illusion." Nevertheless considerable agreement

is possible; there are many things that are widely acknowledged to be "facts," or at least acknowledged to be so probable that any presently-accepted theory must incorporate them. The area that springs most quickly to mind for most people today is probably the whole body of widely accepted scientific facts (meaning primarily the natural sciences). I would include, for example, the idea that more complex forms of life evolved over a period of millions of years from less complex forms as one of the scientific ideas that is so probable that it must be incorporated into any acceptable theological doctrine of creation.

However, there is another type of "fact" that should be even more regulative of our theological formulations: there are a number of ideas that we all presuppose in practice whether or not we espouse them verbally. Even if we verbally deny these ideas, our behavior shows that we accept them. For example, some philosophers have denied that we have any knowledge of causation in the sense that one event influences another event. And yet all of us, including those same philosophers, presuppose in every moment that we are influenced by other events (otherwise we wouldn't get angry at others for stabbing us) and that our present actions will influence the future (otherwise we wouldn't brush our teeth). All those notions that are presupposed in practice by all people, regardless of their cultural backgrounds, have been called "common notions." To deny one of them would be to be guilty of self-contradiction, for one would be denying verbally what one is otherwise presupposing in one's living. *These common notions constitute the most fundamental facts to which any philosophical or theological position must be adequate.* It is not an easy matter to formulate these common notions precisely. In fact, the attempt to approximate them more and more closely is the unending philosophical task. However, some of them can be identified and expressed with enough adequacy to serve as criteria. Any position that clearly denies one of these common notions is *ipso facto* inadequate. One such common notion, I maintain, is that we are partially free and hence partially responsible for our actions; another one is that *genuinely* evil things happen in the world.

(6) One other central assumption behind my theodicy involves the nature of "religion." What does being "religious" or having "faith" involve? Most centrally, it involves what has variously been called "a vision of God," "a sense of the sacred," "a taste of the holy," etc. What is meant by the "holy" or the "sacred" probably cannot be adequately defined, but certain pointers can be given. The holy is that which evokes awe, worship, commitment. It is that which has ultimate intrinsic value, and in relation to which other things have their value. To sense something as being holy is to want to be in harmony with it. This, in fact, is the basic religious drive of human beings—the desire to be in harmony with the holy reality.

What attributes does a reality need to have to be considered holy? Insofar as one is talking of things that have been actually worshiped as holy, there has been great diversity. If we limit attention to what has been explicitly conceived as worthy of worship, then the number of characteristics is greatly reduced, and there is some unanimity on certain characteristics. For example, the various religions agree that the ultimately holy reality must be eternal, and must exist necessarily. Also it must be the ultimately decisive power, at least in regard to matters of ultimate concern. And there is considerable consensus that the divine must be perfect, in the sense defined by Anselm: that greater than which nothing can be thought. Only that which is perfect can evoke our wholehearted worship and commitment.

But there are still important differences among the various religious traditions. In particular, there are differences in regard to which attributes are essential to perfection, and hence which attributes must be possessed to a perfect degree. The tradition in which we stand largely shapes our perception of what a reality must be like in order to be considered holy, perfect, worthy of worship and ultimate commitment. Those who have been decisively shaped by the biblical tradition generally have felt that to be holy a reality had to be morally perfect (as well as eternal, necessarily existing, and perfect in power). In fact this perception has been so central that the word "holy" has tended to lose much of its original meaning and to become virtually synonymous with "morally good." It is the idea that the holy reality is morally perfect as well as perfect in power that creates the problem of evil: if God is perfect in regard to both power and moral intention, it seems that there should be no evil in the world. (My solution to this problem involves arguing that "perfect power" need not be equated with the traditional doctrine of omnipotence.)

(7) I said above that to sense something as holy is to want to be in harmony with it. To make this statement credible, a distinction implicit in it must be made explicit. This is the distinction between a *perception* (what I have been calling a vision, a taste, or a sense) of the holy, and a *conception* (or belief) in something as holy. One may conceptually believe, for example, that the God revealed through the biblical tradition is holy, and hence believe that one *should* live in harmony with this God's will, without really *perceiving* the world in these terms. One will perceive something else to be holy, such as material things or "the bitch goddess success," and it is around this other thing that one's life will be decisively oriented. One's *conception* of the holy will have some affect upon one's attitudes and emotions and hence upon one's outer behavior: for example, one may give some money to the church. But one's attitudes, emotions and behavior will be more decisively affected by one's *perception* of holiness. Insofar as one's conception and perception of holiness conflict, one will be psychically split, unable to act spontaneously on one's beliefs, and unable to support one's spontaneous impulses with conviction. It is the task of preachers, teachers, counselors and finally the individuals themselves to bring their perceptions of holiness into harmony with their beliefs. This presupposes, of course, that the beliefs are *worthy* beliefs, ones to which people's perceptions of the world *ought* to be

aligned. It is the task of the Christian theologian to help people arrive at a set of beliefs that are worthy and that can, at that time and place, be somewhat readily apprehended as convincing, so that the beliefs about the Christian God can become a *perception* of *this* God as the Holy Reality.

(8) One implication of this understanding of the theological task is that a repetition of doctrines that performed this task quite well in previous centuries may fail miserably today. What I have in mind in particular is this: throughout most of Christian history in Europe (roughly the 4th to the 18th centuries), the cultural situation was such that the reality of God seemed overwhelmingly obvious to most people. The understanding of the Bible, the ideas of the leading thinkers, the works of the leading artists, and the authority of the leading institutions all presupposed and reinforced the conceptual belief and perceptual faith in the Christian God. In such a situation the theologian could, when having trouble reconciling Christian doctrines with each other, appeal to "mystery" without defaulting on the theological task. Likewise, when Christian doctrines conflicted with the conclusions of "reason," the theologian could simply appeal to authority (including the "authority" of reason which provided proofs for the existence of God), which supported the Christian doctrines. In other words, the theologian did not need to present a comprehensive view of the world that was *intrinsically convincing*. The *truth* of the Christian position (whatever it was) was widely held to be *externally guaranteed* (through the authority of the Bible, the authority of the Church, and the rational arguments for the existence of God and for the authority of the Bible and/or the Church). In those centuries the theological task could be primarily limited to the refinement of belief and the essentially negative task of responding to objections to this or that doctrine. The problem of evil in that situation constituted no overwhelming problem threatening to undermine faith itself. There was widespread confidence that there *was* a solution, known to God, and there was no overriding need to be able to discover that solution. Theologians often did devote many pages to it, but when they encountered questions they could not answer, there was no sense of desperation. They could calmly say that those remaining problems were "mysteries" which we were not intended to understand.

But in our day, all of this has changed. The results of the historical-critical approach to the Bible that has been carried out in the past two centuries make it very difficult to consider it (the Bible) an external guarantee for any particular doctrines. The same is true for the Church. The "authority" of the Church and its theologians is virtually non-existent. Furthermore, the leading thinkers of the day, especially the philosophers, do not provide a cultural context in which the reality of God is either assumed or commonly supported by argumentation. In *this* situation the evils experienced in the twentieth century constitute a much more serious problem for faith in God than did the evils experienced by people in earlier centuries (and this is true even if one does not believe that the horrendous events of this century exceed the evils of previous centuries qualitatively or even quantitatively).

I will now apply the above points to the task of a theodicy for our times. A theodicy should be part of a total theological position that is intended to be more consistent, adequate, and illuminating of our experience than any of the alternative philosophical and theological positions of the time. Such a theodicy cannot merely show that the evils of the world do not necessarily contradict belief in God's perfect goodness and power. Nor can such a theodicy resort to encouraging us to believe that there is a God of perfect goodness and power *in spite of* the fact that the appearances suggest that some other hypothesis is more probable. Rather, such a theodicy must attempt to *portray* the world so that the hypothesis that the world has been created by such a God seems *more likely* than other hypotheses, so that those who accept this belief can come to *perceive* the world in these terms. In such a theodicy, the evils of the world should not be an embarrassment to the total theological position; they should not be that "fact" to which the theology somehow manages to be "adequate" but which would fit more comfortably within some contrary hypothesis. Rather, the theodicy should ideally be more illuminating of the nature of evil, and the reason for its existence, than other portrayals of reality, including atheistic ones.

These are austere ideals for a theodicy, and I do not pretend that mine achieves them. But they are the standards by which I think a theodicy in our time should be measured. The substantive differences between my theodicy and the others in this volume probably all reflect differences in regard to these formal matters. This does not necessarily mean that all debate should shift from substantive doctrines to formal issues, for there is a dialectical relation between substantive and formal issues. One's substantive beliefs influence one's position on formal issues at least as much as the other way around.

What it does mean is that debates as to the adequacy of various theodicies should not be carried on apart from reflection on the over-all task of Christian theology in our time.

Critiques

Critique by John K. Roth

John Hick promised pie in the sky by and by—a whole one for everybody. Stephen Davis suggested that ignorance is bliss. Now enter David Griffin with his God on a leash. With the exception of Griffin's, all of the theodicies in this book leave us wondering why God created the world as he did. Process theology, however, has "solved" the problem of evil. It does so by paring away God's power, but only in the most flattering ways. Lacking omnipotence though he may be, Griffin's Greek God is a paragon of virtue. Following Plato's lead, this God never does less than the best that his inherently limited powers will allow. Genuine evil does abound, much of it due to freedom abused. More importantly, though, necessity creates the final solution.

His theory, Griffin notes repeatedly, is a speculative hypothesis. It must be tested by experience, judged by its capacity to provide adequate illumination. Still, one should not be deceived. Of the options offered here, Griffin's is the most rationalistic, and he intends to make strong claims for its truth. It is no coincidence that he describes his theory ("including variations on it") as "the *only* hypothesis I have found that makes faith possible in the face of the horrendous evils that occur in our world" (my italics). If Griffin's apology for God—"He's doing the best he can"—is *in any sense* the only one that makes faith possible, that outcome is not without considerable cost. To my mind it requires one to accept principles of necessity that neither should be nor are convincing. Moreover, if Griffin's theory is correct, I am persuaded that religious faith is irrelevant.

Start with Griffin's appeals to necessity. We are told that "each increase in the capacity to enjoy intrinsic goodness is likewise an increase in the capacity to suffer." Indeed this relationship "is a necessary, metaphysical correlation." Such an outlook produces a crucial question: what is the evidence supporting Griffin's claim for necessity? It is not clear that any appeal to empirical facts can provide it, for those facts are contingent. Indeed appeals to empirical facts would seem to provide counterexamples to Griffin's view.

For instance, since a polio vaccine was discovered some years ago, my capacity to suffer that disease has virtually disappeared. Thus, not only is it questionable in principle that my capacity to enjoy intrinsic goodness in any way necessitates a capacity to suffer, but also it is quite clear in fact that my immunity to polio results in a net loss where my capacity to suffer is concerned. Moreover, far from hampering my capacity to enjoy intrinsic goodness, a decrease in my capacity to suffer from disease actually enhances my potential to experience what is good. A multiplication of similar cases may leave Griffin without a necessary leg to stand on, unless he can really persuade us that there is a necessity to suffer from disease in order to maximize good experience.

Another of Griffin's hypotheses about necessity affirms that the "possibility of higher value experiences" necessarily entails higher degrees of freedom, including increased potentialities for destruction. If this theory is correct, it seems to follow that my potential to experience value is somehow dependent on my capacity to commit murder, or even to help unleash a Holocaust. Here I think we need to ask Griffin to tell us what specific values could not be experienced if these destructive capacities were absent. I am at a loss to think of any that would be so indispensable that we could not get along quite well—maybe even better—

without them. If either Griffin or God can persuade me otherwise, I will stand corrected, but I doubt that they can do so without assuming the very necessity that is in question.

Griffin's doctrines of necessity are jeopardized by a lack of direct evidence in their favor. Still, he tries to finesse this difficulty by making an indirect appeal for their validity: his hypothesis, he suggests, will be validated overall by its capacity to illuminate experience. I find Griffin's theory inadequate on these terms, too, and one of the reasons is that his theodicy steals significance from faith in God.

All of Griffin's appeals to necessity intend to buttress the claim that God is doing the best he can. If one really looks at the sorry state of the world with that proposition in mind, then it is obvious that God's best is far from enough. Thus, the problem that Griffin and his God must face is that they are badly overmatched by human recalcitrance. If the propensities for evil that lurk in human hearts and wreak their havoc everywhere were not so vast and unyielding, there might be more reason for optimism, more enthusiasm for joining hands with Griffin's weak and suffering God. History indicates, however, that there has been precious little moral progress resulting from God's persuasive powers. Things may even be heading for apocalypse now. If so, it is not because God has been totally without allies. Over the centuries, many human beings have rallied nobly to their perception of God's call, and they have done so in considerable numbers, although probably not because they thought the God of Alfred North Whitehead was calling them.

Beyond life in this world, God's persuasion might make things decisively better, if not well. Not by accident, however, Griffin's theodicy is silent at this point. He says nothing about resurrection; eschatology is missing. The absence of these ingredients is a crucial gap in his theodicy For it leaves us to ask: in Griffin's view, what are we to have faith about? Surely not that history is suddenly, or even slowly, going to reveal moral progress overall. That proposition would require a leap of faith quite out of character with Griffin's theory. On the other hand, if Griffin decides to add eschatological elements it will be a neat trick whether he can mesh those elements consistently and credibly in relation to his claims about God's weakness and unpersuasive performance in the world to date. I doubt that he can perform it.

By the implications of Griffin's theory, when Elie Wiesel arrived at Auschwitz, the best that God could possibly do was to permit 10,000 Jews a day to go up in smoke. That process continued for another year, but remember that God really was doing all that he could to persuade a different outcome into existence— at least according to David Griffin. A God of such weakness, no matter how much he suffers, is rather pathetic. Good though he may be, Griffin's God is too small. He inspires little awe, little sense of holiness. History shows that this God's persuasive power is too scant to make a difference that is decisive enough, and unless God has the potential to act in that fashion, I think that he neither deserves nor will get much attention. With one hand Griffin offers the hypothesis that God lures us to realize the greatest good that is possible in our particular situations. With a leash of necessity in the other, Griffin removes virtually every good reason for religious faith in God's power to redeem and save. And so someone might inquire:

> "God, are you doing the best you can? Are you bound by necessity's chains? If so, it's sad."
>
> "Suppose I am. Can't I persuade you to help me? Together we can make everything so much better."
>
> "Really?"

Critique by John H. Hick

Griffin's paper is an excellent presentation of a process theodicy. A process theodicy, however, is not a solution to the traditional theological problem of evil, but a denial that there is properly any such problem. For the traditional task is to reconcile the fact of evil—in the forms both of wickedness and of pain and suffering—with faith in an unlimitedly good and unlimitedly powerful Creator. But if, as process theology teaches, God is limited in power, no such reconciliation is called for. The explanation of the undoubted fact of evil is that God is doing the best he can with an independent and recalcitrant material. And, given that God is thus limited, and exists in ultimate duality with an alien realm which partially thwarts the divine goodness, the problem of evil in its traditional form fails to arise.

Accordingly the fundamental criticism of a process theodicy must be a criticism of the doctrine of a limited God. However, it is not feasible to embark upon a discussion of that doctrine within the limits of this brief comment upon Griffin's chapter. In his chapter the only recommendation offered for the notion of a limited deity is that it would enable us to avoid the traditional theodicy problem. I believe, on the other hand, that the idea of a finite God (except as a finite *eikon* of the infinite God) is metaphysically unsatisfying; and also that the theodicy problem provoked by the doctrine of divine omnipotence is capable of an adequate, though not a full, response. I have tried to outline such a response in my own chapter.

Instead, then, of discussing the conception of a limited deity, I propose to comment upon Griffin's distinction, which plays an important part in his discussion, between "genuine" and "apparent" evil. He defines "genuine" evil as "anything that makes the world worse than it could have otherwise been." On the other hand he defines "apparent" evil as evil which "contributes to a greater good." These are presumably being presented as mutually exclusive categories: an evil is either genuine or apparent, i.e., it either makes the world worse than it could otherwise have been, or it contributes to a greater good. But is not this an unreal alternative? It is a tautology that *any* evil, whether it contributes to a greater good or not, makes the world worse than it would have been if that evil had not existed. Otherwise we should not count it as an evil. But it may nevertheless be the case that some or many or all evils ultimately contribute to a greater good in that (a) they are part of the actual process of the universe and (b) this process is leading to the limitless good of the unending joy of perfected spiritual life. In other words, it may be that evil is *both* such as to make the world worse than it could otherwise have been, and *also* part of a creative process which is leading to limitless good. This possibility is indeed affirmed in the kind of theodicy which I have outlined in my own paper.

I therefore feel that Griffin's definition of genuine evil is open to question. The contrary of evil which contributes to a greater good is not evil which makes the world worse, but evil which does not contribute to a greater good; and whether there is any such is precisely the central question raised by the Irenaean type of theodicy. Griffin says, "that genuinely evil things happen in the world is one of the common notions which constitute the fundamental facts to which any philosophy or theology must be adequate." But I do not think that it is common, in the sense of an agreed or obvious or undeniable or uncontroversial statement, that there is evil which is not part of the actual process of the universe, and that the actual process of the universe will not lead to a limitlessly good end-state. Christian faith affirms that the divine creative process is in fact moving towards such a culmination; whereas the contrary is apparently an essential premise of Griffin's argument. His premise leads him to postulate a limited God, whereas the contrary faith of the main Christian tradition presupposes an unlimited God.

Critique by Frederick Sontag

Griffin has done us the service of making it quite plain just what the Process God can and cannot do. Knowing this we can accept or reject that picture of God according to what we think it necessary for God to do. Griffin is clear that he is returning to an ancient notion of a limited God, and I think he is right in seeing that Plato excuses God from evil by making him not responsible for all but only for the good in the world. God does the best he can with materials that were given to him and not created by him. This point is important because much heat has been generated over the supposed borrowing of Greek notions by early Christian theologians. Griffin makes it clear that, at least in this crucial point regarding God, Christian theology departed radically from Greek concepts. The early church fathers held to the omnipotence of God and rejected Plato's more limited deity.

Why did early Christian theology do this, when it compounds the problem of evil? Why do Griffin and other Process theologians now propose a return to a limited deity in order to make the solution to the problem of evil easier? And what is the key issue which determines whether we should follow them in their compromise or not? Early Christianity, I believe, became convinced of God's intention to save humanity, as illustrated in the resurrection of Jesus, and any God who is to do this needs more power than Plato's limited deity possesses. Thus, our decision concerns this: (1) Do we want a specifically Christian deity and thus incur greater problems with evil; and (2) Do God's Christian promises require that he be able to control all things—and thus increase his responsibility for evil—in order for him to have the power necessary to back up Christian promises?

Of course, everything depends upon how one interprets "Christian promises," eschatology, and the resurrection of Jesus. Griffin does not outline the Process stand on these matters, and strictly speaking there is no reason why he should in sketching a theodicy. However, in deciding whether to accept a God of limited responsibility and thus limited power, we must decide what we expect God to do and then outline a doctrine about a God who has power commensurate with his responsibilities and our expectations. Certainly to remove God from direct responsibility for evil only to find that he is incapable of overcoming it, due to lack of control over it, is a questionable advantage. "What God does not create he cannot control," so that our question is whether Griffin's God, who tries his best, is good enough.

Our decision partly depends on how seriously we take the problem of evil. Process theology is the child of modern optimism, an era of anthropodicy rather than theodicy, where we thought that at last we held the power to irradicate evil in human hands. If we remain optimistic about human ability to engineer a new world for ourselves, a limited, benevolent, cooperative God is sufficient, and he has the advantage of not interfering with our human schemes to determine the course of the world. On the other hand, if we do not think human schemes to control or irradicate evil (e.g., Marx) are sufficient, if evil seems pervasive of the very structure of nature and human nature, then we either need a God with sufficient power to control nature and alter it radically, or else we must abandon hope of ever overcoming evil.

But we cannot "have our cake and eat it too"—Griffin is right. The God with the power to save us is a God implicated in the evil of the world, because his vast creative powers make him responsible for the choice of the world as we know it. God's power was also sufficient to create a different world had he chosen to do so. The Process God is confronted with the elements of the world in disassembled form. He makes no basic choices of one world against another but, faced with a surd given, he does his best. Is that enough? And what happens to Christianity's good news? Griffin admits his God is "destructive of the hope that God will totally defeat the powers of evil and make all things new." The Bible does not force us to one view or another, since the Old Testament surely has several views of God, some of them a limited deity—Griffin is right. All these may be "speculative hypotheses," but the issue is: what kind of God does the New Testament require?

In the structure of Griffin's argument, the most crucial issue is step 4: "A morally perfect being would want to bring about a world devoid of genuine evil." Who says so? Why do we assume some simple standard of "moral perfection" and plaster it on to God? God may be bound by no such limitation, although it might be easier on us if he were. Certainly I do not accept any such assumption about God, and I see little evidence God is of such a type, although this assumption might fit certain notions in British ethics. If God was thwarted in the beginning of creation, the same forces which limited him then limit him now, and the Christian hope for a new world fades. If power is always shared, people can thwart God. They have in the past. Is there any evidence they won't continue to thwart him in the future if God does not have the power to overrule them?

Is a "persuading God" enough? We must be optimistic about human progress if we think so. Griffin has given us essentially a "natural theology." God could do no other. He is part of the process, and increasing good requires increasing pain. However, the question is whether the degree of pain and loss is exactly the amount necessary to achieve good or whether the loss involved is excessive. There is little evidence that we live in such a nicely balanced world and thus not much reason to be confident about the overcoming of evil, unless some power can intervene into the process (but it will not be Griffin's God). If God had no choice in the world we have, he has no power to alter it. So we either are optimistic about the direction of natural progress, or else the problem of evil Griffin hoped to avoid by limiting God is back again in the form of our disillusion over the possibility for the human self-elimination of evil in time.

Griffin's God cannot prevent evil; he pleads with us to improve things. No quick change is possible, so eschatology is eliminated, and we are stuck with the natural direction of events. Realizing that masses are difficult to control, Griffin's God works primarily on an individual level. But is that sufficient to do anything but bring momentary patches of light on a canvas painted primarily in shades of grey and black? Such a theodicy makes faith possible, Griffin tells us. But what does this faith trust in? Certainly not in God's power to save us. Why should any theodicy attempt to present itself as being "more likely"? The Christian notion that God acted once, and will act again, to save humankind requires a God of quite unlikely powers.

Critique by Stephen T. Davis

Process Theology is an authentic movement in twentieth century theology, one which seems to be growing in influence, especially among liberal Protestants in America. So it is interesting to see how Griffin, one of Process Theology's leading thinkers, tackles the problem of evil. Instead of denying the perfect goodness of God, as Roth and Sontag do, he denies the omnipotence of God. By way of response, let me first make a preliminary point about "genuine evil." Then I will give three reasons why I think Griffin's theodicy fails.

It is usually quite acceptable for theologians or philosophers to define terms in any consistent way they prefer. Thus I have no objection to Griffin's stipulation that "genuine evil" is "anything that makes the world worse than it could have otherwise been." This does indeed imply, as Griffin notes, that those theists who hold that all evil helps lead to a greater good must deny that "genuine evil" (as Griffin defines the term) exists. That is, they affirm that all evil is only apparent. (Of course many theists—including me—will want to define the term "genuine evil" in some other way, but Griffin is entitled to his technical definition.)

But it is important to notice two things here. First, while nearly every rational person will agree that evil exists (it is not, a la Mary Baker Eddy, "an illusion of the material sense"), it is not true that nearly every rational person will agree that "genuine evil" (as Griffin defines the term) exists. For it may well be true, as some Christians claim, that in the end God will use every event that has ever occurred to help produce the great good of the Kingdom of God. So it seems to me unfair for Griffin to imply that theodicists who deny that "genuine evil" (as he defines the term) exists deny something that nearly every rational person knows, as if their views were on a level with those of Miss Eddy. Second, it is perfectly possible for someone to say of some heinous event (e.g., the Holocaust) *both* that it "makes the world worse than it could have otherwise been," i.e., that God will not use it causally to produce a greater good *and* that God will in the end nevertheless produce a greater good. Such a person can then affirm, even on Griffin's definition, that genuine evil exists.

Let me now turn to my three main objections to Griffin's theodicy. The first has to do with creation *ex nihilo*. It is crucial for Griffin to deny this doctrine, for it is part of his program to say that God's power is limited both by the uncreated, pre-existent material out of which he fashioned the world and by the built-in power over against God that every actual thing has.

I agree that creation *ex nihilo* is not explicitly taught in Genesis. But (1) it does seem clearly suggested in several other biblical texts (e.g., John 1:3; Rom. 4:17; 11:36; Col. 1:16; Heb. 11:3). (2) It is implied both in the biblical notion of the power of God (for whom "all things are possible" and "nothing is impossible") and in the biblical notion of the absolute lordship and sovereignty of God over the world, i.e., the absolute dependence of the world on God. (3) It is a virtually unanimous aspect of the Christian tradition from the earliest theologians till today. (4) There is no suggestion in Genesis 1:1 (*however* the word *bārā'* is to be interpreted) of a pre-existent "stuff" that was not created by God. Nor is this idea taught anywhere else in the Bible. (5) It is difficult to see why Griffin even bothers to deny that creation *ex nihilo* is taught in the Bible since he holds that the modern historical-critical approach to the Bible makes it "very difficult to consider the Bible an external guarantee for any particular doctrines." (Incidentally, I could not agree less with this sentiment.) (6) Contrary to Griffin, I see no necessary connection whatsoever between creation *ex nihilo* and a denial of theistic evolution. I happen to accept both.

My second main reservation about Griffin's theodicy concerns his denial of the traditional Christian view of omnipotence. I consider this doctrine (which Griffin admits is taught in the Bible) essential to Christianity. The God of traditional Christianity can create the stars, part the waters of the sea, heal people of disease, give sight to the blind, and even raise people from the dead. But the God of Process cannot heal people of cancer or of cellular damage due to exposure to radiation. He cannot directly deflect moving rocks, bullets, or automobiles from their paths. In fact, says Griffin, he cannot directly influence inanimate objects at all. While I do not recommend the worship of power per se (an omnipotent scoundrel would not be worthy of worship), I believe Griffin's God is nowhere near powerful enough to merit worship. Could a sick person rationally pray to such a being for healing?

In addition, I am dubious about Griffin's suggestion that every actual thing must have power of its own over against God. Griffin makes clear that this is only a hypothesis—one which he thinks fits the facts and helps solve the problem of evil. But we do notice that there is no argument for it in Griffin's paper. Furthermore, even if it is true it does not entail the much stronger claim that God cannot directly deflect a moving automobile. But even as a hypothesis it does not seem to me to have much to commend it. This is because it seems entirely possible that God has all the power there is. This seems a perfectly consistent suggestion; some theologians have seriously advanced it. Perhaps a rigid predestinarianism is true; perhaps every event that occurs is brought about by God. So I believe Griffin owes us an argument why this apparently coherent picture of the world cannot be a true picture. Furthermore, perhaps God has the power totally to control all events and totally to determine all actual things but does not use it. This is my own view (and the view of many other Christians): God is fully sovereign and omnipotent, but voluntarily shares some of his power with his creatures.

The third reason I do not believe Griffin solves the problem of evil has to do with the future. Unlike Hick's theodicy and mine, Griffin's is not strongly eschatological. And for reasons I will mention, I do not believe the problem of evil can be solved from a Christian perspective without crucial reference to the future. Thus in response to Griffin's view that God *aims, intends, seeks, works,* and *tries* to overcome evil, we must ask: does God have the power, influence, or persuasive ability to make his intention succeed? If he might not succeed (and I believe this is what Process thinkers must say; they cannot be sure but can only *hope* that God will emerge victorious), then, again, God is not worthy of worship. He is a good being who tries his best: we can certainly sympathize with him and perhaps even pity him. Some of us will choose to fight on his side in the battle against evil, and we can all *hope* he will win in the end. But I see no reason to worship him.

God obviously ran a great risk in creating this sort of world—on that, Griffin and I can agree (although we mean different things by "create"). But was the risk worth taking? Evangelical Christians believe it was. They believe God foresees the future of the world, i.e., the coming kingdom of God, and they believe he has revealed that the risk was worth taking. As Paul says, "The sufferings of this present time are not worth comparing with the glory that is to be revealed" (Rom. 8:18). But on Process Thought we do not know whether the risk was worth taking, for we do not know how the world turns out, and neither does God.

I do not know whether Griffin believes in eternal life, but it is clear that eschatological concerns play no role in his theodicy. Consistent with this, he says he cannot imagine that present and future evil is so bad as to make it better that human life had never been created. Is Griffin saying that the intrinsic evils that now exist are so great that they outweigh *any* evil events that might occur in the future? It would seem an exercise in pollyanna optimism if so. What if ten years from now all human beings die, cursing God, after years of horrible physical and mental suffering? Will God's great adventure have turned out worthwhile? I hardly think so. At this point orthodox Christianity seems far more realistic. Good events do indeed occur, evangelicals want to say, but the power of evil is pervasive in the world. The world may not be worthwhile *as it stands:* it needs to be redeemed.

So even if we grant Griffin his view of omnipotence (which I am not willing to do), it seems still to follow that God is indictable for creating the sort of world he created if in the end evil outweighs good. The God of Process reminds me of a mad scientist who fashions a monster he hopes will behave but whom he cannot control. If the monster does more evil than good the scientist's decision to make the monster will turn out to have been terribly wrong. The scientist will be indictable.

Griffin's Response to Critiques

There are numerous issues raised in the foregoing critiques. I will organize my responses to them under nine points. The first four deal with more limited issues, and partly attempt to clear up misunderstandings. The latter five deal with much more wide-ranging issues, including the basic issue of what Christian faith and theology are all about. These points reflect the fact that theodicy is only one part of the total theological enterprise.

(1) Hick and Davis both evidently misunderstood the distinction between "genuine" and "apparent" evil. It may help to introduce a third term, *"prima facie* evil.'' This refers to anything that is taken to be evil at first glance, as it were. The question is whether at least some of this *prima facie* evil is *genuinely* evil, i.e., whether it results in the world's being a worse place than it might have otherwise been, all things considered. If one were to conclude, upon reflection, that there were no genuine evil, one would be asserting that all *prima facie* evil were merely *apparently* evil, i.e., that it was not evil at all. That was the position adopted by traditional theists such as Augustine, Aquinas, and Luther. Roth and Sontag clearly reject this view. The positions of Hick and Davis are less clear. They evidently think they can, without contradiction, affirm that genuine evil exists and yet that all evil will be used to contribute to a state better than which none is possible. Hick's affirmation is clearer, as he speaks of a "limitlessly good end-state.'' If it is "limitlessly'' good, there would seem to be no possible state that would be better. Hence, none of the evil is genuine—it does not result in the world's being a worse place overall than it could have been. Davis is less clear, speaking of "the great good of the kingdom of God.'' If he means this to be the greatest possible state of affairs (or at least *one* of the greatest possible), then he too has denied the genuineness of evil—all evil is merely apparent. But if he means only that the kingdom of God will be a great good, but less great than it could have been, then he should tell us why his God is perfectly good if this God allows the world to come to a worse conclusion than would have been possible. Why didn't his God use the divine omnipotence to bring about the best possible result? This is the dilemma of those espousing omnipotence: they must either admit that God is not totally good, or else deny that any of the *prima facie* evil in the world is really evil. And if they say the latter, I fail to see how their view *finally* differs from that of Mary Baker Eddy (Davis' protest notwithstanding).

(2) This leads into the question of "common notions.'' I claimed that the idea that genuinely evil things occur is one of the "common notions'' of humanity, those things we all know to be true. Hick and Davis demur, saying that not all people agree to this. Of course, a lot of people have *said* that no genuine evil exists. But I defined a common notion as one of those things that all people affirm *in practice,* regardless of what they may *say.* Just as all Humeans reveal in practice that they know that some things causally affect other things, I claim that the emotions, attitudes, and actions of all people manifest their conviction that some things have happened that should not have happened. So, if Hick and Davis do finally deny that any genuine evil occurs, I believe they are contradicting verbally something they affirm in practice.

(3) Roth asks for evidence for my hypothesis that every increase in the capacity for positive enjoyment is necessarily an increase in the capacity to suffer. In trying (unsuccessfully) to provide a counter example, Roth seems to misunderstand the nature of my position. I am simply pointing to the correlations

that *in fact* exist, from the bottom to the top of the evolutionary scale, and then suggesting that these correlations exist *necessarily* (because of metaphysical truths inherent in the nature of things), rather than being due to accident or the arbitrary fiat of a creator. It simply is a fact—at least most of us believe it to be so—that fleas can enjoy more and suffer more than single-cell organisms, dogs more than fleas, humans more than dogs, and normal adult humans more than babies. Increased complexity in the structure of an individual means increased capacity for enjoyment *and* for suffering. The correlation exists universally. I am only suggesting that this universal correlation exists necessarily, so that it would necessarily obtain in *any* world God could create. My suggestion is a speculative hypothesis. But it is more grounded in empirical reality than the contrary hypothesis, accepted implicitly or explicitly by the other four authors. For, they are asserting (Roth and Sontag), or at least assuming (Davis and Hick), that there are possible worlds in which this correlation does not exist. This is an empirically groundless speculation, since *we have never experienced a world in which this correlation does not exist.* Hence we do not know that such a world is really possible. But we know that a world in which the correlation holds is possible, since ours is such a world. Hence *my* speculation is much more modest and rooted in empirical reality, since my speculation is limited to the suggestion that the way things *are* (in terms of this aspect of our world) may be the way things *have* to be. Recognizing that the contrary hypothesis is not only responsible for the problem of evil, but is also based on a groundless flight of fancy, may be enough to free people from its embittering grip.

(4) Davis demands an argument for the hypothesis that all actual individuals have power of their own with which they can resist God's will. In other words, why is not the view that God has a monopoly on power a coherent and hence possibly true view of the world? I have provided some argumentation for this in *God, Power, and Evil,* especially Chapters 7, 14, 16, 17 and 18. To the points made there I will add one similar to the one made above in regard to the correlations: it does seem to be the case that every actual individual has power. And if God be conceived (e.g., on the basis of Christian faith) to be perfectly good, the most natural hypothesis is that this power includes the power to go contrary to God's will. All the authors in this book agree that at least some creatures have this power. My hypothesis is simply that all creaturely individuals have this power *necessarily,* i.e., that creaturely individuals in *any* world God could create would have this power. Again, my hypothesis simply takes a fundamental aspect of the empirical situation and suggests that this aspect obtains necessarily. The other authors, in holding that the freedom of the creatures to go contrary to God's will is due to a voluntary relinquishment of power by God, are indulging in a much more speculative hypothesis. For they do not have any experientially-based knowledge that a world of totally controlled actualities is even possible. Hence, the demand for argumentation falls much more heavily on

their own hypothesis than on mine. The mere fact that they represent the majority viewpoint in the history of Christian thought and within this book does not change this situation, though it tends to disguise it.

(5) I begin now the points that reflect differences in our understandings of what Christian faith and theology are all about. As I argued in my essay, a theodicy is simply one part of an overall theological position. Positively, this means that to defend one's theodicy means finally to defend one's entire theological position. (For example, Davis would need to defend, in the light of the historical-critical study of the Bible in the past 200 years, his assertion that we can still responsibly take the Bible as an external guarantee of the truth of particular propositions.) Negatively, this means that one's theodicy is not necessarily inadequate because of its failure to fit into *someone else's* total theological position. Yet theologians keep forgetting this. Since Roth, Sontag and Davis hold to the traditional doctrine of omnipotence, the fact that the world is pervaded by evil is a severe threat to the notion that there is a God worthy of worship. Because they do not share Hick's faith that divine persuasion will eventually overcome all evil, they can justify allegiance to their God (even in the half-way fashion advocated by Roth) only by expecting an extraordinary act of God in which things will suddenly and dramatically change. They then look at my doctrine of God's power and conclude that it is inadequate since it does not support the kind of eschatological hope that is necessary to solve the problem of evil that was created by *their* doctrine of divine power. Davis sums up their sentiments: "I do not believe the problem of evil can be solved from a Christian perspective without crucial reference to the future." That is true for them. But within my theological perspective God's creative activity can be seen as the expression of perfect goodness apart from any expectation for a radical change in the nature of finite existence, and even apart from any expectation of continued consciousness after bodily death.

(6) Another complex issue concerns the basis from which one constructs a doctrine of God. Sontag and Roth portray me as having a "natural theology" and a "Greek" God rather than a theology based upon the biblical, especially the New Testament, revelation. These are matters of judgment. Is their view that the divine power of the universe is partly good and partly evil less of a "natural" theology than the view suggested by Plato and most of the Bible that God is the source only of good? Is their view of a partly malevolent deity closer to the New Testament than my view, in which a God of perfect love is battling against other powers?

In any case, to take *revelation* seriously means, to me, to take what has actually happened more seriously in forming our doctrines than the ideas spun out of imaginative flights. And what actually happened during the history that the "people of the book" take to be revelatory? God's "chosen" people are constantly defeated. God's prophets are stoned. And the one whom Christians take to be God's decisive revelation was crucified. There is nothing in this picture that suggests that the God served possesses controlling power. Nor does anything in the following two thousand years, including and especially the Jewish Holocaust.

Sontag and Roth think that the resurrection of Jesus supports their doctrine of omnipotence. But what does the resurrection of Jesus reveal, in terms of divine power? At most, that God has the power to renew life after bodily death. It emphatically does *not* reveal that God created the world *ex nihilo,* or that God can change the basic structure of existence as we know it. That doctrine of omnipotence is not based upon historical revelation, but upon imaginative flights designed to fulfill egocentric wishes. Sontag admits as much, saying that "we must decide what we expect God to do and then outline a doctrine about a God who has power commensurate with his responsibilities and our expectations." Should we not instead try to discover what God is like, on the basis of the revelation history provides and our best reasoning on the basis of this revelation, and then reform our expectations in this light?

(7) Closely related is the charge made by Sontag, Roth, and Davis that my doctrine is "optimistic." For this to be a source of reproach, they must mean *unrealistically* optimistic. Their point is that *their* view is much more realistic than mine, as they know, in Sontag's words, that "evil is pervasive of the very structure of nature and human nature," so that a God with only persuasive power could never bring about an end to evil. Hence, they posit a God with controlling power. I cannot but wonder why they find their doctrine less unrealistically optimistic than mine. To expect, after all that has happened which any decent being with controlling power would have stopped, that God is going to act differently than ever before, bringing about a complete change in the structure of existence, seems the height of unrealistic optimism. Again, Sontag is at least candid, saying that a theodicy should be based upon our hopes, not on our ideas of what is "likely."

Since they have no faith in the persuasive power of love to effect salvation, they see my position as providing no basis for hope. It is true that my position supplies no guarantee that we will not destroy ourselves and perhaps all life on this planet. But there would be more basis for hope in this regard if those who worship God would disconnect this worship from the assumption that this God has the kind of power *unilaterally* to prevent this disaster. The complacency promoted by this unrealistic belief is one of the reasons, in my view, that people of good will have allowed the world to get into such a hopeless state. There will be more basis for hope for this world when more people perceive that God's *modus operandi* is to save us *through* our activities, not in spite of them. (There is, I believe, a sense in which our salvation is effected by God alone, without any co-operation being required of us. But salvation in this sense involves saving our lives from ultimate meaninglessness, from making no difference in the ultimate scheme of things. But it is a mistake of utmost seriousness to transmute the intuition of this truth into the baseless doctrine that the re-formation of our individual lives and/or our world will be effected by God unilaterally.)

(8) The differences between me and some of the other authors on the previous three issues reflect differences in regard to what the Christian gospel is, and what Christian faith is all about. Sontag and Roth in particular think there is no "good news" in my position, and that my view makes faith in God "irrelevant." From their perspective (partly for reasons explained above), the good news is that God will save us, in the sense of bringing us into a state of existence in which evil is totally overcome; and this is the content of faith—what God will do in the future. From my perspective, central to the good news is the cry, "Emmanuel—God is with us and for us!" The key question, in this evil-riddled world, in which every movement, every structure, every dimension of existence is ambiguous at best, is whether there is *any* reality which is working unambiguously for good, to which we can give our allegiance without reservation (with our *whole* heart, soul, and mind), which can empower us to overcome the evil within ourselves and the world around us, and the worship of which can integrate our lives and give them purpose and direction. The Christian gospel, as I understand it, is that there is. God is with us here and now, and is totally for us. Accordingly, from this perspective it is Sontag and Roth who deny the good news by transposing the world's ambiguity into the very heart of God. Their God needs help as much or more than we do (which makes their characterization of my God as "pathetic" somewhat humorous). And if what we most need, in order to prevent this whole planet from premature death, is empowerment to co-operate with God's purposes, then it is Sontag, Roth and Davis, with their focus on what God will unilaterally do in the future, who present a faith that is irrelevant.

(9) Most of the other authors agree that my theodicy solves the problem of evil. Their central reason for considering it inadequate is that it does so by portraying a God who is not worshipful. This charge can mean that this God either (i) *does* not evoke worship or (ii) *should* not evoke worship. Unfortunately they do not distinguish these two meanings. In any case, there are several reasons given as to why the process doctrine of God is inadequate.

(A) One such reason is that this God is "limited" or "finite." These terms are acceptable if they are properly understood; but often they are used as synonymous with "imperfect." My God is finite if this means that God is not the totality of reality, that there are other actualities besides God. (The biblical God is clearly "finite" in this sense.) My God is limited if this means that these other actualities have power of their own that cannot be totally controlled by God. (The biblical witness is ambiguous on this point.) But my God is *not* finite or limited if this means that God's power is imperfect in comparison with that of some other conceivable deity. As I stated in the last section of my essay, I conceive God to be perfect in power (as well as goodness), which means having the greatest power it is possible for one being to have. Accordingly, what is at issue is not a God whose power is imperfect in contrast with a God whose power is perfect; rather, what we have is a conflict between two conceptions of perfect power. Insofar as the arguments (referred to in point 4) as to why the idea of a divine monopoly on power is an incoherent idea are convincing, an answer is provided to the claim that my God is not worthy of worship because "not powerful enough"—i.e., one cannot reasonably ask for more than the possible.

Hick indicates that his chief criticism of my theodicy would be directed toward its idea of a limited God. The only suggestion he gives as to what his criticism would be is that this idea is "metaphysically unsatisfying." He gives no hint in his critique as to the direction his argument would take. However, in his *Evil and the God of Love* (pp. 35-36) he provides this explanation: if God were not "the creator of everything other than Himself," God would not be "an eternal self-existent Being." Hence one would have to ask who created God. Unfortunately, this argument itself is metaphysically unsatisfying, since a being could well be eternal and self-existent without being creator of everything else. If that is the worst challenge the process doctrine of God must face, it is in good shape.

(B) Hick and Davis almost seem to think that the mere fact that the traditional doctrine of omnipotence, including creation *ex nihilo,* has been the dominant view in Christian theology settles the issue as to *the* Christian position. But, for example, a good case can be made for the proposition that anti-Semitism has characterized "the main Christian tradition"; this does not make anti-Semitism Christian in a normative sense. So, more argument than an appeal to the past majority opinion will be needed to support the idea that Jews and Christians today should continue to accept divine omnipotence.

(C) Sontag, Davis and especially Roth say that the God of persuasion I portray has not been effective enough in the world to inspire awe and worship. Roth speaks of God's "unpersuasive performance in the world to date." But when I contemplate the creation as a whole, I am rather overwhelmed. When I view the heavens, and the beauty of our own planet, and when I reflect upon the fact that creatures as wondrously complex as ourselves were brought into being out of minute trajectories of energy such as protons and electrons, I am *quite* impressed. I *do* stand in awe before the directive power that could bring about such results out of partially self-determining entities, and a sense of holiness *is* produced in me. So to some extent it may simply be that Roth is more difficult to impress than I am.

However, to some extent it seems that Roth takes an anthropocentric view of things. In saying that there has been little progress, he speaks only of *moral* progress; in speaking of resistance, he speaks only of *human* recalcitrance. This suggests that Roth begins grading God only after human beings have been produced. Perhaps if he would extend his vision a few billion years further back, he would see that we really have come a long way. Further, even during the extremely short period of human history, Roth admits that "many human beings have rallied nobly to their perception of God's call." I wonder why this alone does not impress him.

Davis finds the God of process theology unworthy of worship because this God cannot guarantee that the risk involved in creating the world "was worth taking." If the world were to end in a situation in which "all human beings die, cursing God, after years of horrible physical and mental suffering," it would have been better, Davis maintains, that human beings had never been created. In fact, like many who want to emphasize the necessity for a dramatic eschatological act of God, Davis says "the world is not worthwhile *as it stands.*" So, even apart from the grim scenario he sketches, if he were to be convinced that no such eschatological act were going to occur, he would presumably be one of those carrying a sign reading, "Doom, doom, the world is *not* going to end." Of course, if he seriously finds his own present life intrinsically unworthwhile (it would be presumptuous of him to say that his own is worthwhile but that of the majority of humanity is not), I can only respect his feelings while witnessing that I do not find my own and that of those I know well to be so. Nor can I judge that, for the majority of humanity, it would have been better that they had not lived, even if there is to be no future existence for them. Furthermore, I have distinguished between the kind of power needed to change the very structure of existence, which I think God does not have, and the power needed to renew our lives beyond bodily death, which I think God does have. So, even if one did think that human life were not intrinsically worthwhile, so that a future life for humans would be necessary to justify God's creation of us, it does not follow that God must be omnipotent in the traditional sense to be justified in bringing forth human life.

One of the stranger complaints from Sontag and Roth is that, given the enormity of evil in the world, a deity that is doing its best is not worthy of worship. The implication is that a deity that is *not* doing its best *is* worthy of worship. For example, in reference to Auschwitz, Roth mocks my God with the statement that "the best that God could possibly do was to permit 10,000 Jews a day to go up in smoke." Roth prefers a God who had the power to prevent this Holocaust but did not do it! This illustrates how much people can differ in what they consider worthy of worship. For Roth, it is clearly brute *power* that evokes worship. The question is: is this what *should* evoke worship? To refer back to the point about revelation: is this kind of power worship consistent with the Christian claim that divinity is decisively revealed in Jesus? Roth finds my God too small to evoke worship; I find his too gross.

POSTSCRIPT: In writing this response, it became obvious that many of the criticisms to which I was called to reply were made in triplicate: from Davis, Roth, and Sontag. They have common objections to process theology. This is probably not coincidental: Roth and Sontag have written books together, and

Roth and Davis have adjoining offices. Also, all three did their doctoral work in philosophy and presently teach in philosophy departments, whereas my graduate work was more concentrated in biblical studies, history of Christian thought, history of religions, and modern theology. This probably has something to do with our different evaluations of the normative status of propositional formulations of Christian faith coming from the early centuries of Christianity.

It also became more obvious than it previously was to me how much Hick and I have in common. We both see God as relying solely upon persuasion to effect our salvation—we do not expect God one of these days to give up on this method and to resort to coercive measures. We both place our faith in the attractiveness of the divine, agreeing with Whitehead that "the power of God is the worship He inspires."[4] The crucial difference between us is that Hick continues to insist that God has that other kind of power, i.e., the coercive kind. And this is the idea that creates all the objectionable aspects in his theodicy. Since Hick, unlike Roth, Sontag, and Davis, believes that God will never *use* this coercive power, I wonder what value is derived from continuing to maintain that God *has* it.

5 Anthropodicy and the Return of God

FREDERICK SONTAG

Growing up in a Baptist church in Long Beach, California in the 20s and 30s did not raise the problem of evil in any vivid form. Although it was the time of the boom of the 20s and then the depression of the 30s, you cannot say life was very difficult, once you have traveled in India and compared conditions there. Long Beach was dominated by retired Iowa farmers and U.S. Navy personnel. It was also permeated by the Protestant dream of building a new society free from foreign corruption. The demise of this dream was not crucial, since the problem of evil was raised for me first as an intellectual puzzle.

It was the problem of God which made evil an urgent issue. My Baptist God was straight out of the Old Testament and philosophically not very sophisticated. Thus, the dazzling array of metaphysical descriptions of the divine nature I encountered in studying philosophy offered him a considerable challenge. However, as I began to revise my notions of God, I discovered that few shared my concern, particularly if they were philosophers. Theologians had not yet risen to pronounce God dead, but modern philosophers seemed little concerned with him.

The first book I wrote on evil had not been projected to take up that topic. Responding to an invitation to teach at the Collegio di Sant' Anselmo in Rome just after Vatican II, I was asked to lecture on atheism, but I discovered that the greatest source of atheism in the modern age is the failure adequately to account for evil. In a post-scientific age, I came to agree, we no longer accept the world as necessary, and so we know God could have corrected any of its defects, just as we have learned to. Sartre rejected God in the name of human freedom, but others deny God because they realize evil is not always voluntary.

There has been a tendency, reflected in the introduction to this volume, to accept the nature of God and the problem of evil as fixed concepts and to argue from there. Given the widespread skepticism about God today, our basic problem is that we do not know how to think about God. Accounting for evil, I became convinced, does stimulate thought about God. We do not know what God is like; our concept of him is not fixed at the beginning. Rather, as Augustine remarked, where God is concerned, thought takes the form of attempting to arrive at the concept. Of course, some have wanted to eliminate the problem and convert the issue into one of accepting the definition of God as given and then trying to decide about the concept.

Moreover, "anthropodicy" has taken over from "theodicy." That is, many no longer try to explain evil in the context of God but accept as their premise that evil stems solely from the human condition. It is to be accounted for and corrected at that level. Thus, until an adequate concept of God is worked out, many avoid seeing evil as an issue for theology at all. The problem of evil today is one of convincing people that theodicy is important or possible. Evil is linked to the question of atheism and no longer is a side issue stemming from a prior belief in God. Some Christians, of course, still come at the problem due to a growing religious perplexity, but we must recognize the number who do not. We do not begin with God and then discover the problem of evil. Rather, evil blocks our consideration of God in the first place.

Lecturing in Rome, I offered a contemporary solution to this dilemma. I was pressed by my Benedictine students to "give an answer."[1] I argued that, in the present day, understanding evil holds the key to forming an adequate concept of God, rather than God being discovered separately and then explaining evil. We have inherited numerous arguments for the existence of God, but today we learn about God by following the arguments that lead away from his existence. We ask: why do men and women deny God today, and is there a concept of God which can meet their objections? I concluded then that you could not have a God without having a devil. That is, any notion of God likely to last today must include and account for the negative and destructive forces we encounter, not simply the positive and the helpful. Beginning with the devil may provide a better guide than any positive idea of God could.

The best empirical evidence for God's existence turns out to be what drove many to deny it. God is often hidden, but evil is felt and seen by all. Thus, any useful theism must begin by accounting for God's frequent silence, particularly in the face of evil. However, a hidden God lends support to atheism, since only a God apparent to all could put an end to disbelief. In the post-scientific age, our major problem is that we possess the power to correct many of nature's defects and so realize the world in which we live is not necessary but is the result of choice. We must either reject God or admit we are dealing with a deity who could have speeded the relief of human suffering but did not choose to do so. He does not come forth clearly to reveal his reasons for doing so and to defend his decisions.

Our task would be simpler if we dealt with only one concept of God. Some philosophers and theologians act as if this were the case, and argument would be easier if it were. Actually, we deal with as many concepts of God as there are arguments for God's existence, so that our first job in dealing with the problem of evil is to decide what God is like, or which notion we are going to use. Furthermore, this situation tips the scales slightly in favor of atheism, since only if our notion of God is fixed could our discussions about theism be conclusive. Thus, those facing the problems of evil have a better than even chance of not finding a concept of God sufficient to deal with the doubts evil's presence raises. Economically speaking, God has produced a rather wasteful order. The destruction included is not cost efficient for the good which comes out of it. An easy God is easy to find, a hard God hard to find.

In an era of "the death of God," we have learned that concepts of God do not stay vital indefinitely. They tend to fade and lose their attractive power. This gives us an added difficulty where evil is concerned, since a once effective solution does not necessarily retain its ability to convince. Yet the passing of one concept can lead to the birth of another more vital for that age. The difficulty is that there is nothing necessary about this process. God may be lost entirely in a time of transition, particularly if the sense of evil is strong. Of course, Kierkegaard and Sartre stressed humankind's essential freedom and aloneness in the world. If this is our primary experience, it may lead to God, as it does for Kierkegaard, but it just as easily leads to the rejection of God, as it did for Sartre.

Although we find a renewed interest in the problem of evil today, theologians in a post-Kantian age are often reluctant to say much directly about God. In the face of such reticence to speak about God, it is difficult to account for evil, at least in terms of a concept of God. An anti-metaphysical bias blocks the basic reconstruction of the first principles we need if we are to form new concepts of God. This restricts us to the existing notions under challenge. However, when evil becomes a major force on the horizon, as it did in the Jewish holocaust, we discover that evil presses us toward new concepts of God in the attempt to account for its force (cf. the writings of Elie Wiesel). If evil ruthlessly destroys but not all of existence disappears, we are left to account for why everything is not destroyed. "Since the devil exists, God also exists."

We have all been apologists for God too long. How do we know God wants us to argue to free him from all responsibility for evil? He certainly is strong enough to take responsibility for any world he cares to create, as he tried to explain to Job. We need to redirect our questions and address them directly to God. We are involved in a "divine scandal"; we have discovered, by increasing our own power, that God had the power to choose a better world but deliberately chose the world we experience, including its horrors as well as its virtues. We are hampered in working out a solution, because our ability to do so depends on our philosophical assumptions. Not all philosophical premises enable us to construct a new concept of God. Some make it difficult if not impossible.

The features you take to be crucial in the divine nature are decisive in shaping the answer you give. For instance, if freedom and will are paramount in God's life, his relationship to the natural world will not be fixed, nor will his actions necessarily be bound by our notions of rationality. How we treat the future versus the past is important too, although any forecast of the future introduces an element of uncertainty into our answers.

We need to learn to live with probable and less than certain answers. If we claim God's nature to be controlled by love, we only heighten the tension, since evil and destruction in the world are hardly evidence of love. Locked in the problem of evil, old notions of God are destroyed, but new ones can emerge. But we must challenge God for answers to the problem of evil ("God, Why Did You Do That?"), since, left to itself, the natural world simply evidences destruction and gives no answers. Thus, it is we who are forced to construct answers for God, since he has not provided us with any definitive explanation of his behavior. Rather, people have constructed religious literature with many answers, but we get one answer only if we construct it out of the material offered.

II

As an example of the problem we face in dealing with evil, consider the introduction to this volume. Davis opens by saying that theism means the belief that this world was created by "an omnipotent and perfectly good personal being." That is just the problem: we have no such agreement that this is what theism means, nor do we agree what "omnipotent" and "perfectly good" mean. Philosophers are notorious for arguing over the statement of the question, but the answer we give to the problem of evil depends entirely on the meaning of "omnipotent" and "perfectly good." For instance, God might possess all power but voluntarily surrender control for a time over parts of creation. He might be good, but not necessarily in the ordinary meaning of the term, and this would allow evil to be consistent with good. He may be perfect, but we have no agreement about what this means.[2]

When Davis suggests that "perfectly good" means that "God never does what is morally wrong," this is difficult to understand. God may allow destructive evil into the world when he does not have to, which goes against what some mean by "morally right," but he might be good in some sense of that term. Thus, God may cause suffering even if there are no overriding moral reasons for him to do so. There may be a demonic side in God, as I have claimed, but this does not make the problem of evil easy to solve, as Davis suggests. If God is free, he is not forced, and the incorporation of destruction in our natural order is not a necessary decision. The alternatives are far from neat and easily defined, as Davis suggests.

If God is good, Davis tells us, "he must be willing to prevent evil." But that is not necessarily true. Everything depends on how the divine will is analyzed, which is no less difficult to do for God than for human beings. However, Davis strikes the crucial issue for all of us, I believe, when he indicates that the problem for theism is not that evil exists, but that *"too much* evil exists." All explanations of the necessity for, or the good we derive from, destruction work only up to a point. Our world is not perfectly balanced so as to allow just the right amount of destruction for contrast or effect. Some losses are extreme and serve no discernable purpose. Evil is purposeless, wasteful destruction, but those involved in religious life point to the desirable effects of evil. This does not explain why this power is more extreme than necessary.

If our problem were neatly defined, with all definitions clear and everyone in agreement about the nature of God and the crucial terms involved, our situation in regard to evil would be different. But we have no single agreed notion of God, and the disagreements we have rest there. Such is the problem of evil. We must discover what God is like before we can proceed very far, but this is our area of greatest disagreement. The meaning of crucial terms is not given to us, although there are classical suggestions in the literature. We may offer our own definitions, but we cannot hope for a universal solution, since we never agree on the statement of the problem at the outset.

III

I arrived at this position by leaving the protection of the seashore of Long Beach for the contentiousness of philosophy and metaphysics. At the same time, I have never left my Baptist Church there, in that I still realize religion attracts for just the opposite reason: it offers solutions. The average philosopher involved in religion is interested in the apologetic task. Experiencing evil threatens the security of the religious answers one has found, and he or she is forced to offer "answers" which appear certain and thus protect his religious security. A few who are religious can live in uncertainty and maintain faith nevertheless. But the average religious person asks for certainty to guard his faith, whether this comes in the form of a charismatic individual, an inerrant book, or a secure religious tradition.

The irony is that God may not prize certainty and definite answers as much as we do, which means our solutions to the problem of evil tell more about human spiritual needs than about God's. The search for a solution to the problem of evil turned, for me, into a quest for a glimpse into the divine psychology. Much has been and can be learned, as my two books on the subject testify. But where God is concerned, Nicholas Cusanas is correct: all our learning is a "learned ignorance." When God is involved, our answers can never be final, and each step opens further steps ahead. The mystic can live with this openendedness. The average believer, and the philosopher, search for something more final by way of an answer.

My assumptions then, are: (1) That the nature of God is our chief problem, and that we begin with no agreement here but rather start a long search. We can arrive at an individually satisfactory description of God, even if it is provisional, but we cannot expect this to be universally accepted. (2) "Good" and "omnipotent" have no single agreed meaning, particularly where God is concerned. It is our problem to find out what good might mean in God's case in the light of evil and destruction in the world. God may have full power, but he has limited it, or restrained it, for certain time periods. (3) Intellect and goodness alone do not determine divine action. Will and emotion play a role in the divine life, which complicates our analysis of the motives behind God's decisions. His response to our question, "God, Why Did You Do That?" may be, "Because I wanted to."

(4) The religious person, particularly the Christian, often feels he or she has been given an answer to the problem of evil in the form of the religious belief he or she finds attractive. Often, however, this is not an immediately visible solution but the acceptance of a promise to act in the future "to make all things whole." Such a future interruption in the course of nature cannot be ruled out, although neither can it be argued that the present state of affairs seems naturally destined for that outcome. In fact, the reverse is the case. The promise to alter the future is often accepted just because the present course of events does not offer a hopeful outcome. This reversal or radical change may happen, but it cannot be appealed to as an answer in the present. It is only a hope that the future will be different from what we now see.

(5) Various philosophical approaches lead to various solutions, so the problem of evil is "answered" only if we accept the metaphysical assumptions which may always be challenged by us or someone else at a later date. St. Thomas deals with evil. Leibniz solves the problem, but if we do not accept the context within which they set it up, the solution will not hold. The religious believer is in the same situation: his conversion to certain forms of belief, his community and religious practice, offer to solve the problem of evil. But this remains valid only as long as his religious situation remains stable, and it does not hold for anyone who does not accept the same religious convictions. This is particularly true if these depend on God acting differently in the future than he does in the present.

(6) God has purposefully placed us in a situation of less than optimal advantage and subject to more waste and destruction than any purpose can account for. We have not been given good odds for success. This does not prove that there is no God but simply that we are dealing with a God capable of harshness more extreme than some people would use. This does not prove that love will not dominate in the end, or that God may not save those he has promised to. But love like that does not dominate the present. It evidently does not dominate every divine action either, e.g., creation, and it leads to an unexpected outcome. The religious believer attempts to see God as one would like God to be, and God might be that way in the future. But his present actions stand in sharp contrast.

(7) We do not start with God, but pursuing the problem of evil may reveal more of what God is like than the decent gods of religious optimism. Ironically, had the believer seen the world and human beings as predominantly good in the first place, he or she would not have been driven to religious belief. Once a future solution is accepted, we tend to turn it around and interpret all of life as if the future divine actions were already accomplished. The individual life may be changed, even dramatically so, but that is quite different from breaking the hold of destructive evil on the world. However, as our early religious optimism breaks down in some holocaust, our depth of understanding of God may be increased, which brings us back to where we started. Where God and evil are concerned, we constantly start all over again.

(8) I assume that all solutions offered to the problem of evil are subject to the same uncertainties and contingencies, no matter how rigorous their logical format may appear. However, the argument of the skeptic or atheist is also subject to the same uncertainties. All answers pro or con depend upon some description of God's nature, about which we do not agree and cannot achieve finality. The history of our inconclusive discussions testifies to this situation. Any individual or group may reach a statement satisfactory for present purposes. New insight into God is always open, and those who deny the possibility of seeing God doom themselves to no answer. However, if God remains the most difficult object one can approach, the problem of evil offers us both the greatest challenge as well as the opportunity for insight.

IV

Let me explain my own theodicy by analyzing what a Christian might mean if he or she said to the doubtful philosopher, somewhat contemptuously: "I have found Jesus, and that's my solution to the problem of evil." In the first place, there is no need to deny that the individual convert to Christianity has experienced a great change from his or her former life. The issue is whether such an experience can be universalized, and whether Jesus' life in fact provides an answer to our experience of evil and senseless destruction. For anyone who comes to share the Christian's experience, Jesus can provide an answer to the problem of evil, but not for those excluded from this experience.

In terms of Jesus' life and words, the stumbling block to accepting this as a solution to the problem of evil lies in the crucifixion and the centrality it has in Jesus' mission. Clearly if God used Jesus to overcome evil in the world, he either could not or did not accomplish this in a way that avoided evil and loss. Jesus, tradition claims, was blameless. Yet he did not become a successful leader in the world but was put to death. Of course, the balance to this loss is the resurrection. God did not allow human evil to work its destruction. He reversed it by restoring Jesus' life. However, although this belief is at the heart of the Christian faith, it does not solve the problem of evil, because Jesus' restoration is not yet universalized. The Christian simply accepts God's action in one instance as a sign or promise of what God will do for others at some future time. For the present, death and destruction and evil continue unabated.

By way of further explanation of my own theodicy, let me offer some reflections on "Russian Roulette."

The Academy Award winning motion picture, *The Deer Hunter*, has one major theme. It cóncerns an avid deer hunter who, after fighting in Vietnam, can no longer kill a deer. The major moral of the story is that war is hell; it destroys people, phychologically as well as physically. However, the underlying symbolism in the story really involves the game of Russian roulette. The heroes of the drama are first forced to play this deadly game by their North Vietnamese captors. Then, the suspense is acted out again in a deer hunting mountain cabin after the hero's return. Finally, the game is played at the climax of the movie when one of the central figures loses at Russian roulette while playing for high stakes in a Saigon gambling den. Certainly war is a game of Russian roulette, the story teller wants to say. But one could extend this and claim the symbolism intends to tell us that all human life has the aspect of an endless game of Russian roulette. We play with loaded guns, and we never quite know when they will destroy us. To paraphrase Shakespeare: all the world's a deadly game, and all the men and women merely players.

Theologically, *The Deer Hunter* should cause us to ask: does God play Russian roulette with the world? In fact, did God invent the game without consulting us on the rules? Christians in particular, and many religious folk in general, prefer to see God as all-kind and good and loving. This is a comforting picture of divinity, and our primary religious instinct is to seek security and an escape from the terrors of the world. Yet, such religious sentiment leaves the vicious Vietnamese captors and the merciless Saigon gamblers unexplained. The chance aspect of all life must find its explanation in God too, or else none of the games we are forced to play make ultimate sense.

We must face it: any God powerful enough to alter the course of nature in order to save people is also one strong enough to force a game of Russian roulette on us all, when he could have withheld such terror from the program for human life. Of course, for a time in the modern age we thought salvation would come out as an end product of the natural process itself. Evolution and the new controls of science would combine to produce it for us, many enlightened ones thought. The dangerous drift of the twentieth century toward terror and destruction has largely removed that modern optimism. This means we are left either with no prospect of being saved from destruction or we must face the fact that the God who can save us is the same one who decided to play Russian roulette with creation.

Of course, Christians shouldn't be surprised to find themselves facing a God of immense power who is capable of playing dangerous games. God could have saved the world by fiat, but, they claim, he chose Jesus as the instrument instead. Such mild methods and calm words ended in crucifixion, not in the overt victory and political power the mob expected; and the Jews were justifiably furious at being left in political bondage. God is the God of Pilate, and the Roman soldiers, and the howling Jewish mob, as well as the God of a savior. The path God chose for salvation was neither without bloodshed nor its precarious and dangerous aspects.

One of the standard excuses theologians use to prevent God from sharing his part in the responsibility for human destruction is the pious answer that all the danger we go through is designed to teach us lessons of courage and to offer us our share of freedom and responsibility. The problem with this answer is that we have learned that God's engineering is not perfect. We could enjoy freedom and learn from difficulty in a world much less harsh than the one we inhabit. God's design is not "cost-effective." We pay too high a price in destruction for what we learn from terror. In his *Dialogues on Natural Religion*, David Hume has one of his spokesmen say that, judging from the faults in the design of the world, we must be up against an idiot God, or at least one not fully competent in exercising control to produce what he wants. We need not be as extreme in our judgment as Hume. But, counting the number of human beings forced to play Russian roulette with their lives each day, we must be dealing with a God who created a world far more precarious and destructive than necessary to achieve any goal theologians have so far attributed to him.

John Hick admits that he himself has not experienced a very harsh world. Thus, evil and destruction appear to him to be nicely moderated for educational purposes, and he expects God's final reward to compensate eventually for every present injustice.[3] This solution may do for pagans, but it is an inappropriate Christian argument. By definition they are not supposed to be satisfied with their own comfortable existence but concerned about those around them for whom life is a forced game of Russian roulette. As far as God's making all things right in the end, the issue is why he made the conditions more destructive than necessary in the first place. What can compensate for inflicting terror and human loss more extreme than any edifying educational scheme for humankind can justify?

God exercised power to set us on a course more dangerous than necessary, knowing it would be destructive for many too weak mentally or physically to protect themselves. Yet a God with such strength of will and such immense exercise of power, although presently more destructive than necessary, has the control over events needed so that their course can be broken and reversed — if he so chooses. Such a God is also one not bound to abide by reason's laws, since he did not do so in fixing the path of creation in the first place. He avoided Aristotle's Golden Mean and left such neatness to a few aristocratic people. But God can upset the imbalance in our accounts and forgive us all if he will.

A God who plays Russian roulette with the world is not necessarily one who lacks compassion or an ability to express love. Yet, if his central nature is that of love, this needs to be revealed to us specifically, since it is not evident in the wars that swirl around us. Human life viewed in the raw is much more like a merciless game of Russian roulette. Nor does the direction of human life presently seem any more headed away from destruction than toward it. A God who decides to play Russian roulette probably also likes surprise endings and an element of suspense in his dramas.

If God's ways are not our ways, and if he is not bound by the restrictions of Kant's moral law, he need not bother to balance our accounts at the end of the game. There is no particular reason why the good must win in the end, since they lose a majority of the time now. This is not to say that the meek may not inherit the kingdom of heaven, but it is to say that the conditions under which we live life were not designed to achieve a happy ending as a natural consequence. God never promised us a rose garden, nor does the script call for all the scales to be precisely balanced in the final act. Life points as much toward an abyss as toward the omega point Teilard de Chardin seems to discern on his horizon.

The infant destroyed by the hand grenade, the veteran who lives out life without legs, will not in the end find their accounts balanced out perfectly with the ones whose luck held in Russian roulette. If Jesus' promise is correct, there may be new life ahead for those who choose to express love over violence, but one couldn't guess that from the precarious conditions under which we are presently forced to live. If terror disappears in some future life, in heaven we will still discuss the mystery of why God chose a life more violent and precarious than he can justify by any goal we presently see.

Life inside churches is pleasant enough, although sometimes acrimonious and frequently less than perfect. But the God who created religious sanctuaries must be the God who created the terrors outside too, else he will be powerless ever to bring such devastating power under control. "Tiger, tiger, burning bright. Did he who made the lamb make thee?," we ask with Blake. And the answer is yes. The lord of love is also the Lord of the jungle. The God of Jesus also gave Caesar the power to destroy. God who decided not to limit the power of destruction on earth is also God who has the power to save us. He who forces us into a game of Russian roulette may also sacrifice himself in love and yet survive destruction.

In *The Saviors of God*[4], Kazantzakis portrays God as needing human help if he is to be saved. The search for God and the struggle to help God involve sheer agony for people, not the bliss some comforting preachers offer us each Sunday. To struggle for God is also to struggle with God, and it can be a bloody battle. Kazantzakis thinks that, if we have too much hope, this dulls one's desire to engage in battle, because as long as we hold on to religious hope we avoid the struggle to help others. We have "found it" – for ourselves. God may be more powerful than Kazantzakis thinks, but it is hard to discern that from the way the tide of the human struggle to improve life is moving at the moment.

Carl Jung thinks God's incarnation in Jesus is his way of atoning for the terror and destruction God originally allowed into human life. God's treatment of Job was unfair[5], Jung thinks, and certainly Job is portrayed as not having deserved his fate at the hands of Satan. More traditional Christologies, such as Saint Anselm's, portray the incarnation as God's ingenious plan to save one who has done all the wrong as contrasted with God's morally impeccable behavior. Yet surely Jung's point has some validity in the modern era, once we are forced to admit God's culpability in electing a more dangerous and destructive world than can be justified. The discovery of chloroform and modern medicine need not have been so long delayed. Pain at times teaches us something, but as often as not it simply destroys or deadens our senses. Jung excuses God by saying that, in his primitive days, God was not aware of the injustice in the world's design. But if Jung is wrong and God was aware when he chose a world of Russian roulette, God does bear an immense burden of responsibility on his shoulders. In opting for a perilous plan, God must have known he retained the power of ultimate control. He who made it can break it, but nothing in our dangerous present life tells us when or how that might happen. We cannot, of course, be sure all destruction will cease one day, that is, unless we believe Jesus' unlikely tale.

V

Although less comforting than some, I believe the kind of strenuous theodicy I propose is, or ought to be, attractive and tenable, to religious or non-religious, because we live in a time of holocaust and not one of serene religious optimism. For us, today, it is not quiet speculation but devastating destruction that has raised the question of God. Descartes' arguments intrigue some who have a philosophical turn of mind and are disposed to consider proofs for God. Saint Anselm's approach to God remains a constant source of intellectual controversy, too. But for the public at large, it is the recent tales of horror and mass destruction that raise the question about God most vividly. This is particularly true for Jews who suffered the most dramatic and publicized holocaust at the hands of the Nazis. However, we all know that holocausts go on in other lands involving peoples not quite so marked by religion. Thus, we must abandon the idea of "progress" and any notion of the gradual uplift of humanity along a scale of increased sophistication. We realize that horror comes from the intellectually advanced as well as from the primitive. Destruction knows no time or place. It is as much at home in universities as in primitive villages.

Where God and the holocaust are concerned, passing through wanton destruction does not automatically remove belief in God, although it certainly does not make belief automatic either. The letters and records of those who undergo these experiences indicate that some disintegrate and lose all semblance of belief, while some have their belief in God transformed but maintained and deepened. As we might suspect, nothing remains quite the same after the whirlwind of destruction has passed by. However, the torrent of writing, TV spectaculars, etc., now out on the holocaust indicates that such a devastating experience can be productive. It is hard to imagine Solzhenitsyn without the Gulag archipelago. Would Elie Wiesel have become a storyteller if he had been left to grow up quietly in a remote village and had not been uprooted by the winds of destruction?

Still, the productivity of such an experience – when it does not destroy those involved totally – is not my particular point. What kind of God is compatible with such an experience of waste and destruction and the degradation of human life? I want to ask. If one lives beyond such a total death experience, a new view of life and God is bound to result. Most obviously, all easy and sweet views of God disappear, as do all notions that religious belief will protect the believer and grant him his heart's desire. In any holocaust, the good suffer with the bad, the pious along with the disbeliever.

It is the status of evil in God's nature which forces us to reconceive divinity. Some faults in our world can be explained by claiming that they are not seen as evil in God's sight but only in ours. However, such an event as a holocaust surely does not appear "good" to God in any sense of the word. All our attempts to make evil out to be only the product of our limited human perspective, unknown by God as such, fail. Either God understands devastation just as we do or he is of no religious service in trying to explain that experience.

The notion that such waste of human life serves God's ultimate purpose in any simple way is equally repugnant. The fully rational God of Descartes, Spinoza, and Leibniz also become useless to us. Rational principles fail to explain mass destruction, although an appeal to the benefit of experiencing evil may give us a plausible account of minor ills. It is hard, if not impossible, to work a holocaust into a rationally devised scheme. We must be dealing with a God whose nature involves a wider latitude than rational principles, if they did dominate his life, would allow. Furthermore, any view of the world's process as being necessary or predestined by God is not only unhelpful but actually repellent where holocausts are concerned. It is shocking even to consider that God not only knew but plotted such destruction from eternity. We may hide some mysteries in the inscrutability of God's nature and plan, but not a holocaust.

"Freedom" and "will" as divine attributes become essential to any picture of a holocaust God. "Contingency" and "chance" are equally important. We must be dealing with a God who takes great risks and whose mode of control is at best quite loose. We face a God with a policy of non-interference, one who consciously created humans with a greater capacity for evil and destruction than any aim to enhance good can account for. And God did this by rejecting other options open to him, some of which are preferable from a human point of view. Such a God, certainly, is not easy or comfortable to believe in, but that is not so great a difficulty for organized religion as it might seem. Easy and obvious as Descartes' God is, few have come to believe in God on the basis of rational necessity alone. Only a God more difficult for us to deal with seems likely to account for a harsh world, once our romantic views of life have been exploded by passing through a holocaust.

Does this mean that Christians must abandon all notion of God as loving or as entering into human life to share it? Not necessarily, but it certainly means that our notions of love must be rethought. Love becomes as much a mystery as a pleasure. Romanticism is ruled out where God is concerned, since even intense suffering is not excluded in a divine scheme. Love either does not or will not always intervene to prevent destruction. God may enter into human experience, but all overtones of triumphalism in religion must be abandoned, at least at this point in time. God's presence often goes unrecognized, and surely it has little effect on the course of public life and political events. We cannot interpret the notion that God "rules the world" in any literal way. Divine rule must involve both what we cannot see and a future as yet unrealized.

A holocaust returns a sense of mystery to life that is never to be dispelled. We must be careful about thinking that the depth of mystery in our experience of God "explains" anything. At best it postpones understanding and at worst it destroys it. The rationalizing impulse is to get rid of mystery, but that assumes all phenomenan have an overt and rational explanation, which is what Freud thinks true of the psyche. Of course, mystery simply means that a final explanation now exceeds our powers, whereas the rationalist posture is that nothing exceeds the grasp of a modern scientifically based reason. We must assert in opposition: the way God operates is something one must be God to fathom fully.

Neither the world nor God is in the grip of any fixed necessity, since what is fixed in its course can be explained without residue. In our experience we find that there are, in the life of God as well as humans, indeterminate events and contingencies only resolved by the future decisions of someone's will. The exercise of power knows no fixed channels, since it spills so easily over into destruction. Rationality in itself leads to evil as well as good, a possibility the rationalist prefers to deny. Our reason calculates, but neither in God nor in human nature is this sufficient to specify right action. We are capable of setting aside any conclusion reason offers and acting in contradiction to it. God's will and power move in considerable independence from the calculations of his reason. God's attraction to what is good does not dictate his action in any simple sense. What is venturesome exerts a certain independent attraction on God.

Evidently, God moves neither easily nor automatically toward intervention in our affairs. His powers of restraint, then, exceed ours considerably. We need not decide that God is indifferent to human tragedy, but we know that, even in the face of extreme need, he can restrain his impulse to intervene physically. Whether God becomes spiritually present and available to us is another matter.

If he does, this may be comforting to some, but it produces no mass effect on all humanity, only on a few. If God works individually and not on the scale of history and cultures, his effect in the world is minimized or at least reduced. Ironically, God's present influence comes nowhere near equalling the power exercised by tyrants. It is hard to side with a God who binds the application of his own power where destructive evil is concerned, although nothing precludes God's future intervention in a more public manner. However, belief in such a possibility does not rest on any evidence of a decisive divine performance in the past.

In the presence of a holocaust God, danger always threatens. If we believe God can or will save us from such danger, this conviction will have to rest on evidence other than a holocaust. In the midst of a rain of destruction, some become more certain that God supports them, but this does not prove that all human beings will be removed from danger or spared the loss of life. Some involved in the Nazi holocaust reported a strange increase in their sense of closeness to God, but seldom were their lives spared as a result. The holocaust God may not demand blood sacrifice, in some primitive sense, but evidently he allows it. His sense of time and urgency cannot be ours. God converts some of us to his perspective in the midst of a holocaust, although the only result we see is loss or destruction. He has great power and strength of will, and he needs it. The question we are left to decide is whether this is strong enough to rescue us from the jaws of hell at the time of the world's end.

Postscript

The modern age hoped to eliminate God from its dealings with the problem of evil and next to eliminate human evil itself. Marx has one proposal; any number of social sciences or humanistic religions have others. But if my theodicy is at all correct, these attempts to deal with evil without God have now failed. So have the attempts to relieve God of all responsibility for evil, or to see God as purely good and loving. A God of some wrath and even violence has returned. This once again replaces anthropodicy with theodicy, but our major problem is how to fathom God, not evil. We see destruction all around. We live through holocausts. We are forced to play Russian roulette with life, and we think God does the same with the world itself. God has returned, a God of might and power and awesome majesty.

Now we must decide whether the reappearance of such a God of power helps or hinders the writing of a theodicy. Certainly no happy endings can be written. God does not ghost write Frank Capra-style movie scripts where the best person always wins. The advantage of the return of such a mysterious God is that part of the burden is taken off us for our situation in the world. And this is a God with sufficient power to alter our situation radically, if he chooses to intervene at a later time. God may intercede in individual cases in the present and thus lead us to hope for an altered future, but our gamble is on how much trust to place in such promises.

Critiques

Critique by John H. Hick

I think Sontag is right in holding that our response to the problem of evil is bound to affect our conception of God. And we have to accept that – putting it in Irenaean terms – the divine creative process, of which we are a part, is sometimes as harsh, as painful, as bloodstained, as destructive and crushing as it is sometimes joyful, beautiful, creative and excitingly fulfilling. The cost of the creation of perfected spiritual life is as great as the sum of all the evils of human (and perhaps also sub-human) experience. And since God's creative action, which is coterminous with the entire process of the universe, thus embraces both good and evil, it is clear that the ultimate source of both must lie in God himself.

But the big question is whether this evil is an aspect – and a necessary aspect – of the temporal creative process, and as such eventually to be transcended; or an element in the eternal life of God's heavenly kingdom. If the former, then it is an open possibility that the creation will prove to have been "cost-effective." At certain points Sontag seems to accept this, but also seems to regard the idea of the future kingdom of God as too uncertain to be taken into account. I, on the other hand, think that we are entitled, indeed obliged, to take it into account in a Christian theodicy.

Is there in his chapter a tendency to caricature an eschatological theodicy and, so doing, to avoid taking it seriously? I can make my point here by responding to a personal reference in Sontag's paper; for he uses an autobiographical remark in my own *Evil and the God of Love* to interpret this kind of theodicy. He says, "John Hick admits that he himself has not experienced a very harsh world. Thus, evil and destruction appear to him to be nicely moderated for educational purposes, and he expects God's final reward to compensate eventually for every present injustice." What I had written, concerning those who are overwhelmed by the weight of evil, is: "And if I had myself experienced some deep and engulfing personal tragedy, drawing me down into black despair and a horrified rejection of life, I might well share that negative response." This is not quite to say that one has not "experienced a very harsh world." Everyone who has lived with any openness through the central and more recent decades of the present century has experienced a very harsh world; and I have, like so many contemporaries, been involved in a world war, and have worked in hospitals, witnessed physical agony and death, shared the experiences of refugees and felt their despair, and served in devastated areas amidst extreme human need. My optimistic theodicy is not based on ignorance of the reality of evil but on a Christian faith in the reality and love of God. Further, that theodicy is not adequately represented by the idea of a "final reward to compensate eventually for every present injustice." The idea of compensation suggests a just proportion between present suffering and future happiness: the more pain now the more compensating joy in heaven. The Irenaean type of theodicy postulates something rather different: the future fulfillment of the divine purpose of forming human animals into children of God. This creative process is indeed harsh: it is human life as it actually occurs. But the end achieved — far beyond this present earthly life — may be the limitless good of the eternal enjoyment of perfected existence; and if so, this may well justify all the pain and struggles of the journey. It will not, however, take the form of compensation to those who have suffered; for those who enjoy the life of heaven will not be, unchanged, the sinful and egoistic creatures who are now suffering, but the perfected persons whom they are eventually to become. The key is not compensation but perfecting. And that perfecting will be partly through suffering, and participation in the suffering of others.

Critique by David R. Griffin

The positions of Sontag and Roth are so similar that I intend all the points in my critique of Roth to be relevant to Sontag also. However, the two men differ in what they emphasize; in this response to Sontag I will focus on a point common to their positions that is especially evident in Sontag's essay. This is the assertion that *every* aspect of the structure of our world must be thought to have resulted from God's decision. In other words, contrary to my hypothesis, there are no aspects of this structure that simply reflect "the nature of things," that are metaphysically necessary, that would characterize any possible world. It is on the basis of his speculative hypothesis that there are no such necessities that Sontag concludes that God must be somewhat ornery. For example, he says that God "deliberately chose the world we experience, including its horrors as well as its virtues," that "God has purposefully placed us in a situation of less than optimal advantage and subject to more waste and destruction than any purpose can account for," and that God "decides to play Russian roulette."

Furthermore, Sontag's speculative metaphysics leads him to conclude that God does not intervene in the world to prevent grotesque evils *not* because God *cannot* intervene in a coercive way, but because God can "restrain his impulse to intervene physically," and has adopted a "policy of noninterference." These statements clearly reveal Sontag's metaphysical assumption that noncoercible power of self-determination is *not* a metaphysical characteristic which would necessarily be exemplified in any world God could create.

On what basis does Sontag justify his speculative hypothesis? It is interesting that he begins by saying that we should not take the definition of God to be given and that we should work out a new concept of God. Yet what has Sontag done except simpl, accept the traditional concept of divine omnipotence, according to which God has "full power," the "power of ultimate control"? Sontag, like Hick, takes this idea as given. Unlike Hick, Sontag cannot believe that the structure of the world, taken to be completely God-given, always works out for the best; hence he concludes that God is partly malevolent, not always being guided by an aim toward goodness.

Insofar as Sontag provides an argument for this hypothesis of divine omnipotence, it is fallacious. The argument (stated more fully in his books) is essentially this:

> *(1) We have been able to overcome some of the sources of suffering (e.g., by discovering chloroform, and by finding a cure for smallpox).*
>
> *(2) Therefore we know that these defects in the world were not necessary.*
>
> *(3) Therefore we know that God could have prevented them in the first place.*
>
> *(4) Therefore we know that God deliberately chose to make the world more destructive than it had to be.*

The fallacy in this argument involves the covert oscillation between two meanings of "necessity." Sontag illegitimately jumps from the fact that something is not necessary to the conclusion that the *possibility* of it is not necessary. For example, it is clearly not necessary that a child will use its freedom to murder someone. But if you decide to bring a child into the world, *it will necessarily be a possibility* that this child will use its freedom to murder someone. Likewise, it was not necessary (I would agree with Sontag) for smallpox ever to have appeared on the face of our planet; but it does not follow that the *possibility* of smallpox's appearing was not necessary.

Sontag probably slides over this crucial distinction between necessary actuality and necessary possibility because he does not think it to be a metaphysical truth that any world God could create would be composed of actualities with creativity or freedom, i.e., with the noncoercible power of self-determination. That is, Sontag thinks that God could have created actual worlds in which all the creatures would be totally controlled by God. If one assumes that creaturely freedom is a purely contingent feature of our world, then one can ignore the difference between necessary actuality and necessary possibility: it is only if creatures necessarily are partially free to choose X, Y, or Z that the *possibility* of X is necessary even if it is not necessary that X be actualized.

But this means that Sontag's argument is circular, question-begging. His argument for God's total responsibility for all the features of our world is based on the premise that there is no metaphysical feature about the world for which God is not responsible – namely, inherent creaturely freedom. This is clearly expressed in his statement that "The chance aspect of all life must find its explanation in God too." The contrary metaphysical hypothesis, basic to my position, is that the "chance aspect" of all life, and indeed of all actuality, is rooted in the very nature of things, not in a cosmic volition. Both our positions put the power to decide at the base of the universe; but I suppose that the existence of a plurality of deciders lies in the nature of things, whereas Sontag supposes that only one decision-maker exists necessarily. The ultimate difference between these two suppositions is the difference between a wholly good deity and a devilish one.

One way to choose between two initial assumptions is by evaluating their logical conclusions. Sontag says that his view of a partly devilish deity is less "comforting" than the view of God as all-kind, good, and loving. The sophisticated reader, knowing the charge that ideas of God are usually wish-fulfillments, is evidently supposed to draw the conclusion that Sontag's "less comforting" view is more likely true. But the major reason Sontag prefers omnipotence-without-total-goodness to total-goodness-without-omnipotence is that he finds the former view more comforting. For example, he stresses that his God "has the control over events needed so that their course can be broken and reversed – if he so chooses;" and he says God must have created the terrors of this world, "else he will be powerless ever to bring such devastating power under control." If either doctrine is more characterizable as a wish-fulfillment than the other, it would seem to be the doctrine of divine omnipotence.

In any case, besides the critique addressed to Roth, my central question about Sontag's position is, how can he claim to "know" that God is responsible for all the structural features of the world? How does he rule out the possibility that there are metaphysical features of reality that are beyond divine decision, features which make the possibility of the various types of evil in our world necessary (i.e., necessary *if* the various types of positive value realizable in our world are to be possible)?

Critique by Stephen T. Davis

My oldest son once owned a masculine doll called "G.I. Joe." If you pulled out the wire on G.I. Joe's chest and let it go G.I. Joe said, "I've got a tough assignment for ya." I feel that writing a critique of Sontag's article is a tough assignment for me. The very wide differences between his approach and mine – in the assumptions we make, in the methodology we follow, and in the conclusions we reach – make it difficult for me to get a firm grip. I note that his rejection of the notion of God's perfect goodness is even more resounding than Roth's and that his unwillingness to commit himself to belief in a happy eschatological future is almost total. Both points place his theodicy far from mine, for I believe in both divine goodness and the Kingdom of God and consider them essential to Christian theism.

Perhaps it will be helpful if I center my remarks on the notion of theological methodology. First I should call attention to the deep strain of theological skepticism in Sontag's article — there are many concepts of God, he says, and we do not know which is correct. Concepts of God change rapidly; what sort of God one believes in depends on factors like where one lives, what assumptions one makes, and what definitions one uses. So ''the nature of God is our chief problem;'' ''we do not know what he is like.'' God hasn't explained himself to us, and so ''where God is concerned, our answers can never be final.'' Thus, Sontag says, we should not begin with a fixed notion of God and then approach the problem of evil; rather we should use the fact of evil to help us form an adequate concept of God.

While I believe a certain degree of theological skepticism is healthy — theology consists of fallible statements of human beings, not God — I regard Sontag's extreme skeptical position as dangerous. There are two reasons for this. The first is a lesson we learn from the history of philosophy — commitment to an official position of skepticism can blind people to the fact that they hold certain opinions quite firmly. And this might well be true of Sontag. His skepticism about God seems somewhat selective; he seems to be quite sure of at least some propositions about God, as if they were not subject to the dictum that ''we do not know what he is like.'' Here are a few representative samples:

> *(1) God chose to create a world far more dangerous and precarious than was strictly necessary for his purposes.*
> *(2) Freedom, emotion, and will play important roles in the divine life.*
> *(3) God is adventuresome, takes risks, limits his power, and controls the world loosely.*
> *(4) God's sense of time and urgency are not the same as ours.*
> *(5) God is not bound by reason's laws.*
> *(6) God is wrathful, violent, and capable of extreme harshness.*

Now it may well be that this is no particularly damaging criticism of Sontag. Perhaps he will say that all these propositions are held by him only tentatively and that they may well have to be rejected. But if this is the case I wish simply to record my desire to be the first to insist that (1), (5), and (6) be rejected.

The second danger in Sontag's theological skepticism is that it might prevent one from seeing that God *has* somewhere decisively revealed himself to us, if indeed he has. I agree with Sontag that what view of God one holds depends in large part on the assumptions one makes, and here there appears to be a very major difference between him and me. While Sontag's article is apparently an exercise exclusively in what once would have been called natural theology, I believe that God has indeed decisively revealed himself to us. God speaks to us, I believe, primarily in Jesus Christ and also in the Bible (as interpreted in the Christian tradition). And so while I agree that all statements about God can be questioned, I do not agree that "we do not know what he is like."

This difference between Sontag and me rears its head in the very different approaches we take to the problem of evil (see his comments on my introduction to this volume). While I agree that Christians must be prepared to allow the existence of evil to raise thoroughgoing and challenging questions about their concept of God, I view the problem of evil for the Christian primarily as subsumable under this question: can one rationally retain the view of God given in the Bible and in Christian tradition in the light of the existence of the evil one sees in the world? Sontag, on the other hand, makes no reference at all to revealed truth and is apparently not particularly interested in the problem of evil as I formulate it. He begins with the premise that we do not know what God is like and tries to use the existence of evil in the world to construct an adequate notion of God.

This makes me wonder what Sontag thinks of the Bible and the Christian tradition. It makes me wonder how he arrives at the propositions about God he accepts. It makes me wonder why (if we are to base our concept of God on evil) Sontag's semi-demonic God is to be preferred to Griffin's God who can't control evil or even to Hume's "idiot God." It makes me wonder whether Sontag recommends worshiping or trusting God. In short, I have very deep misgivings about Sontag's way of doing theology.

Let me briefly mention two other points. First, philosophers are all familiar with the distinction between the popularity or appeal of a statement or argument, on the one hand, and its truth or soundness, on the other. Yet this is a distinction Sontag seems to slip over. An effective solution to the problem of evil, he says, "does not necessarily retain its ability to convince." "We cannot hope for a universal solution, since we never agree on the statement of the problem at the outset." "All answers pro and con depend upon some description of God's nature, about which we do not agree and cannot achieve finality." But while I agree that there is no universally accepted statement of the issue, notion of God, or solution to the problem of evil, that fact *by itself* does not show that no existing definition or concept is adequate or that no existing solution works. It may well be that some people have produced or can produce a tenable definition of God and sound solution to the problem of evil. And if they have done so they have done all they can do as philosophers or theologians. The question of how many people agree with them is quite another matter altogether. The popularity of a given theodicy may well depend on when and where it is presented, but not its soundness. Truth is not decided by majority vote.

Second, there are several firm conclusions in Sontag's paper which I do not accept and which make me wonder how he can be so sure of them. For example, how do we know the destruction God allows in the world is not cost-efficient for the good which comes out of it? For surely we do not know what goods will come out in the end. How do we know God has deliberately placed us in a world "subject to more waste and destruction than any purpose can account for. "For surely we do not know all God's purposes. How do we know that people who suffer horribly in life "will not in the end find their accounts balanced out perfectly with the ones whose luck held?" For surely we do not know how accounts will be balanced in the eschaton. How do we know that God's present influence in the world comes nowhere near equalling the power exercised by tyrants? For surely we do not know what God is doing in the world or how he does it. I strongly disagree with each of the statements mentioned above; I wonder how anybody could sensibly claim to know them, let alone a theological skeptic like Sontag.

In the final analysis, I confess I am unable to offer any decisive refutation of Sontag's austere and bleak vision of God and the world. In fact, I am inclined to agree that if one ignores what Christians traditionally claim God has revealed about himself, Sontag's view of a semi-demonic God is one conclusion one might naturally reach. (Another is the theory that God is finite, and, as noted above, on natural grounds alone it is hard to see how one is to be preferred to the other.) Thus Sontag's theodicy seems to me to constitute a very good reason for Christians to think seriously about such matters as revelation and religious authority before trying to solve the problem of evil.

Critique by John K. Roth

Apologies for God have been made too long. With that thesis Frederick Sontag strikes a blow against the chains of necessity. After the theodicies of Hick, Davis, and Griffin, this challenge is a breath of fresh air. It is not, however, without problems. To consider them remember that the first article in this book stresses protest, while Sontag's features Russian roulette. These two emphases belong together, but it is not clear that Sontag agrees. Therefore, I would ask him to address this question: if God forces us to play Russian roulette, how are we best advised to relate to him?

One reason for raising this question concerns the method behind Sontag's theodicy. Note three elements that pertain to the first part of my question. Together they probe the existential status of Sontag's God. First, Sontag cannot say often enough that we lack agreement on the meaning of terms such as "omnipotent" and "good" and indeed on the concept of God itself. Thus, large doses of subjectivism, relativism, and pluralism ooze into his theory. Second, Sontag nevertheless believes that there is "empirical evidence for God's existence." By neatly turning natural theology upside down, he locates this evidence in evil itself. Third, Sontag goes on to make strong theological claims. For example, he states unequivocally (if not inconsistently) that "God has purposefully placed us in a situation of less than optimal advantage and subject to more waste and destruction than any purpose can account for."

Sontag intends to do more than offer a mere opinion in the latter case. Thus, if the pluralism of meaning with which he starts is really as extensive as his comments suggest, what warrant is there for his claims about empirical evidence and the truth of his view of God? As it appears in this book, Sontag's theodicy is essentially a metaphysical construction, as opposed to a view fundamentally rooted in Scripture or religious tradition. To make this theodicy stand as a sound theory on its own terms, we need greater clarification about Sontag's epistemology. Either that, or Sontag will need to appeal more directly to a scriptural and religious base. Unless Sontag brings together more intelligibly his relativism, his claims about empirical evidence, and his unequivocal assertions about God, we cannot assert with much confidence, at least from a metaphysical point of view, whether we are dealing with Sontag's God of Russian roulette, or with a God very different, or with none at all.

If Sontag's theodicy is a metaphysics resting on a spongy epistemology, it also lacks a needed ethical component. That is, Sontag has little to say about how we ought to relate to a God of Russian roulette. "We must face it," he tells us, God appears to be "strong enough to force a game of Russian roulette on us all, when he could have withheld such terror from the program of human life." But *how* should we face it? How should we face God and each other if Russian roulette is the name of the game? With despair, joy, outrage, love, indifference, all or none of the above? How?

"We need not decide that God is indifferent to human tragedy," Sontag tells us later on, "but we know that, even in the face of extreme need, he can restrain his impulse to intervene physically." Fine, but assuming that God has the impulse to intervene, restrained as it surely is, what should we go on to say about our heavenly Father? Sontag suggests that there may be a decisive transformation forthcoming, one that will reveal the dominance of God's love. But he emphasizes even more strongly the fact that we lack evidence of that dominance now. Christian hopes, to cite a specific example, are essentially rooted in promises derived from Jesus' "unlikely tale."

I can identify with Sontag's description of God's relation to humankind. At the same time, I am uneasy about the cavalier manner in which the affair is left. Sontag advises that "we are involved in a 'divine scandal.'" The only problem is that he seems not to take the scandal very seriously from a moral point of view. He tells us that God's nature includes demonic elements, and with a deft bit of understatement points out that "it is hard to side with a God who binds the application of his own power where destructive evil is concerned." Should we side with such a God? Or should we stand against him? Or are these stances best intermingled? Sontag does not say. I wish he would, because I think he should.

Accurate though his metaphysical description may be, it has the effect — unintended, I am sure — of legitimating evil too much because it protests so little against the God of Russian roulette, says so little in defense of those who lose in the brutally wasteful game. In fact, at one point Sontag reverts to the ancient apologetic theme: God may "forgive us all if he will." Will not a God of Russian roulette need to seek forgiveness, too? Not to say so, even to remain silent on the question, is in effect to side with naked power. Is that where Frederick Sontag wants to be?

The moral dilemma in Sontag's metaphysical theodicy is that he fails to take his own charge seriously enough: we have been God's apologists for too long. Sontag is very interested in constructing a theory about God. But he is too little concerned to wrestle with God in ways that might enjoin a version of Elie Wiesel's honest insight: namely, that the best human concern can be for God, not to mention being for men, women, and children, only by being *against* God, too. Granted, Sontag holds that we must challenge God by asking, "Why Did You Do That?" In his reply, such as it is, Sontag's God says, "because I wanted to," and the game of Russian roulette rolls on, unrelenting. Now it is Sontag, not God, who is silent. He does not say what the best response to such an enigmatic God would be. This silence is curious, disturbing, for in addition to being a metaphysician and a teacher, Sontag is also ordained to preach the Christian gospel. Can he instruct us Christians, then, as to how we can best relate to his God of Russian roulette? Should the response be "love your enemies and pray for those who persecute you" — or something else?

Like the other essays in this book, Sontag's focuses on the Holocaust. "Such an event," he writes, "surely does not appear 'good' to God in any sense of the word." To that observation he adds another: "Either God understands devastation just as we do or he is of no religious service in trying to explain that experience." Apparently the meaning of "good" is not as vague and relative as Sontag's earlier principles may imply, and therefore we confront again the issue of what he thinks our best relation to his God would be. Unfortunately, I can guess. Sontag will resort to pluralism, subjectivity, and relativity all over again: everyone for himself or herself. If that is the outcome, it does not displease me altogether, although it would still be helpful for Sontag to speak out more directly and share the sense of *his* relation to a God of evil.

Can Frederick Sontag be provoked out of his metaphysical serenity? Clearly he banks on some decisive intervention by God. He is also fond of speaking about persons who, in the midst of incredible destruction, experience "a strange increase in their sense of closeness to God." Where do these ingredients leave us? Sontag thinks that we are not going to find it easy to be at peace with God. But then where are we? What should be our reactions to roulette, for the sake of our own lives and God's as well?

Sontag's Response to Critiques

It is difficult to decide which is the harder task: *Encountering Evil* or encountering one's colleagues about evil. Our purpose in working together was to confront evil, and we have done that in the sense that each has propounded his own theory about it. But when we come to deal with criticisms of that theory, each tends to respond in terms of his own basic assumptions, rather than stepping back to question those assumptions. We treat each other on our own terms, which I suppose is the way philosophy and theology have gone on for quite some time. On the other hand, evil means precisely that destructive force, that mystery whose effect when we experience it is to challenge all our defenses, if it does not destroy them first. When we treat evil as if it could be easily explained, we do it an injustice, not to mention violating the memory of all those who were destroyed by its power. Yet most of us seem to demand an explanation which will take away all mystery. But is this appropriate where evil is concerned?

John Hick replies that "the cost of perfected spiritual life is as great as the sum of all the evils of human . . . experience." But to say that simply repeats his argument and does not deal with the charge that this neat balance may not obtain. We have little evidence that our "perfected spiritual life" (are we achieving that?) costs precisely the price of the sum of the evils we experience. Can we be assured that life will balance out so neatly, or are we even sure that God is concerned to make it do so? Is evil to be transcended?, Hick asks. Then it may prove cost effective in God's heavenly kingdom. Certainly this is a possibility, and a Christian must take God's future promise into account now; Hick is right. I simply deny that, in itself, this proves that "all's right with the world." Hick wants to base his theodicy on the reality of the love of God. Alright, but I deny that love as we experience it is always sweet and kind. Certainly anyone who is Christian should agonize over those who do not feel love as strongly as Hick does.

Life may be harsh, and the end achieved may be a "limitless good of the eternal enjoyment of perfected existence." But Hick is right that this does not imply a perfect compensation. Perfecting us may be done partly through suffering and by participating in the suffering of others. The problem is that Hick breaks off here, as if that solved the problem of evil. On the contrary, it only compounds it, because our suffering is more intense, more destructive, than we can find any grounds to justify. His appeal is always to the future. And I neither deny nor limit what God may accomplish. Certainly accepting such a nice future involves faith, but a belief in things unseen is not a convincing answer now — except for the one who believes. Faith is not an argument to convince the unbeliever but a belief where no argument suffices.

David Griffin objects to my metaphysics, that is, that *every* aspect of the world results from a contingent divine decision. He opposes this with his own, that certain aspects of the world are metaphysically necessary and would characterize any possible world. It is easier to believe that some structures are necessitated, since one does not have to justify why they are that way but can simply accept them. However, this notion is part of Griffin's limited God who works within a given structure but does not control it. Both his and mine are possible metaphysical perspectives, and Griffin could be right. The question at issue, I insist, is what kind of God you want, or what kind of God Christian promises require. If we relieve God of conscious choice, we can accommodate ourselves to the unpleasant facts of life more easily, but we also limit God's degree of control. We cannot have it both ways. Why should "non-coercible power of self-determination" be a characteristic necessarily exemplified in any world God could create? Why should we limit God to that, even if our world fits that description?

It is my conviction that I have not simply restated the traditional concept of divine omnipotence. Although what I want to assert is descended from that theory, the freedom of will I assign to God alone makes my version depart from tradition. I do take the divine power as a given, but not in the sense that other views are not possible (that is obvious), but in the sense that I believe Christian hope (e.g., the resurrection) requires it. Also my exploration of the notion of divine perfection leads me to believe that the tradition disagrees on what perfection means.[6] It need not mean unchanging, but traditional theologians did try to reserve ultimate power to God as the core of his perfection. Nevertheless, I do not want to say that God is "partly malevolant." He is guided by goodness, but that goodness is less serene and allows more latitude than we might like.

I puzzle most over Griffin's charge of my oscillation between two types of necessity. "Necessary actuality" versus "necessary possibility" is Griffin's distinction, not mine. Life will be full of charges if we are all guilty simply for not holding to another theologian's pet distinctions. However, Griffin does see that I reject his notion that God must create a world with certain necessities. I do indeed assume that creaturely freedom is a contingent feature of our world and that God could have created a necessary world, which is in fact what many theologians have believed. Thus, the worst crime I can be accused of is not thinking Griffin's view of necessity is necessary for us all. Griffin wants to root the chance aspect of life "in the very nature of things." But I should think the fact that a host of philosophers and theologians have rejected this doctrine would be sufficient to make Griffin see that nothing in the world forces us to adopt his metaphysics.

Yes, I do believe only one decision maker exists necessarily, and a chorus of theologians before me have argued that way. However, I deny that God's decisions are necessary, and so distinguish myself from Aquinas, Spinoza, Leibniz, and others. The result of this is to cast a pall of contingency over the world. However, our world is God's choice, not an order God had to create. I do not think this makes God devilish in any simple way, just as I do not think wholly good is the easy concept we wish it to be. My position certainly does make God responsible for the devilish aspects we find in the world, and it requires that any sense of goodness in God be compatible with this. But God did not have to create a world so opaque to final interpretation as ours if he did not want to.

Griffin would like to force me to choose "omnipotence-without-total-goodness" as opposed to "total-goodness-without-omnipotence." He says I must find this "more comforting," else he cannot see why I would make such a choice. But I thought it abundantly clear by now that I believe, where God is concerned, that few choices are "comforting." Evil most of all, if we confront it, offers little comfort to anyone. Hick does take comfort in the future and God's promise of a new world. However, that comfort does not come from confronting evil but from turning to a future solution. The question of whether my interest to have God retain the power to bring evil under control is wish fulfillment is beside the point. Is it required for the God who resurrected Jesus from the dead?, I ask. Other critics think I am not Christian enough. Griffin evidently thinks a God with Christian characteristics is chosen because he satisfies one's dreams. And so he may, he does so only rarely in the present.

How can I claim to "know" that God is responsible for all the structural features of the world, Griffin asks? I would not claim to know such a thing with finality; metaphysics is an uncertain business. But I do think this a defensible metaphysical outlook and that it has certain virtues as a theological base. I do not, I cannot, rule out the possibility that there are features of reality beyond divine decision. It would be easier if we could necessitate evil in that way and then accommodate ourselves to it. I just do not think this solution does justice to the sense of contingency one feels about life in the world. I believe with Duns Scotus that there can be no genuine contingency in our decisions unless there is first a contingency in God's. Besides, to necessitate evil means that God as well as we are stuck with it, unless we believe in slow human progress, which I do not. What is contingent at its core can be changed. God must bear the responsibility for his original decisions, but at least they are not beyond his power to alter later.

I don't quite understand why Davis finds it hard to deal with someone whose assumptions are not his — unless he feels that all Christians should think alike. (I think they should *act* alike.) He claims I am unwilling to commit myself to belief in a happy eschatological future, but that is not true. I simply claim that such a "happy future" is not predictable from the present facts and does not dissolve the problem of evil. I do believe in divine goodness — Davis misses the point. I just do not think what good means is either evident, simple, beyond debate, or excludes evil. The kingdom of God is essential to Christian theism, right. But I do not think we quite know what it is like or how it will arise. And above all, we do not know that it provides a ready-made theodicy. I distinguish quite sharply between theodicy, the theological-metaphysical enterprise, and the life of faith.

This does not mean that these two lives can or ought to be in contradiction, although Tertullian and Kierkegaard find this quite natural. However, I do not feel that either the Bible or tradition provide a ready-made, single theodicy. We must account for the fact that a wide number of those who claim the title Christian hold varying theologies, and I will not allow Davis to define me out of this group. The attempt to set the limits of acceptable Christianity by the use of doctrine is a futile enterprise, as history attests. This does not mean that one cannot claim to have a Christian revelation, or that the biblical documents do not contain God's word, or that one can believe anything one wants. Jesus is a norm for Christians. But the unfortunate fact is that the norm does not have the rigor of a sophisticated theological doctrine. Far from it. Why does Davis feel his Christianity is threatened if he and I do not agree doctrinally?

Of course, he claims I am a theological skeptic. But that is not a term I would choose as an accurate description for what I am trying to work out theologically. I do not believe we have the ability to establish one true doctrine, short of force. But certainly I believe partial knowledge is possible, if not full certainty, and that each of us should work to arrive at a defensible position. That is not skepticism, unless we use the term for all who accept a bit of mystery in divining God's purpose. (Skepticism and mysticism have always been close.) As I said, I believe with Cusanus that we do learn more about God, except that ironically, what we learn of God deepens our sense of mystery rather than dispells it. Why, then, is my position dangerous? It is so only to the one who demands certainty and finality as a basis for faith, which of course ironically makes real faith unnecessary. Socrates was regarded as dangerous, too.

I am indeed quite sure of some propositions about God. I have been at work on this problem for twenty-five years at least, perhaps fifty, and have a right to show some results for the effort. But I do not think my conclusions easy to arrive at or that others will necessarily agree. I was asked for my position, and I stated it. When I say, "We do not know what God is like," I think it obvious that I mean in the sense of final certitude or the removal of all mystery ("Now we see through a glass darkly . . . "). I offer such insight as I have into the divine nature without a demand for compliance. Has God "decisively revealed himself?" If that was his intent, he had poor metaphysical-theological advice in planning the event, since we have been at odds about interpreting it ever since. If God intended to create uniformity of doctrine, he made a sorry mess of things. He should have called on Wittgenstein or Russell for advice on how to achieve clarity. The biblical documents do not come up to their standards.

Such a situation does not prevent me from saying that God has revealed himself (I believe he has) or that the biblical documents contain the word of God. All this has not been done with Papal finality, I contend, but rather with a hiddenness that forces much onto the interpreter. I think I can maintain the view of God given to me in the Bible and in Christina tradition in the light of evil as I see it and do so quite nicely, thank you. I just do not believe this equivalent to accepting Davis' special theological views. Yes, I expressly omit reference to revealed truth in discussing theodicy. I was asked for my theodicy, not for a confession of faith, and the latter does not determine one's solution to the former. I do not claim that we do not know what God is like. We know a great deal, perhaps too much when we put it all together. But we do not know what God is like *finally*, I argue, although Davis is welcome to think he does if he wants to.

What do I think of "the Bible and the Christian tradition?" A lot of things, one of which is that they do not give us a definitive theology and thus leave room for faith, as both Kant and Hume said. Worship or trust God? The God I have discovered — or been discovered by, if you like — demands a great deal of trust, much more than Davis' secure God. Worship? That should be done with awe and a sense of majesty and mystery. That is worship; all the rest seems like self-gratification. But all of this is a bit beside the point in developing a theodicy. Yes, someone might produce a final "sound solution" to the problem of evil. The history of theology does not make this appear very likely, and I myself doubt anything like that can be stated by human beings. Popularity of doctrine is not the test, I agree. How the situation has gone in the past only gives us a clue for the present, our hopes and dreams of a final theory notwithstanding.

We do not know all God's purposes, Davis and I agree. But then surely we cannot use some conjecture about God's purpose as if it provided a secure solution. Davis may disagree with my statements, but that does not prove me a skeptic or that Davis' view of God alone defines what is sensible. And as far as sensibility goes, God seems little more likely to side with sweet reasonableness than with Kierkegaard or Nietzsche. "Semi-demonic" is not the way I would describe God. However, given Davis' need for security in doctrine, a God who keeps him in suspense or makes unreasonable demands on him might seem so. I think Christians should think about revelation and religious authority before trying to solve the problem of evil, as Davis suggests. I just do not see how we can expect this to furnish us with one theory, although it may give us some guidelines. Has Davis given any reasons, other than accusations, why my view of God does not fit the biblical account just as well as his?

John Roth, too, seems to forget that we were asked to write a theodicy, not to construct a systematic theology or lead the world away from sin. In fourteen books and a hundred odd articles, I have tried to deal with some of the questions he asks, but it would be ludicrous to try to deal with all these issues in a few pages. How are we to relate to God? That is for each person to explore, seeking whatever guidance from church, Scripture, other human beings or the Holy Spirit as he or she sees fit. You may trust God as Job did, if you can, but Job did not make the mistake of arguing that, in the midst of destruction, he just knew that the future would be a bed of roses. Jesus, of course, is how millions claim to relate to God, but that is Christology (or preaching – and there is a difference), not theodicy. Jesus may be an answer, but first we must understand the problem God has posed for us in theodicy. Subjectivism and relativism do not seem to me very good terms for what I propose, although I readily accept and advocate some form of pluralism.

There can be empirical evidence for, and some truth in, the view of God I suggest. This just does not mean that one and only one view of God is confirmed, as some have hoped. A view "rooted in Scripture and religious tradition?" I did not intend to write a biblical theology but I see nothing in conflict with that in what I suggest. As far as tradition goes, I have a host of mystics on my side, although I admit that Norman Vincent Peale is far away. Tradition too covers a multitidue of sins and only when accompanied by an accepted principle of selection (e.g., a Pope) does it yield unanimity. Religious experience is like that, I feel. Should we side with God or stand against him? In such a difficult matter, I should think a little of both appropriate, but I am sure that God has not left us a handbook governing divine-human relations. That is what is meant by "the long search." Do I legitimate evil because I do not protest enough? Job knew evil, and he also knew when silence was an appropriate response.

Protest to God? I doubt he needs to be told or shocked into awareness. Protest to people? I should hope so, but that is not a theodicy. The best response? I don't think there is one and only one, and I surely think God can deal with individuals vs. masses and will judge us as such. Should I instruct Christians on how to deal with God? That is for preachers, and I hope even they will not be too dogmatic about this. Instructing men and women on how to find God or come into relation with him via evil? Yes, that is theodicy, but the response we each give is not mine to determine. As a man Roth wants me to give him guidance which even God has declined to give. What is my own relationship to a God of evil? Kierkegaard said all too much for all of us about his special relationship to God. That is presumptuous. And besides, some of us – not all – are tested by being forced to wait in silence. If Roth knows enough to speak out (to put himself first by declaring his relationship to God), more power to him. But people have also destroyed each other in their certainty over God, and I fear that more than I prize certainty and public displays of piety.

Again, we each have spoken to our own concerns. We have responded to what strikes us in what is written more than to the substance of what is said. I would urge my critics, as I did on my first page, to look at the wide-spread atheism abroad today and account for it. My critics make it out as if everyone in the world is a passionate believer and that I alone am a hold-out. Such is not the case. If traditional theodicies, or Scripture and tradition, are sufficient, why has God drifted so far from so many in the modern world? The promise of "all's well that ends well'' has lost some of its power in today's world, it seems. I write to those who do not – who cannot – come at the problem of evil as simply a problem of belief. In this situation, to make God appear too obvious, too comfortable, too secure, flies in the face of the apostasy and religious agony that has broken out over the last centuries.

Postscript:

The Problem of Evil
and the Task of Ministry
JOHN B. COBB, JR.

The problem of evil faces everyone. It faces pastors in a double way. Not only do they experience evil in their own lives. They are also called to minister to others at points in their lives when they experience evil with peculiar poignancy.

I

An all too common experience for pastors is ministering to parishioners who have learned that they have terminal cancer. The parishioner, in our day, does not usually turn to the pastor for healing from the disease, although interest in the relation of faith and healing has been renewed. The parishioner turns to the pastor more often with the question, Why? For thousands of years religion has been associated with the explanation of evil, and consciously or unconsciously, whether encouraged by the express theology of the pastor or not, persons in their suffering turn to those they perceive as representatives of religion.

There are many possible responses. In our psychological age many pastors have decided that it is better not to try to give any answer at all. The pastor's task is to be present with the sufferer, to "hear" her or him, to let the parishioner know that the fear, anger, and loneliness that are felt can be expressed and will be accepted. I do not dispute the validity of this approach. In many cases it is no doubt the best that is possible.

The question, Why?, can be appropriately understood and dealt with psychologically. But to treat it only that way is to fail to take the questioner with full seriousness as a human being. A pastor who has not reflected about the question, who has nothing to say, will have a truncated ministry.

One type of answer that can be given is the scientific one. One can discuss what is known of the causes of cancer and seek to understand how they have operated in this case. I for one believe that this kind of explanation has an important role to play, that many of us benefit emotionally and spiritually, as well as intellectually, from knowing what is going on, evil though it may be. But this is not the kind of answer for which the parishioner turns to the pastor.

A second type of answer developed in India under the heading of karma. Everything that happens has a reason and not only a cause. In this sense, ours is a rational universe. When good things happen to us this is because we have so acted as to deserve them in this life or an earlier one. The same is true with respect to evil things. At first blush it seems extremely cruel to the cancer patient to speak of such a moral law in the universe. But the situation is more complex. There are many who can deal better with evil when they understand that it is just than when it seems wholly irrational. In the Indian setting one knew that to experience this evil now meant that some of the accumulated bad karma was working its way out. There would be less need to suffer in the future. If one bore the present evil well, one could accumulate good karma. These ideas have been less explicitly developed in the West, but they have their appeal. We expect to reap what we sow. Also there are parallel currents of thought today. The pastor may be persuaded, for example, that there is a connection between the personality and emotional temperament of the parishioner and the onset of cancer. In some sense the cancer is the wages of sin. If so, instead of railing against fate or God, it may be healthier to recognize one's own responsibility for what happens in the body. Indeed the body may be able to resist the cancer better, and the spirit may be more serene if, even at this difficult point in life, there is repentance.

But not all pastors believe this. Assuming we are in the Christian context, the pastor is expected to be one who can speak rightly of God. The thought of God has always been bound up with the experience of evil. But the relation, even among Christians, has been multifarious. This has been well illustrated in the preceding essays.

In the theistic context one explanation of evil that has been prominent in the past but is absent from this book is that it comes as punishment. Among those who ask Why? there are many who suspect that they are being punished, and many pastors over many centuries have encouraged that suspicion. For the theist the relation between sin and suffering did not work its way out in karmic fashion, but was mediated by the all-knowing and all-just God. Thinking in this way could add intensity to feelings of responsibility and urgency to the importance of repentance. Whether theologically encouraged or not, it could give to the sufferer some sense of meaning in the suffering and also the hope that paying this price now could reduce the likelihood of future punishment. By providing a Person as the source of the suffering, it opened the way to the possibility that by penitence, prayer, and good works, the sufferer could persuade God to mitigate the suffering.

Perhaps some of the essayists would allow for this as an explanation in some contexts, but clearly all of them agree that there is much suffering that is not punishment. One may contract cancer because of genetic predisposition or because of environmental conditions over which one has no control, while the polluters go scot free. Hence these essays direct us to other explanations.

In John Hick's essay we have a modern formulation of another major theme in Christian reflection about God and evil. We may understand evil as a necessary part of God's plan for soul-making. The pastor who thinks in these terms will look on this illness as an occasion for spiritual growth, growth for the patient but also for the family, and for the pastor too. The explanation will not be that God has singled out this person for cancer so that this growth can occur. The question, Why me? cannot be given a theological answer. But the pastor can explain why there is cancer in the world and how God intends that we respond to it. Happiness and enjoyment are not the aim of life. Spiritual growth is. Hence, what appears at first glance as unmitigated evil can be an occasion for the most important good. And even if in this particular case we cannot believe that any good will come of it, we can nevertheless believe in the goodness and mercy of God. We can believe that the death which this cancer will bring is not the end of life but only the transition to other lives, that eventually we will all be perfected. The pastor who can communicate this conviction effectively to the sufferer will make an important difference in her or his life.

Other pastors may be dissatisfied with Hick's response. True, much evil can conduce to growth, but much does not. Like Stephen Davis they see no signs that the course of history on this planet expresses the sort of spiritual growth of which Hick speaks. The hypothesis that this will occur after death is too ad hoc. In any case, there is no biblical warrant for Hick's position. Like Hick, the Bible is committed to a final salvation, but for the Bible this is not the outcome of millenia of growth. In the twinkling of an eye everything will be changed. Furthermore, Hick's expectation that all will ultimately be brought to fulfillment conflicts with biblical teaching that judgment makes an ultimate difference. The pastor cannot simply reassure everyone that all will be well in the end. The most important matter always, but especially as a parishioner approaches death, is to call for the faith through which one's ultimate destiny is determined. Should the suffering raise doubts about the goodness and power of God, the pastor can show that these are not contradicted by the evil in the world, even by the murderous cancer. All such evil is caused by the sins of free creatures, either human beings or fallen angels. God has allowed all this sin because only through this full freedom can the good be achieved. But all is for the sake of the good. Although we often cannot see how evil works for good, we can believe that it does. Therefore we can have faith in God, and because of our faith God will save us.

But not all pastors agree with either of these accounts. For some it seems that not only is this cancer an unjust and unmitigated evil that will conduce to no one's good but also that there is much senseless evil of this sort which cannot be explained as necessary for, or the result of, either human or angelic freedom. As noted in the introduction to this book, the Holocaust has become a symbol of such evil. Of course a few people may have grown spiritually or otherwise profited, because of the Holocaust. It may have helped many to outgrow immature forms of faith, for example. But it was far from "cost efficient," as our writers like to say. Pastors who agree with John Roth cannot assure the parishioner that there is positive meaning in cancer. Instead they will side with another aspect of the parishioner's feelings, anger. The parishioner is likely to feel guilty for this anger, especially when it is admittedly directed against God. These pastors, in agreement with Roth, will encourage the expression of this anger and share in it. God deserves our rage. Nothing God will ever do will justify this pointless evil, this waste of a woman's or a man's life. Nevertheless, the pastor will have another message as well. Despite God's responsibility for evil—God's guilt—we can believe that God is also a God of love. This world of unjust suffering does not have the last word. The sufferer's hopes for a new life beyond the grave are safely grounded in the resurrection of Jesus Christ. These pastors will not try to soften the paradox of God's injustice here and the confidence in God's graciousness beyond. Both elements are part of the Christian's faith and experience. Neither should be softened. Our task is not to achieve a smooth harmony of these apparently conflicting beliefs but rather to let both have their full expression in faithfulness to what we see and believe. This kind of pastoral ministry will also have its effect.

But a pastor might agree with Sontag that even this would not do justice to the meaning of this evil. It would leave too intact the understanding of God that had seemed appropriate in sunnier days. It would be bringing in a second theme alongside the loving power of God without fundamentally reconsidering the whole idea. The patient needs to be encouraged to face the meaningless evil of the cancer with no softening of its horror through a pre-existing belief in God. On the contrary, a new way of thinking of God must be forged precisely through the contemplation of the cancer and its destruction of life. The results may be confused and confusing. But they will be honest. The only God in whom one can really believe is the God who has allowed, even caused, this cancer. If one would call this God good, one must come to a new understanding of goodness. If one would speak of this God's love, one must transform the understanding of love. One may still hold that this strange and seemingly cruel God will some day change and bring about a radically different world. That hope can be grounded in Jesus Christ. But in acknowledging the power and freedom of God to act ultimately in grace, one must not forget that the God in whom one places this hope is the one who now sends cancer without reason.

Still other pastors may agree that the fact of cancer and its unredeemable evil must be taken with utmost seriousness and agree that we should rethink what we mean by God in the light of this and many other evils that do not contribute to any overriding good. But does that necessarily mean that we must rethink God in the light of the assumption that God is the cause of such genuine evils? That would be required if our basic conception of God were as the Supreme and All-determining Power. But is that what is revealed in the cross of Christ? The power of that cross has been the power to draw people to it, not the power of compulsion. It is a power that does not prevent suffering and death or hostile rejection, but it is not the power that causes those evils. Even in the midst of those evils it continues to work for good. The pastor who believes this may follow Griffin's thinking and encourage the sufferer to take with utmost seriousness all that can be learned about cancer cells and their perverse behavior, as well as all the human sins, including but not limited to the patient's, that have contributed to their growth. But that is not where God's work and presence are to be found. Instead God is to be found in the life forces within the body that struggle against the cancer, even though they are losing. And more important, God is to be found in the sick person's own experience, sharing the agony, struggling against despair, guiding toward serenity in the face of death, and finding opportunities to express love even in these terrible circumstances. God is suffering with the sufferer, not causing the suffering. God is in those who watch helplessly as the sufferer dies, trying to transform their impotent rage into constructive determination to do what they can to prevent the suffering of others. The parishioner who experiences God in this way can die with the knowledge of God's presence and love.

This review of the five positions taken in this book is intended to show that indeed it does matter what we believe about God and evil. But it also shows the burden that is placed upon the pastor in a time when those who write books on the subject diverge so much from one another. By what criteria should we decide what to say to one who is dying of cancer?

One possibility is to return to the psychological criterion with which we begin. What will be psychologically most beneficial to the sufferer? The tone of these essays indicates how much nonphilosophical factors shape the positions of philosophers. These are based more on their individual religious needs and their judgments about the needs of others than on rational considerations. In their critical responses to Griffin, for example, there are few challenges to the consistency of his doctrine of God with the facts of evil. But there are vigorous protests that his description of God is not religiously moving or metaphysically satisfying. If religious satisfaction is so important for the philosophers, the pastor will be excused for judging that what is needed in the relation to the sufferer is a word that will satisfy. Of course, it is not wise to speak words that one does not find persuasive oneself simply because of what one judges the other to need. A dying person wants honesty of communication. The decision as to what is satisfying to the pastor is as important as the judgment of what the cancer patient needs to hear.

Still the question of what is satisfying is not a merely psychological one. We cannot be satisfied by beliefs that do not ring true to us. There are many factors that influence what "rings true." Familiarity and compatibility with other beliefs are two. Logical consistency and consistency with facts are others. All of these are operative in these essays. All are important to pastors. It is not my task to guide them as they select among the positions offered here.

II

It is striking that it has been possible to find in one academic community five philosophers of religion who have devoted extended attention to the problem of theodicy. I suspect that they have jointly written more on this topic in the past two decades than all the theologians in North America combined. At first glance that may seem odd. We are accustomed to thinking that theodicy is a theological question. Why is it discussed primarily by philosophers?

The answer, I think, is found in Davis' introduction. There he points out that theodicy as a problem is dependent on theism as a belief. He then proceeds to explain what theism is. He sees that there are two ways of understanding the term "theodicy." Though he eventually adopts a broader definition, I am interested in the implications of his first, more narrow, definition—a theodicy is any attempt to retain rational belief in an omnipotent and perfectly good God in spite of evil. By this definition, of course, only Davis and Hick qualify as writers of theodicies. But though Roth and Sontag, in developing their positions, modify theism, it is clear that they take their bearings from it, and to a lesser extent this is true of Griffin as well. Accordingly all discuss the problems of theodicy even if, from the point of view of Davis' first definition, the arguments of several are in themselves not theodicies. The philosophical climate in this country is congenial to this endeavor, for even though most philosophers do not themselves believe in or care much about God, many recognize the effort to display the consistency among *prima facie* inconsistent beliefs as a legitimate, and intrinsically interesting, activity.

The theologocial community is quite different. There the influence of the German Protestant tradition is primary. In that tradition since Kant few philosophers or theologians have called themselves theists, or taken their bearing from theism. Theism means for the Germans the doctirne of a supreme being, personally conceived, acting upon the world from without. Also, the term is only used for doctrines of this sort that have a metaphysical cast. The Germans associate with theism just the sorts of speculations with which this book is replete, including the speculation about God's purposes and intentions behind the act of creation. And they have rejected all that for 150 years. The philosopher, Lotze, is an exception, but Lotze's influence has been in the personalistic theism of the Boston school, not in Germany. Even in the United States that tradition is no longer vigorous.

In the English-speaking world there is a broader use of the term theism which virtually equates it with any belief in God. In that sense, of course, most theologians are theists. But Davis is right that it is not belief in God as such but a particular kind of belief about God that generates the problem of theodicy. It would be hard to imagine Ebeling or Moltmann or Tillich wrestling with the sorts of issues dealt with in this book! For most German theology of the nineteenth and twentieth centuries a doctrine such as *creatio ex nihilo* would be taken as an important symbol but hardly as a literal theory of how the universe began. That topic would be left to natural scientists. But the English-speaking theistic philosophers of religion take up this question quite literally. It is the literal belief in creation out of nothing which leads to many of the problems of theodicy. They do not arise when it is viewed symbolically as a way of emphasizing the "absolute dependence" of human beings on God.

Of course I am exaggerating the contrast. Among German language theologians, even among those who reject the label theist, there are some who clearly hold all the tenets required by Davis. Karl Barth is forced by his understanding of God to deal with the question of evil. Emil Brunner even more clearly qualifies as a theist by Davis' criteria and cannot avoid the problems of theodicy.

I do not want to be understood as taking sides on this question. I am not a theist by Davis' definition, but because I recognize important affinities I usually call myself one, even when I know the term is offensive. I am glad that philosophers have continued to discuss the inherited doctrines of the church in a literal-minded way. I often fear that we theologians try to create a world of images in which to shape life without sufficiently considering how these images are grounded in reality. The idealistic tradition in philosophy made that all too easy. One reason pastors have turned to psychology for help in answering (or not answering) the question, Why?, is that most theologians give them no help. On the other hand, I am astounded—and somewhat put off—by the audacity of philosophers including some who have contributed to this volume who undertake to tell us what God was thinking before there was a world! I would prefer that pastors not take their cue from that.

III

Pastors do not face the problem of evil only in their ministry to those who are dying with cancer. The attitudes of all Christians are shaped by their awareness of the great evils of our time for which Auschwitz serves so effectively as a paradigm. As Sontag notes, the problem of belief in God is not merely one that comes in personal crisis. It is a cultural problem. The pastor must speak to people for many of whom the awareness of evil has shaken belief deeply. There is a general sense that belief in God is on the defensive. People speak of "still" believing. In concluding this postscript, I want to add my comments to those of the others in the effort to understand our situation.

The problem of evil in Western society arises for many people out of shock at the contrast of what they feel *should* be the situation and what they discover actually occurs. That shock is not felt in the same way in India. Buddhist cultures have long recognized the universality of evil in the world and have taken this as the starting point of reflection. It does not contrast for them with the way things *should* be, for there is no reason to suppose that things should be better. In the West, however, as the legacy of the biblical doctrine of creation and God's announcement that everything is very good, there is a deep-seated feeling that things *should* indeed be good. This is shared by many who no longer consciously believe in God.

The contrast of what is with what should be arouses outrage. Indeed, the presence of the spirit of outrage is taken as a norm. One who is not outraged betrays the human spirit. In these essays, too, we find that norm operating. Each writer finds it important to show that he feels the outrage, and yet several are criticized for the threat which their positions imply to that spirit. For Roth this is the central note.

There is no doubt about the value of outrage. It evokes action to mitigate the evils. It gives intensity and meaning to life. It breaks up the stultifying complacency of too much religious life and forces attention again and again to the facts. It stimulates fresh thinking and exposes the deadness of many of the inherited solutions to our intellectual problems.

However, there is another direction possible for us. Richard Rubenstein, whose book made such a deep impression on Roth, has rejected outrage as a way of thought and life. He does not do so by papering over the evils of Auschwitz. In many ways his accounts are still the most devastating. But he rejects the deep-seated assumption that things *should* be better. Why should they? Of course, he would *prefer* that things were different. But since he no longer believes in the theistic God, he recognizes that things are as we should expect them to be. Indeed, one senses that he is now more surprised by the elements of goodness in social behavior than by the ruthless rationality of the death camps.

This deep shift in his perceptions expresses itself in his accounts of Christianity. Most Christians and Jews who deal with the history of our relations express outrage at the way Christians throughout the centuries have persecuted and murdered Jews. Given our basic assumptions, there is every reason that they should be outraged. But in Rubenstein's account the matter appears differently. He expects that people who have power will use it for their advantage. He sees that the very existence of the Jews in the midst of Christendom threatened the Christological basis of the whole culture. He is not surprised that Christians villified Jews and often killed them. What appears surprising is that as long as Europe was Christian it did not exterminate the Jews. Some Christians at times even established a reasonable *modus vivendi* with some Jewish communities.

I do not report Rubenstein's account in order to make us Christians proud. The best we can say for ourselves is that we did not quite descend to the level of the Nazis. When we judge our behavior in relation to our teachings, we have full cause for outrage.

What I do want to point out is a new possibility for the future, which would be a return to the way of thinking of our earliest ancestors in the biblical faith. In recent centuries we have begun with theism. We have tried to reconcile the facts of the world to the doctrine with which we have begun. The facts have forced the doctrine on the defensive. The strongest defense now possible of an entirely traditional theism is Davis' claim that the facts are not absolutely, logically incompatible with theism. The reconciliation is attained only by a series of seemingly *ad hoc* hypotheses. Davis does not pretend that his position is plausible to anyone who is not convinced on quite other grounds that theism is true.

Perhaps, even if theism in an unqualified or somewhat qualified form is true, another strategy may prove better. Perhaps we need to look again at the world without the optimistic expectations generated by the theistic hypothesis. Let us see how selfishness, cruelty, and stupidity are everywhere triumphant. Let us recognize with Rubenstein that the triumph of rationality only makes our mutual destruction more efficient. Let us recognize the likelihood that we will destroy ourselves as a species. Let us take Auschwitz not simply as the paradigm for genuine evil but also as the paradigm for the way the world as a whole and in general is.

When we look at the world with our present expectations established by theism we are rightly outraged. But when we look at the world with expectations established by Auschwitz, we will also find much to astonish us. There are many patterns of human relations in which people seem genuinely concerned for the good of others in a community. Sometimes there are concerns that transcend even the welfare of the community. Some people are self-critical and change their ideas when evidence is pointed out to them even though it is humiliating to do so. Beauty is prized for its own sake. There are cases of people laying down their lives for the sake of friends or nations. One man voluntarily took hemlock rather than betray his convictions about obedience to the law. Another accepted crucifixion out of love for God and humanity. What can all this mean? Must there not be something at work other than narrow and brutal self-interest and absolutization of one's own group? Can we not call that God?

Perhaps if we begin there, we will gain more credibility in a world that has grown weary of the defenders of theism. Perhaps we would ourselves have more confidence. Of course, that will be only a beginning. By itself it will not tell us much about the nature of God's activity or how powerful God is. Perhaps people would someday be led again, marveling at how, out of such unpromising materials as we human beings, God accomplishes so much, to speak of God's power in ways not unlike those of theism. Perhaps they will not. But just as the ancient biblical affirmations of God's power grew out of the people's experience with God's gracious acts, so once again we might learn to praise God out of our own real experience and vital historical memories. It would be a refreshing change from defending doubtful dogma.

In the course of Christian history it was an article of faith that the world was good. People knew it was good because it was created by God. In times when people lived far closer to suffering and death than most of us, the goodness of life was felt and prized keenly. Perhaps its very precariousness added to the sense of its goodness. Eventually the sense of the goodness of life and of all being became stronger than the belief in God which had grounded it. In the eighteenth century one believed in God because the world was so good! Later one could believe in the goodness of the world and forget about God. But that sense of the world's goodness and life's goodness is fast fading now. One would judge from these essays that even those who hold to the doctrine of creation out of nothing do not believe that the world as now constituted is good. They seem to think that to declare the goodness of creation as it now is would conflict with their dominant principle of outrage. For all the writers except Griffin, the possibility of holding that creation is good seems to depend entirely on belief that something very different will someday come out of it or replace it, something so good that it will entirely or in part counter-balance the present evil.

I am not sure that they really mean what they seem to say. If creation is as evil as that, then death seems a great mercy and it is hard to see why we should be outraged by the Nazis mercifully ending the lives of so many Jews! Surely there must be some lingering sense that it is better to be born and to live a full life than not to be born at all or to be killed early. And surely that judgment is not *wholly* dependent on eschatological hope.

But the question is not easily settled. There is a perplexing relation between God, the goodness of life, and hope for the future. The three go together, seeming to support each other and yet to depend upon each other. I find it doubtful that those who do not find life more a blessing than a curse can believe in God. Why speak of the giver of life as God if life is essentially a curse? Yet I agree that for most of us in the West life without hope is hardly a blessing.

The hope that makes life a blessing can take many forms, but all of them ultimately depend on belief in God. We cannot believe in God unless we experience life as a blessing. We cannot experience life as a blessing if we have no hope. We cannot have hope unless we believe in God. We need all three, and if we break the chain at any point, the whole will dissolve. We must not let our sense of outrage destroy our belief in the goodness of life. Wiesel is a better guide than Roth here. But if, as I have suggested, we set aside the whole complex of ideas, if we take Auschwitz as the paradigm of reality and learn to marvel again at the strange occurrences which do not fit that paradigm, will that marveling be enough to restore the sense of the fundamental goodness of being alive? I am not sure. That is a risk we may have to take.

Notes

INTRODUCTION

1. *Dialogues Concerning Natural Religion* (New York : Social Sciences Publishers, 1948), p. 198.

CHAPTER I

1. See, for example, Frederick Sontag and John K. Roth, *The American Religious Experience* (New York: Harper & Row, 1972), and also our jointly authored sequel, *God and America's Future* (Wilmington: Consortium Books, 1977). Related themes are discussed in my *American Dreams: Meditations on Life in the United States* (San Francisco: Chandler & Sharp, 1976) and in my article, "William James and Contemporary Religious Thought: The Problem of Evil," in *The Philosophy of William James,* Walter Robert Corti, ed. (Hamburg: Felix Meiner, 1976).
2. The impact of Elie Wiesel on my religious thought is traced best in my book *A Consuming Fire: Encounters with Elie Wiesel and the Holocaust* (Atlanta: John Knox Press, 1979).
3. G. W. F. Hegel, *Reason in History,* trans. Robert S. Hartman (Indianapolis: The Bobbs-Merrill Co., 1953), p. 27.
4. I am indebted to my colleague, Stephen T. Davis, the editor of this book, for suggesting this concept of "cost-effectiveness" in relation to God.
5. Albert Camus, *The Rebel,* trans. Anthony Bower (New York: Vintage Books, 1956), p. 297.
6. I quote from an article by Paul Dean, "Coming to the Aid of the Boat People," which appeared in the *Los Angeles Times* on July 23, 1979. See section IV, pp. 1, 4, and 5.
7. Richard L. Rubenstein, *The Cunning of History* (New York: Harper Colophon Books, 1978), p. 67.
8. William Styron, *Sophie's Choice* (New York: Random House, 1979), p. 392.
9. *Ibid.,* p. 483.
10. Ben J. Wattenberg, *The Real America* (Garden City: Doubleday & Company, 1974), p. 9.
11. *The Cunning of History,* p. 91 (Rubenstein's emphasis).
12. John Hick, *Evil and the God of Love,* rev. ed. (New York: Harper & Row, 1977), p. 386.
13. Over the years, my views on God's power and his relation to evil have been strongly

influenced by the work of Frederick Sontag. See especially his books *The God of Evil* (New York: Harper & Row, 1970); *God, Why Did You Do That?* (Philadelphia: The Westminster Press, 1970); and *What Can God Do?* (Nashville: Abingdon, 1979).

14. Elie Wiesel, *The Trial of God*, trans. Marion Wiesel (New York: Random House, 1979), p. 133.
15. Quoted from the King James Version.
16. Elie Wiesel, *Messengers of God*, trans. Marion Wiesel (New York: Random House, 1976), p. 235.
17. C. G. Jung, *Answer to Job*, trans. R. F. C. Hull (Princeton: Princeton University Press, 1973), p. 99.
18. Elie Wiesel, *The Oath*, trans. Marion Wiesel (New York: Random House, 1973), p. 78.
19. *Messengers of God*, p. 235.
20. Quoted from the Jerusalem Bible. See also Ps. 22:1.
21. The sentences quoted in this paragraph can be found in *The Varieties of Religious Experience* (Garden City: Doubleday Image Books, 1978), p. 470.
22. Quoted from the Revised Standard Version.
23. Annie Dillard, *Holy the Firm* (New York: Bantam Books, 1979), pp. 58-59.
24. In selecting these phrases, I have drawn from the Revised Standard Version, the Jerusalem Bible, and Today's English Version.
25. Elie Wiesel, *A Jew Today*, trans. Marion Wiesel (New York: Random House, 1978), p. 136.
26. *Messengers of God*, pp. 35-36.
27. Fyodor Dostoyevsky, *The Brothers Karamazov*, trans. by Constance Garnett (New York: Modern Library, n.d.), Bk. V, chap. 4, p. 254.
28. See Greenberg's essay as published in *Auschwitz: Beginning of a New Era?*, ed. Eva Fleischner (New York: KTAV Publishing House, Inc., 1977), p. 23.
29. Quoted from Jankiel Wiernik, "One Year in Treblinka," in *The Death Camp Treblinka*, ed. Alexander Donat (New York: Holocaust Library, 1979), p. 149.
30. *Ibid.*, p. 148.
31. Elie Wiesel, *One Generation After*, trans. Lily Edelman and the author (New York: Avon Books, 1972), p. 214.
32. Elie Wiesel, *Night*, trans. Stella Rodway (New York: Avon Books, 1969), p. 14.

CHAPTER 2

1. R. Held and A. Hein, "Movement-produced stimulation in the development of visually guided behaviour", *Journal of Comparative and Physiological Psychology*, Vol. 56 (1963), pp. 872-876.
2. Fyodor Dostoyevsky, *The Brothers Karamazov*, trans. by Constance Garnett (New York: Modern Library, n.d.), Bk. V, chap. 4, p. 254.
3. Erich Fromm, "Values, Psychology, and Human Existence," in *New Knowledge of Human Values*, ed. A. H. Maslow (New York: Harper, 1959), p. 156.
4. John Hick, *Death and Eternal Life* (New York: Harper & Row, and London: Collins, 1976).
5. *The Confessions of St. Augustine*, trans. by F. J. Sheed (New York: Sheed and Ward, 1942), Bk. I, Chap. 1, p. 3.
6. Hick, *Death and Eternal Life*, chap. 13.

CHAPTER 3

1. Sadly, there is no space here for me to explain why I do not say *"the* normative guide."
2. See, for example, J. L. Mackie, "Evil and Omnipotence," Nelson Pike (ed.), *God and Evil* (Englewood Cliffs, New Jersey: Prentice-Hall, Inc., 1964), p. 47.
3. Some free will defenders argue that free will in itself is such a great moral good that it will outweigh any possible bad consequences that follow from it. But this claim seems both false and unnecessary to the FWD. What if in the end *no* free moral agent chooses to love and obey God? I hardly think God's policy can fairly be called wise if this were to happen, even if free will, as claimed, is in itself a great moral good.
4. Alvin Plantinga has so argued. See *God, Freedom, and Evil* (New York: Harper and Row, 1974), p. 61.
5. *Ibid.,* p. 25.
6. John Hick argues along these lines. See *Evil and the God of Love* (New York: Harper and Row, 1966), pp. 68-69.
7. Mackie, p. 56.
8. See Plantinga, *God, Freedom, and Evil,* pp. 34-44 on this.
9. *Ibid.,* p. 58.
10. I am indebted to my friend and colleague John Roth for making remarks that led me to see that the EPE is distinct from the LPE.
11. I should point out here that a "universe" is not the same thing as a Leibnizian "possible world," and so my claim that there is only one universe is not falsified by our ability to imagine various possible worlds. There is only one actual universe, and all possible worlds are conceived of and talked about in it. Imagined possible worlds are only possible (not actual) states of the actual world. Inductive arguments can only be based on past *actual* states of affairs, not possible ones. Thus this argument might or might not count as a good inductive argument: "I have seen thousands of tigers and they all had stripes; therefore it is probable that the next tiger I will see will have stripes." But this one will certainly not count as a good inductive argument: "The next tiger I see will probably have no stripes, because I can imagine possible worlds that contain nothing but stripeless tigers."
12. Hume has Philo make this sort of statement. See *Dialogues Concerning Natural Religion* (New York: Hafner Publishing Company, 1959), p. 73.
13. *God, Freedom, and Evil,* pp. 48-53.
14. Peter Geach, *Providence and Evil* (Cambridge: Cambridge University Press, 1977), p. 58.

CHAPTER 4

1. Rather than rejecting *creatio ex nihilo,* some theologians (e.g., Nicholas Berdyaev) distinguish between two interpretations of *nihil:* absolute nothingness *(ouk on* in Greek) and relative nothingness *(mē on).* Then they affirm the doctrine in the second sense. That is a perfectly acceptable approach, and one which I as a Whiteheadian can take, since a pure chaos would have no order, and the first type of order is the ordering of momentary events into series of "enduring objects," such as electrons. Since when we speak of a "thing" we normally have an enduring object in mind, there would be no-thing in a state of pure chaos. However, the doctrine of *ex nihilo* has usually been used to affirm creation out of absolutely nothing, often with the specific intention of

denying creation out of chaos. It is in this sense that I employ the term in this essay.
2. Even this expanded statement would not be adequate for all positions, since some theologians do not consider God to be ''a being.'' But this problem does not arise for the positions articulated in this book.
3. Defenders of the hybrid free-will defense have another major problem which my more consistent affirmation of creaturely freedom avoids. According to their position, since God freely created human freedom, God could interrupt it at any time. Hence they must explain why God does not interrupt it to prevent at least some of the more horrendous moral evils that occur. This problem, along with that of accounting for natural evil, tends to lead them finally to deny that any events are *genuinely* evil.
4. Alfred North Whitehead, *Science and the Modern World* (New York: Macmillan Co., 1953), p. 192.

CHAPTER 5

1. Frederick Sontag, *The God of Evil* (New York: Harper and Row, 1970); and *God, Why Did You Do That?* (Philadelphia: Westminster Press, 1970).
2. For my analysis of the problem see *Divine Perfection* (New York: Harper and Row, 1962).
3. John Hick, *Evil and the God of Love* (New York: Harper and Row, 1978), p. 386.
4. Nikos Kazantzakis, *Saviors of God* (New York: Simon and Schuster, 1969).
5. Carl G. Jung, *The Answer to Job* (New York: Meridian Books, 1960).
6. Frederick Sontag, *Divine Perfection* (New York: Harper and Row, 1962).

Bibliography

What follows is a list of the major writings on the problem of evil of the five main contributors to this book.

1. JOHN K. ROTH

A Consuming Fire: Encounters with Elie Wiesel and the Holocaust. Atlanta: John Knox Press, 1979.

God and America's Future (with Frederick Sontag). Wilmington, North Carolina: Consortium Books, 1977.

Problems of the Philosophy of Religion. Scranton: Chandler/INTEXT, 1971.

The American Religious Experience (with Frederick Sontag). New York: Harper and Row, 1972.

'William James and Contemporary Religious Thought: The Problem of Evil,'' *The Philosophy of William James.* Edited by Walter R. Corti. Hamburg: Felix Meiner, 1976.

2. JOHN H. HICK

Christianity at the Centre. London: SCM Press, 1968, and New York: Herder & Herder, 1970. Revised edition, *The Centre of Christianity.* London: SCM Press, 1977, and San Francisco: Harper & Row, 1978.

"Coherence and the God of Love Again," *Journal of Theological Studies,* Vol. XXIV, Part 2 (1973), pp. 522-528.

Evil and the God of Love. London: Macmillan, and New York: Harper & Row, 1966; 2nd ed. 1977.

"Freedom and the Irenaean Theodicy Again, *Journal of Theological Studies,* Vol. XXI, Part 2 (October 1970), pp. 419-422.

"God, Evil and Mystery," *Religious Studies,* Vol. 3, No. 2 (April 1968), pp. 539-546. Reprinted in *God and the Universe of Faiths.* London: Macmillan, and New York: St. Martin's Press, 1973.

Philosophy of Religion. Englewood Cliffs, N.J.: Prentice-Hall, Inc., 1963; 2nd ed. 1973.

"Remarks on the Problem of Evil," *Reason and Religion,* ed. Stuart C. Brown. Ithaca and London: Cornell University Press, 1977.

"The Problem of Evil," *The Encyclopedia of Philosophy.* New York: The Macmillan Co., and The Free Press, 1967, pp. 136-141.

"The Problem of Evil in the First and Last Things," *Journal of Theological Studies,* Vol. XIX, Part 2 (October 1968), pp. 591-602. Reprinted in *God and the Universe of Faiths.*

3. STEPHEN T. DAVIS

"A Defense of the Free Will Defense," *Religious Studies*, Vol. VIII, No. 4 (December 1972), pp. 335-344.

"Assurance of Victory," *Pulpit Digest*, Vol. LXI, No. 449 (May-June 1981), pp. 65-69.

"God the Mad Scientist: Process Theology on God and Evil," *Themelios*, Vol. 5, No. 1 (September 1979), pp. 18-23.

"Why Did This Happen to Me?''—The Patient as a Philosopher," *The Princeton Seminary Bulletin*, Vol. LXV, No. 1 (July 1972), pp. 61-67.

4. DAVID R. GRIFFIN

"Divine Causality, Evil, and Philosophical Theology: A Critique of James Ross," *International Journal for Philosophy of Religion*, Vol. 4, No. 3 (1973, pp. 168-186).

God, Power, and Evil: A Process Theodicy. Philadelphia: Westminster Press, 1976.

"Philosophical Theology and the Pastoral Ministry," *Encounter*, Vol. 33 (Summer 1972), pp. 230-244.

Process Theology: An Introductory Exposition (with John B. Cobb). Philadelphia: The Westminster Press, 1976.

"Values, Evil, and Liberation Theology," *Encounter*, Vol. 40, No. 1 (Winter 1979), pp. 1-15.

5. FREDERICK SONTAG

God and America's Future (with John K. Roth). Wilmington, North Carolina: Consortium Books, 1977.

"God and Evil," *Religion in Life*, Vol. XXXIV, No. 2 (Spring 1965), pp. 215-223.

God, Why Did You Do That? Philadelphia: The Westminster Press, 1970.

The American Religious Experience (with John K. Roth). New York: Harper and Row, 1972.

The God of Evil: An Argument from the Existence of the Devil. New York: Harper and Row, 1970.